Educational Diversity

Also by Yvette Taylor

WORKING-CLASS LESBIAN LIFE: Classed Outsiders

LESBIAN AND GAY PARENTING: Securing Social and Educational Capital

CLASSED INTERSECTIONS: Spaces, Selves, Knowledges

THEORIZING INTERSECTIONALITY AND SEXUALITY (*co-edited with S. Hines and M. Casey*)

FITTING INTO PLACE? Class and Gender Geographies and Temporalities

SEXUALITIES: Reflections and Futures (*with S. Hines*)

Educational Diversity

The Subject of Difference and Different Subjects

Yvette Taylor
London South Bank University, London, UK

First published 2012 by
PALGRAVE MACMILLAN

Palgrave Macmillan in the UK is an imprint of Macmillan Publishers Limited,
registered in England, company number 785998, of Houndmills, Basingstoke,
Hampshire RG21 6XS.

Palgrave Macmillan in the US is a division of St Martin's Press LLC,
175 Fifth Avenue, New York, NY 10010.

Palgrave Macmillan is the global academic imprint of the above companies
and has companies and representatives throughout the world.

Palgrave® and Macmillan® are registered trademarks in the United States,
the United Kingdom, Europe and other countries.

ISBN 978–0–230–29342–7

This book is printed on paper suitable for recycling and made from fully
managed and sustained forest sources. Logging, pulping and manufacturing
processes are expected to conform to the environmental regulations of the
country of origin.

A catalogue record for this book is available from the British Library.

A catalog record for this book is available from the Library of Congress.

10   9   8   7   6   5   4   3   2   1
21   20   19   18   17   16   15   14   13   12

Printed and bound in Great Britain by
CPI Antony Rowe, Chippenham and Eastbourne

Contents

Section 2   Higher Education, Higher Standards?

Section 3   Boundary Conditions

Figures

Acknowledgements

This collection is based on a seminar series initiated by Yvette Taylor while a senior lecturer at Newcastle University, UK: Educational Diversity: the Subject of Difference and Different Subjects (2010). Thanks are paid for the internal funding received for the series and to all those who participated in it. Chapter 14 was originally published as Taylor, Y. (2009) Facts, fictions, identity constrictions: Sexuality, gender and class in higher education, *Lesbian & Gay Psychology Review*, Special Issue **10(1)**: 38–47 and thanks are paid for allowing reproduction here.

Foreword

Doing Diversity Differently

Diane Reay

This edited book, which grew out of a seminar series on educational diversity, is itself a diverse collection, spanning all stages of education and every aspect of diversity. Diversity has a problematic genealogy within education, and it has been used ideologically by the Right to both countermand and undermine the equalities agenda, and by government and policy makers to sanitise and sweeten unacceptable neoliberal policies. Diversity, often linked to choice, was frequently the justification used to introduce greater and greater levels of marketisation within education. Within this right-wing rhetoric, what the UK needed was increased levels of diversity in the supply of education in order to respond to the diversity of demand among students and their parents. In this ideological deployment, diversity is not an issue that requires attention in and of itself; rather, it becomes a means to something else, in this case neoliberal educational policies promoting free markets and choice in education. Those of us who remember the powerful influence of Chubb and Moe's (1990) book *Politics, Markets and America's Schools*, and the subsequent UK White Paper 'Choice and diversity' (DfE, July 1992), which became law in 1993, will recall the law as the first major attempt to put Chubb and Moe's right-wing, neoliberal doctrines into operation in Britain. Since then, the concept of diversity has gone through a number of twists and turns, and it has certainly gone global as a number of the chapters in the book demonstrate. But in its many guises, it has too rarely been twinned with equality rather than choice. This book then is a very welcome departure: a real attempt to retrieve diversity as a key equalities issue.

What many of the chapters do extremely well is highlight how diversity in its mainstream conceptualisation marginalises social class. The conundrum those of us on the Left have to struggle with is that social class is no longer seen as a social justice issue; social class inequalities have become naturalised – they are just how things are. This naturalisation of socio-economic inequalities was most clearly evidenced in the recent actions of the Liberal–Conservative coalition government. In November 2010, Home Secretary Theresa May scrapped the socio-economic duty from the Equalities Act. This duty demanded that public bodies consider the impact of policy on people from poorer backgrounds, in the same way that they currently need to consider the impact of policy decisions on women, minorities, the disabled, and lesbian, gay and transgender people, as well as take into account the influence of age and religion. In the 2010s, the fallacy that Basil Bernstein pointed out 50 years ago – that education can compensate for society – has been superseded by the fallacy that aspirations can compensate for social class. So the dominant discourse is that anyone, no matter how disadvantaged, can succeed if they want success enough. And if ability and effort are all that matter now, then social class disadvantage has become an anachronism. This eliding and downgrading of social class has ironically occurred at a historical juncture when an increasingly stratified society has produced unprecedented levels of poverty and wealth. This collection constitutes a very welcome challenge to such dominant thinking. In chapters as varied as Michelle Addison's account of the (re)making and (un)doing of identities of value within higher education (HE) (Chapter 13), Val Gillies' critical account of new behaviour management practices in schools (Chapter 2), and Yvette Taylor's moving account of combining classed, gendered and sexual identities as an academic (Chapter 14), the authors' abilities to think across and between intersections that include social class alongside other axes of difference is a clear challenge to contemporary elisions.

This collection constitutes a concerted engagement with how divisions and differences are addressed and responded to, an attempt to look beneath the neoliberal rhetoric and marketing hype, and grasp the realities. As Kimberly Allen and her colleagues point out when discussing student work placements (Chapter 10), too often doing diversity operates simultaneously as a means of evading rather than addressing equality. In Bourdieusian terms, it becomes a way of capitalising on difference and generating a profit, rather than recognising and respecting it. As Jenny Shaw and Kath Bridger elaborate (Chapter 7), student diversity in HE is often seen as a problem that needs to be contained or a series of concessions grudgingly made. The oppressiveness of such an approach is brought vividly to life by Sara Ahmed, who looks at embodying diversity as a Black feminist (Chapter 11). In a beautifully crafted discussion, she makes crystal clear how damaging the diversity agenda can be when it narrowly constitutes a programme of tokenistically ticking boxes and counting heads. Her poetic account of doing diversity (or perhaps more accurately being 'done over' by diversity) encapsulates the problematic paradox that diversity has become in the twenty-first century.

This powerful theme of the damage of 'doing diversity' in a perfunctory tick-box manner that permeates many of the chapters resonates with my own research with Gill Crozier and David James (2011), where we found that the White middle classes placed a very high value on diversity. However, this high value was all about resourcing the White middle-class self, a means of enhancing educative potential. As Ainscow et al. (2007) point out, 'national policies to promote choice and diversity are working within and compounding existing patterns of inequity and social division'. Unfortunately, despite the rhetorical flourishes around difference and diversity, it is sameness that routinely gets more highly valued. So there was much talk about the wonderful advantage of ethnic diversity but in terms of an advantage that accrued only to the White middle classes. This is ethnic diversity as a form of capital to be consumed or invested. Threaded through the discourse of valuing diversity is a powerful theme of the value to be gained from diversity. This consuming of the diverse Other by more powerful mainstream subjects is touched on in a range of different chapters in the book, but is most apparent in Sara Ahmed's narrative of appropriation (Chapter 11). Positioned as a Black feminist trying to find an equitable space in the academy, she asserts: 'Our difference becomes their diversity.'

Over and over again in the chapters, diversity is seen as working against rather than reinforcing equality. One of the most important messages we gain from the book is that, for too often and in too many educational contexts, diversity has been deployed as a sticking plaster to cover up unacceptable levels of inequality. It operates as a superficial veneer rather than an in-depth engagement with unfairness and injustices, and it is evident in myriad educational practices that span the primary classroom to the university seminar. As the chapters in this book admirably, if rather depressingly, demonstrate, at too many times and in too many places doing diversity becomes a way of not doing fairness and social justice – a sop rather than a solution.

The book also, more hopefully, shows us a way forward. A number of the chapters focus specifically on ways of reclaiming diversity. Both Kay Inckle (Chapter 9) and Damien W. Riggs (Chapter 12) write about reworking diversity through radical pedagogic approaches. And as Inckle points out, 'when classrooms become communities where everyone is equally embodied, vulnerable and valued, diversity is realised'.

Both authors reveal the imperative to grasp back the diversity agenda, to replace the tokenistic rhetoric with a sustained and substantial commitment to putting right what has been wrong for far too long. In order to do that, we need to uncouple diversity from choice and the vacuous performativity that neoliberalism promotes, and harness it in the interests of equality and social justice. Over the last 30 years, the celebration of diversity has become little more than an excuse for papering over the growing gaps in the social fabric, for disregarding the vast inequalities and injustices that permeate social differences. Yet what this book reminds us is that both difference, the new mantra within sociological theorising, and diversity, the new mantra in relation to British educational provision, are still always about inequalities. The book reveals the enormous potential for enhancing the common good, as well as individual wellbeing, when we make the effort to do diversity in socially just ways.

References

Ainscow, M., Crow, M., Dyson, A., Goldrick, S., Kerr, K., Lennie, C., Miles, S., Muijs, D. and Skyrme, J. (2007) *Equity in Education: New Directions*. Manchester: Centre for Equity in Education.

DfE. (1992) *White Paper Choice and Diversity: A New Framework for Schools*. London: HMSO.

Chubb, J. and Moe, T. (1990) *Politics, Markets and America's Schools*. Washington: Brookings Institute.

Reay, D., Crozier, G. and James, D. (2011) *White Middle Class Identities and Urban Schooling*. Basingstoke: Palgrave Macmillan.

Foreword

Space, Affect and Value: A Commentary on Educational Diversity: The Subject of Difference and Different Subjects

Jon Binnie

It is a great privilege to be invited to write this commentary on educational diversity. In this piece, I wish to explore how some of the key arguments explored in the individual chapters could be brought into productive discussion with one another. From the context of UK HE, this collection of essays could not be more timely, as the impact of the trebling of undergraduate tuition fees is being felt in the changing demography of student cohorts and shifts in undergraduate recruitment between different disciplines. As Yvette Taylor highlights in her introductory essay (Chapter 1), equality and diversity work in UK HE is threatened by cutbacks and austerity. For instance, the 'Aimhigher' programme introduced by New Labour, which sought to widen participation in HE among young people from disadvantaged socio-economic backgrounds, was scrapped by the coalition government in the Comprehensive Spending Review in 2010. The Education Maintenance Allowance, which provided financial support to students from poorer backgrounds, has also been scrapped. Sarah Evans' focus on the application process to UK higher education institutions (HEIs) (Chapter 6) provides a helpful summary of the current UK policy context. Some essays reflect on the transformation of UK HE under New Labour, and critically examine how equality and diversity were framed during this era. The chapters in the book cover a range of contexts for critically examining how differences are reproduced within educational spaces. They bring to the fore the experiences of teachers and lecturers (e.g. Inckle, Ahmed and Riggs: Chapters 9, 11 and 12), of students (Hodges and Jobanputra: Chapter 8) and of administrators, cleaners and workers in educational spaces (Addison: Chapter 13). The collection is interdisciplinary, with contributors coming from sociology, psychology, geography, social work and gender studies. Some essays focus on specific disciplines – for instance, Hodges and Jobanputra's examination of the experiences of Black and minority ethnic students (Chapter 8), as well as gay and lesbian students within UK university psychology departments; while Allen et al. (Chapter 10) examine how inequalities may be produced through the practice of diversity within creative sector work placements. A common concern in a number of these chapters is the degree to which material inequalities are commonly reproduced through the practice of diversity management. For example, Allen et al. suggest that despite the fetishism of difference within the creative sector, interviews with placement providers show little recognition of inequalities within the workplace. While diversity may be espoused by these providers, inequality was often relegated to the realm of the unspeakable. Sara Ahmed (Chapter 11) addresses the costs of challenging institutional practices of diversity management that can reproduce rather than counter blatant inequalities. *Educational Diversity* challenges and unsettles any comfortable, taken-for-granted notions that HEIs are spaces where inequalities are adequately addressed in the name of social justice. Indeed, these essays address the political economy of diversity within educational spaces. Allen et al. suggest that issues of social justice tend to get sidelined when diversity is promoted for narrow commercial interests within HEIs.

In critically addressing the way in which diversity can be used as a tool of neoliberal governance within HEIs, some chapters examine the politics of language in the field of diversity management. Diversity is a non-threatening or challenging word, unlike what Sara Ahmed describes as 'stickier' words, such as racism and inequality. She is critical about diversity management strategies within one UK HEI, suggesting that the term 'diversity' is used in some contexts because it is a 'cuddly term' that is non-threatening and can therefore encourage workers within HEIs to participate in this type of activity. Elsewhere in her chapter, she argues that practices of diversity within HEI organisations can reproduce violence and silencing around racism, suggesting that 'diversity becomes a technology for not hearing'. While 'diversity' is critiqued as a 'cuddly' term by Ahmed, Val Gillies (Chapter 2) argues that the slippery term 'inclusion' can likewise work to obscure power relations and reproduce inequalities within UK inner city comprehensive schools. Ahmed is critical of the way in which a superficial and cynical engagement with diversity work can appropriate and capitalise on difference to market the university as diverse 'images of "colourful" happy faces', to thereby commodify diversity as an asset, while failing to address institutional racism directly. She examines the way that diversity can be mobilised as a brand and marketing tool to add value to the institution. Her essay explores the disjuncture between the 'feel good' of marketised diversity and the failure to address institutional racism. In terms of addressing institutional inequalities directly, Shaw and Bridger argue that an approach based on 'mainstreaming' is one way of addressing inequality and diversity needs to be incorporated within all aspects of an HEI's day-to-day operation and institutional culture. They suggest that this is preferable to a strategy that focuses on providing measures targeted at specific students with additional learning needs.

The essays by Inckle, Ahmed and Addison (Chapters 9, 11 and 13) explicitly address how diversity is embodied within institutional spaces, arguing that within institutional practices of diversity management, some bodies are expected to carry the burden of diversity more than others. Diversity strategies can therefore leave some identity categories un-marked. From a Black feminist perspective, Sara Ahmed notes that certain bodies are weighed down with the institutional burden of diversity, and that in an institutional racist context Black bodies 'symbolise the hope or promise that whiteness is being undone'. Ahmed suggests that even the presence of certain bodies within HEI spaces can produce anxiety and tension and can be a source of troubling bad affect. Narrating her experience of attempting to address institutional racism within one UK HEI, she argues that her engagement with diversity work paradoxically resulted in the loss of her voice and that 'to embody diversity is to be prohibited from even speaking about racism'. Building on Ahmed's (2004) discussion of the politics of emotion, Michelle Addison's essay focuses on the classed labour practices of workers within an elite UK HEI. She argues that workers within UK HEIs have to conform to certain forms of embodied worker identities of the 'happy worker' in order to fit in to the work place, and that those who cannot conform to middle-class norms, or those who challenge inequalities directly, may be marked as troublemakers. Ahmed's and Addison's essays demonstrate that there are personal and professional costs in embodying difference in ways that do not conform to institutionally sanctioned formations of diversity. In contrast, Kay Inckle sees her own embodied identity as female, queer, disabled and 'visibly non-normative' as a pedagogic tool that can open up safe spaces for the critical discussion of difference within the classroom. She rightly acknowledges that the dangers of reifying experience of pain and being marked as non-normative can be used to silence others in the classroom environment. Drawing on queer and crip theory, she argues that her own embodiment can be a means of challenging different but intersecting forms of normativity. She suggests that the act of making the non-normative body visible within educational spaces, while not without costs, can embody the 'desire for an intimate, engaged and transformative teaching and learning experience [as a]...radical act which opens up new possibilities for knowing and being'. Inckle states that an embodied pedagogic approach to diversity entails making her vulnerable within HE teaching spaces, but she is upbeat about how this can creative possibilities to produce safe pedagogic spaces to facilitate deep learning.

A number of writers in *Educational Diversity* draw attention to the way that HEIs may mobilise certain constructions of diversity in order to capitalise on diversity. They examine how some forms of difference become valued, while others are excluded and pathologised as troubling and abnormal. In her essay on behaviour support units (BSUs) in British inner city comprehensive schools, Val Gillies (Chapter 2) argues that these units are a means of addressing and containing 'troublesome difference', with pupils removed from mainstream classrooms with the aim of making them 'includable'. She claims that, despite the rhetoric of inclusion, the individualistic therapeutic framework mobilised within these units can pathologise certain forms of difference that are treated as abnormal. For example, she notes how the behaviour of one male student whose interest in cheerleading transgressed gendered norms was labelled as 'eccentric and socially incongruous'. Michelle Addison's essay examines questions of value and how the intensification of neoliberalism within UK HEIs has led to the greater valuing of elite worker identities. Likewise, Sarah Evans (Chapter 6) examines how applicants to university from working-class backgrounds navigate the admissions process – through the writing of the personal statement on their application forms, how they try to communicate their extra-curricular activities and how they present themselves at interview. The students in her study were often unclear about how to fit their life experiences into successful narratives that would impress university admission tutors and help to gain admission into elite HEIs. She argues that while university admission tutors are meant to take the class backgrounds of applicants into account, the process still often favours the possession of certain forms of cultural capital and works to the disadvantage of working-class students, particularly those who seek to maintain their authenticity as working class.

Some essays explicitly engage with the politics of emotions and affect. In doing so, they make extensive reference to Sara Ahmed's (2004) pioneering work on the politics of emotion. For instance, Michelle Addison notes how 'class can be a raw emotional process' for the respondents in her study of class and value in UK HEIs. Gillies' essay draws attention to the way that emotions have become a subject of study within UK schools with an emphasis on teaching students to manage their emotions. Her study of BSUs in three UK inner city comprehensive schools demonstrates how this focus on emotional literacy and what she terms 'psychologised assessments of personal competence and wellbeing' can occlude explicit addressing of wider social, economic contexts that structure and frame student conduct. Interviews with teachers working in BSUs showed that the therapeutic focus on emotional regulation of the individual meant that institutional barriers to learning and structures of racism, sexism and homophobia were often overlooked in attempts to understand disruptive behaviour, meaning that policies aimed at inclusion led to further exclusion. Worse still, Gillies argues, BSUs often reproduced racialised and gendered narratives about students whose conduct they sought to regulate.

The role played by space and place in the governance of embodied difference and the practice of diversity management is a theme of a number of essays in this book. For instance, in her Foucauldian examination of the history of deaf education in the Irish Republic, Elizabeth S. Mathews (Chapter 4) shows how in the post-war period the classification of students led to the spatial separation of partially deaf and profoundly deaf students. In one school, these two sets wore different uniforms and were taught in separate parts of the building. She argues that the contemporary practice of mainstreaming deaf and hard-of-hearing children without sufficient resources to support their learning through the use of sign language may be the ultimate step in their subjectification.

These essays are predominantly written from a UK or Irish perspective. However, we need to recognise how debates on diversity play out in different contexts. This is important because, as Damien W. Riggs argues in a discussion of pedagogy and the colonisation of indigenous land in South Australia (Chapter 12), where we literally stand can itself be highly contested. Yu-Chieh Hsieh, talking about policies to address inequalities around gender and sexuality in Taiwanese schools (Chapter 5), is one of the few contributors to address educational diversity from a non-UK or non-Irish perspective. Her valuable insights, such as that boys were seen as higher achievers than girls, run counter to research on educational diversity in Western contexts. Hsieh's essay demonstrates that the need for more comparative work in the area of educational diversity could add much to the thoughtful discussions of educational diversity in this collection. More analysis is needed of how policies towards diversity management travel across national borders and across different scales of policy making more generally. The critical study of diversity management within HE could benefit from taking on board Nina Glick-Schiller and Ayse Caglar's (2009) critique of what they term 'methodological nationalism', by which they mean the narrow, exclusive focus on the nation-state as a container for social processes. Methodological nationalism may curtail the possibilities for insights that could be learned from comparison with elsewhere and how policies and practices of diversity management travel from one geographical, political context to another. Internationalisation is a key policy focus of many UK HEIs that also relates to diversity (Brooks and Waters, 2009). It would be productive to interrogate the strategic goal of internationalisation alongside questions of equality and diversity, and how HEI policies in these areas may dovetail, or be in conflict.

The collected essays in this volume constitute a form of a coalitional politics of solidarity by critiquing and challenging discourses of diversity management in different contexts. These essays examine class, gender, race, sexuality and disability, often from an explicit intersectional approach. However, it would also be productive for future research in this area to more explicitly engage with questions of age, generation and the lifecourse, as in the UK there is evidence to suggest that the changing fees regime in HE is leading to the further exclusion of mature students from HE spaces. *Educational Diversity* is a timely and critical intervention into debates on social justice and the future direction of education. The essays in this collection will provoke and inspire those working in education to rethink and transform their pedagogical practices and working environments.

References

Ahmed, S. (2004) *The Cultural Politics of Emotion*. Edinburgh: Edinburgh University Press.

Brooks, R. and Waters, J. (2009) International higher education and the mobility of UK students. *Journal of Research in International Education*, 8(2): 191–209.

Glick Schiller, N. and Caglar, A. (2009) Towards a comparative theory of locality in migration studies: Migrant incorporation and city scale. *Journal of Ethnic and Migration Studies*, 35: 177–202.

Contributors

Michelle Addison is a final-year PhD student (funded by the Economic and Social Research Council (ESRC)) at Newcastle University and a visiting scholar at the Weeks Centre for Social and Policy Research, London South Bank University. Her research explores the classed and gendered contours of employees' workplace experiences as they come to be mediated, expressed and realised through emotion. Her study looks at workplace identity (re)formation, (mis)recognition and resistance, querying which identities come to be valued and rewarded while drawing attention to those who are silenced and marginalised. Previously, Michelle worked as a researcher in the private sector and as a research assistant on the ESRC-funded study 'From the coal to the car park?' with Yvette Taylor (see Taylor, Y. and Addison, M. (2011) Placing Research: 'City Publics' and the 'Public Sociologist'. *Sociological Research Online* **6(4)**). Michelle co-authored (Re)constituting the past, (re)branding the present and (re)imagining the future: women's spatial negotiation of gender and class. *Journal of Youth Studies*, Special Issue Young People, Class and Space **12(5)**: 563–578 (2009) and co-edited (with Yvette Taylor) the 2010 special issue of *Journal of International Women's Studies*. She is currently working with Yvette on a co-edited book entitled *Queer Presences and Absences* (forthcoming, Palgrave Macmillan).

Sara Ahmed is Professor of Race and Cultural Studies at Goldsmiths College. She works at the intersection of feminist, queer, critical race and postcolonial theory. Her publications include: *Differences that Matter: Feminist Theory and Postmodernism* (1998); *Strange Encounters: Embodied Others in Post-Coloniality* (2000); *The Cultural Politics of Emotion* (2004); *Queer Phenomenology: Orientations, Objects, Others* (2006); *The Promise of Happiness* (2010) and *On Being Included: Racism and Diversity in Institutional Life* (2012). She is currently working on a book on the will and willfulness.

Kimberly Allen is a senior research fellow at the Institute for Policy Studies in Education at London Metropolitan University. A sociologist of education, she is interested broadly in educational inequalities, but with a particular focus on young people's career aspirations and transitions, and how these are shaped by social class, gender, 'race' and place. She has researched and written about issues of exclusion, equality and diversity in the creative industries. Her doctoral research (funded by the Arts and Humanities Research Council) explored young women's experiences of performing arts education and their aspirations for employment in the creative industries. Kim has also written about the relationship between celebrity culture, young people's educational identities, and classed and gendered regimes of selfhood. She has worked on and led a number of research projects on educational inequalities funded by government, local authorities and charities. With Professor Jocey Quinn, Kim co-directs the Economic and Social Research Council funded seminar series 'New Perspectives on Education and Culture' (http://educationandculture.wordpress.com/).

Jon Binnie is a reader in human geography at Manchester Metropolitan University. His research interests focus on the geographies of sexualities in the urban and transnational context. He is the author of *The Globalization of Sexuality* (Sage, 2004), *The Sexual Citizen: Queer Politics and Beyond* (with David Bell, 2000) and *Pleasure Zones: Bodies, Cities, Spaces* (with David Bell, Ruth Holliday, Robyn Longhurst and Robin Peace, 2001). He is also the editor of *Cosmopolitan Urbanism* (with Julian Holloway, Steve Millington and Craig Young, 2006) and is currently completing a monograph on transnational activism and sexual politics in central and eastern Europe with Christian Klesse.

Kath Bridger is a director of BSV Associates Ltd, a company that she founded with her colleague Jenny Shaw in 2009, providing independent research and consultancy support to the HE sector. She worked previously as Director of Access and Widening Participation at the University of Bradford, and Diversity and Business Manager for the Open University, as well as in a number of senior roles in widening participation, including Regional Director for Aimhigher across the Yorkshire and Humber Region. Kath led the UK-wide Higher Education Academy-funded study 'Mainstreaming widening participation and promoting student diversity: What can be learned from a business case approach?' (2006), and wrote the resulting toolkit for UK institutions. She was subsequently the research partner to the HE Academy Change Programme 'Developing and Embedding Inclusive Policy and Practice in Higher Education' (2010), which worked with ten institutions to mainstream inclusive policy and practice. Most recently, she has worked with Supporting Professionalism in Admissions, researching the relationship between widening participation, contextual data and fair admissions practice. She is an expert in diversity issues and has provided strategic advice to a range of organisations to support their diversity aims. Her area of interest is in identifying and supporting the implementation of tools and techniques that result in improved equality outcomes and inclusive practice in the HE and further education sectors.

Sarah Evans is Engagement Development Manager for Social Sciences at the British Library. In this post she works with curators to promote the value of the social science collections to academics and members of the public through collaborative research, projects and events. She is particularly interested in the oral histories, magazines and zines held at the British Library. Sarah is also a sociologist and completed her PhD at the University of Kent in 2008. Her thesis examined the aspirations of a group of young, educationally successful working-class women. Her interests include social class, psychosocial methods, feminism, intimate relationships and education. She lives in London with her partner and young son.

Val Gillies is Professor of Social Research and a co-director of the Families and Social Capital Research Group, Weeks Centre for Social and Policy Research, London South Bank University. She has researched and published in the areas of family, social class and at-risk youth, producing a range of journal articles and book chapters on parenting, social policy and home school relations as well as qualitative research methods. She has also written *Marginalised Mothers: Exploring Working Class Parenting* (2007). Current projects include ESRC research with secondary-level pupils at risk of school exclusion, and a historical comparison of accounts of parenting from the 1960s.

Ian Hodges is a senior lecturer in psychology at the University of Westminster and teaches psychotherapy and counselling, critical psychology, qualitative research methods, psychology of sexuality and social psychology. He studied psychology and sociology at the University of Reading and undertook his PhD research at Goldsmiths College, London, supervised by Professor Nikolas Rose. His thesis (1998) was entitled 'A Problem Aired: Exploring Radio Therapeutic Discourse and Ethical Self-formation'. He has a longstanding interest in psychotherapy and counselling, especially in relation to the lack of clients' and patients' voices in research and the use of constructionist and narrative approaches in psychotherapeutic practice. He is also committed to documenting and understanding the experience of minority students in HE and works with colleagues as part of the Westminster Diversity in Education Research group. He has undertaken training in group analysis and psychoanalysis, and he is currently training in existential psychotherapy and counselling. Ian has been a member of the British Psychological Society (BPS) Standing Committee for the Promotion of Equal Opportunities and Treasurer for the BPS Psychology of Sexualities Section.

Sumi Hollingworth is a senior research fellow at the Institute for Policy Studies in Education at London Metropolitan University. Working at the nexus of sociology, geography and youth studies, she researches inequalities of social class, race and gender in education. She has a particular interest in young people's educational transitions and access to work and career opportunities, and has a commitment to feminist research practice. She is a co-author of *Urban Youth and Schooling* (2010) with Louise Archer and Heather Mendick.

Yu-Chieh Hsieh is an assistant professor in the Department of Geography at Chinese Culture University, Taiwan. She completed her PhD at Loughborough University, UK. As a graduate student of the Graduate Institute of Building and Planning in National Taiwan University, she was involved in research projects on urban planning, the sex industry and education policy. After completing her graduate study, she was a hig-school teacher in Taiwan for two years (2003–2005). This inspired her PhD project entitled 'Gender Equity Education in Taiwan: Policy, Schooling, and Young People's Identities'. Her thesis explores the intersection of the role of education, young people's agency, and the formation of their gender and sexual identities in the Taiwanese policy context. Her current research interests focus on geographies of education, young people, and gender and sexuality.

Kay Inckle runs practitioner courses and is currently writing her third book, *Safe with Self-Injury: A Practical Guide to Understanding, Responding and Risk Reduction*, to be published in 2012. Recent publications include: The first cut is the deepest: A harm-reduction approach to self-injury. *Social Work in Mental Health* **9(5)**: 364–378 (2011); Scarred for life: Women's creative self-journeys through stigmatised embodiment. *Somatechnics* 1(2): 315–333 (2011); and, with Andrew Sparkes and James Brighton, A cripp(l)ing blow: Disability, sex and sport, in Jennifer Hargreaves and Eric Anderson (eds), *Routledge Handbook of Sport, Gender & Sexuality* (forthcoming).

Sanjay Jobanputra is a senior lecturer in psychology at the University of Westminster. He is also the course leader for the part-time psychology pathway. His teaching includes modules on prejudice, counselling and consciousness. He completed his first degree in psychology in 1985. After receiving his MSc and CQSW from Royal Holloway and Bedford New College (University of London) in 1989, he worked in a number of community-based projects as a drug worker, alcohol advisory worker and HIV/AIDS social worker. Within the context of identity politics and giving voice, Sanjay's PhD explored the experiences of Black and minority ethnic students studying psychology in HE. He has continued research in this area over the past 20 years and has spoken regularly at conferences. He delivered a number of workshops for lecturers on the theme of diversity in the classroom, organised by the Higher Education Academy. He was also an invited keynote speaker at the Psychology for All educational conference in 2009. Sanjay has been on a path of conscious self-development for more than two decades. He is involved with the Academy of Self Knowledge, which focuses on the contemporary relevance and application of wisdom teachings for self-knowledge and self-transformation. This broad interest is also reflected in his current research, which explores the relationship between mindfulness, life satisfaction and self-efficacy.

Elizabeth S. Mathews is an associate lecturer at the Institute of Technology, Tallaght, where she teaches social care practice degree students a variety of subjects, including applied sociology, research methodology and disability studies. She is also the current coordinator of the Deaf Education Centre in Dublin. This is a new initiative aimed at providing information, advice and support to members of the deaf community, parents and professionals on all aspects of deafness as they relate to education. It also has a research remit to investigate and contribute to educational attainment for deaf and hard-of-hearing children. She is a graduate of the National University of Ireland. In 2005 she travelled to Washington DC to undertake a master's in deaf education at Gallaudet University, sponsored by the Fulbright Deaf Studies programme. Returning to Ireland, she commenced a PhD with the National Institute for Regional and Spatial Analysis and the Geography Department at National University of Ireland, Maynooth. Her thesis was titled 'Mainstreaming of Deaf Education in the Republic of Ireland: Language, Power, Resistance' (2011). She recently wrote the 'Proposal for Access to Initial Teacher Education for Deaf and Hard of Hearing People' and is working closely with the Department of Education and Skills in Ireland to create the first training programme for deaf people to become primary school teachers.

Jocey Quinn is a professor of education at the University of Plymouth. Her key research interest is the inter-relationship between education and culture. She is particularly interested in both HE and the learning that takes place outside formal education: in community contexts, in the home, at work, in creative activities, in nature, and in volunteering and activism. Her work has focused on lifelong learning and issues of social exclusion and knowledge transformation, exploring changes in what counts for knowledge and who has access to it. Recent publications include *Learning Communities and Imagined Social Capital: Learning to Belong* (2010), *Powerful Subjects: Are Women Really Taking Over the University?* (2003) and *Education and Culture* (forthcoming). She has led a range of national and international research projects funded by research councils, major charities and government bodies. Her current work includes co-ordinating the ESRC seminar series 'New Perspectives on Education and Culture' (http://educationandculture. wordpress.com/).

Diane Reay is a professor of education in the Faculty of Education, University of Cambridge, with particular interests in social justice issues in education, Pierre Bourdieu's social theory, and cultural analyses of social class. She has researched extensively in the areas of social class, gender and ethnicity across primary, secondary and post-compulsory stages of education. Recent funded research projects include primary–secondary school transfer, choice of HE, pupil consultation and voice, working-class students in HE, and White middle-classes and comprehensive schooling. She is currently focusing on issues around social mobility and what constitutes a socially just educational system. Her most recent book (with Gill Crozier and David James) is *White Middle Class Identities and Urban Schooling* (2011).

Damien W. Riggs is a senior lecturer in social work at Flinders University, where he teaches gender and sexuality, mental health and child protection. He is the author of over 100 publications in these areas (and their intersections), with titles including *What about the Children! Masculinities, Sexualities and Hegemony* (2010) and (with Clemence Due) *Representations of Indigenous Australians in the Mainstream News Media* (2011). He is the editor of the *Gay and Lesbian Issues and Psychology Review*, a publication of the Australian Psychological Society.

Anthea Rose is a research fellow at the Institute for Policy Studies in Education at London Metropolitan University. Her research background spans the education sector, from compulsory schooling to adult education. She has a particular interest in the role that education plays in promoting social justice and inclusion for those often excluded, such as lone parents, BME groups and those from the Traveller, Gypsy and Roma communities. She is specifically interested in issues of gender, the family, literacy, technology and education. She has worked on a range of projects covering diverse educational policy areas, such as school improvement initiatives, school leaders in international development, the use of technology in schools to support parental engagement, the role of supplementary schools in raising achievement for underperforming groups and the implications of the Prevent agenda in further education. Anthea has published widely for a range of audiences: academic, practitioners and policy. She has also carried out cross-disciplinary research in the community, voluntary and third sector, and criminology.

Jenny Shaw is currently Head of Higher Education Engagement for the UNITE Group, a trustee of the UNITE Foundation and an associate director for BSV Associates Ltd, having worked in the UK HE sector for 16 years. She has held senior widening participation and strategic partnership roles at three institutions and has acted as a consultant to several others. During her career she has spearheaded a number of leading-edge initiatives for institutions across the diversity of the UK sector. At Middlesex University she helped to develop the institution's strategic approach to work with business and the community, developing innovative new curriculum offers attractive to a broader range of the regional population. Later, at York St John University, she led the Aimhigher programme for York and North Yorkshire. Her most recent full-time appointment was as Director of the Yorkshire and Humber East

Lifelong Learning Network based at the University of Hull. She has since worked as a consultant with the Equality Challenge Unit, Supporting Professionalism in Admissions, the Higher Education Academy and JISC Techdis. Jenny has also worked extensively with the voluntary and community sectors, specialising in strategic support for community-based and grass-roots organisations. As well as contributing to practitioner and academic journals, she has presented at a number of international conferences, contributing to edited collections on the subject of widening participation and student diversity. She was an editor of the European Access Network's newsletter for five years.

Vanita Sundaram is a lecturer in education at the University of York. Her areas of research interest and expertise broadly cover issues of inequality, rights and inclusion. More specifically, her work deals with factors influencing access to and participation in education, including gender, sexuality, trauma and disability. She has recently completed research on young people's understandings of violence and implications for school-based violence prevention. She is currently working on projects related to anti-violence and sex education, gendered learner identities and academic motivation, and the role of religion and ethnicity in community cohesion. She supervises doctoral projects on women in leadership positions in HE; the experiences of lesbian, gay, bisexual and transgender students in HE; and the professional inclusion of internationally educated teachers in the UK.

Yvette Taylor is Professor in Social and Policy Studies and Head of the Weeks Centre, London South Bank University. She has held a Fulbright Scholarship at Rutgers University (2010–2011) and the Lillian Robinson Fellowship at Concordia University (2009). Her books include *Working-Class Lesbian Life: Classed Outsiders* (2007), *Lesbian and Gay Parenting: Securing Social and Educational Capitals* (2009) and *Fitting into Place? Class and Gender Geographies and Temporalities* (2012). Edited collections include *Classed Intersections: Spaces, Selves, Knowledges* (2010), (with S. Hines and M. Casey) *Theorizing Intersectionality and Sexuality* (2010) and (with S. Hines) *Sexualities: Reflections and Futures* (2012). She has published articles in a range of journals, including *British Journal of the Sociology of Education, European Societies, Sociological Research Online, Sexualities, Feminist Theory.* Yvette is currently working on an ESRC standard grant 'Making space for queer identifying religious youth'.

Alison Wilde is a lecturer in education at Bangor University. Her primary research interests are related to two main areas: educational inclusion and disability; and the depiction and reception of images of disability and gender in a range of popular media, including film, television and children's literature. She has researched and published on disability, soap opera/television drama, celebrity and reality TV, audience and identity, gender, educational inclusion, disabled families, disability and pregnancy, social care and research methods. She is currently supervising MA dissertations in areas related to inclusion and accreditations of special education need and in disabled people's access to dramatic arts. She is currently working on projects related to disability culture/arts and disabling cultures in schools.

1
Educational Diversity: The Subject of Difference and Different Subjects

Yvette Taylor

'Diversity' has become a key term in contemporary social theory, politics and practice and is often used as both a description of complex social realities and a prescription for how those realities should be valued, assessed and managed. In considering diversity in education, this collection of essays explores the relationship between new equality regimes and continued societal inequalities, exploring change, ambivalence and resistance as negotiated, lived-in and differently inhabited in and through policies, institutional practices and everyday interpersonal encounters. Legislative requirements sit alongside easy rhetorics and uneasy realities. The New Labour UK government (1997–2010) recognised and formalised six equality strands (age, disability, religion, race, sexual orientation and gender) with fresh legislation that addressed equality issues (Equality Act, 2010)[1]: these are negotiated at the EU level and, indeed, internationally, with a raft of recent 'diversity' legislation reconfiguring mainstreamed-marginalised identities. Yet these strands of equality and diversity are threatened in a climate of welfare cut-backs, economic crisis and an overhauling of higher education. As 'diversity' is increasingly invoked in changing educational landscapes, it is pulled in different directions: as capital, cure, caveat and check. We hear how diverse institutions can respond to tough times of educational cut-backs and economic crisis, to buffer their diverse subjects, as resilient, capacitated future-workers. These pronouncements frequently invoke a sentiment of 'to be improved', as a rejection of elitism via 'internationalisation' and 'widening participation', whereby students are propelled into diverse, enhanced futures (Taylor and Allen, 2011). Diversity stories and sentiments are told despite the reality of unequal opportunities, entries and futures.

Widening participation in higher education is now used to justify maximum top-up fees (e.g. 2010 Browne Report in the UK; European Union's 2020 Strategy, see Taylor and Scurry, 2011). Diversity is promised and praised in the carving out of another market as a showcase of inclusiveness, extending the call for the 'non-traditional' to participate. But the massive price-tag signals the insincerity of such attempts. The National Scholarship Programme as a Conservative-Liberal invention which provides (limited) bursaries to stimulate participation from 'disadvantaged' groups does not alter overwhelmingly middle-class, white compositions. There exists an uncomfortable conflation and separation between groups of pupils, students and staff who are, on the one hand, problematically held up as embodying diversity while, on the other, required to change, adapt and become 'traditional' somehow at 'home' in the educational setting. Certain groups are both invested with a hopeful potential in standing for and embodying institutional initiatives while still being positioned as deficit and failing, manifest in linguistic, material and cultural (in)competencies (Evans, 2010; Wakeling, 2010; Allen and Taylor, 2011). We witness this on the now happy included 'diverse' student on certain university webpages, which, like a Benetton advert, seemingly represents institutional success at 'doing' diversity (Ahmed, 2009). This is impossible for many post-1992 universities to do precisely because there is no singular measure or embodiment of diversity. Instead, diversity is a lived-in reality, a sound and sense in and around campus rather than something which can be captured and displayed for use (Taylor, 2011a).

This necessitates comparisons between different educational structures, spaces and subjects in changing times, with neutralising neoliberal language encouraging students to invest in their own futures, building their individual human capital as 'responsible', accumulating subjects, rather than as members of groups that are differently able to do this. For example, university education is still marketed as the correct choice to make for those who want to better themselves, highlighted in the 'Aimhigher' programme, run by the Department for Education and Skills under the previous UK New Labour government. In asking socially disadvantaged people to 'aim higher', such policies reproduce a narrow focus on dispositions and attitudes, decontextualising continued embedded institutional inequalities as attitudes and ambitions. This is a heightened tension in a climate of tuition fee increases, where students are to invest in their own futures and manage their debts (Taylor, 2008; Evans, 2010). Non-traditional students, subjects and even staff are to prove their new viability to endure, reshaping the university as an agent in the production and mobilisation of better social futures (including, it would seem, as a regenerator of the city, the public and the economy; see Taylor, 2011b).

At the same time as expanding and securing undergraduates, universities now support large numbers of postgraduate students and postdoctoral research staff, seeking – and being compelled – to 'become' in higher education. In new funding regimes we hear of 'at risk' institutions, redundancies, short(er)-term contracts, increased teaching and administration, and fewer research opportunities. Like undergraduate students, staff groups inhabit (and constitute) the university in overlapping waves of fixed and short-term populations, which are increasingly diverse in terms of class, gender, ethnicity and nationality (Ahmed, 2008; Wakeling, 2010). And where there is a generalised uncertainly about the prospects of universities, it seems that 'failures' recast certain futures, as the 'top universities' and 'top students' are seen to come forward as resilient and able to deal with the blows. In doing so, certain claims may be cemented, where the 'shake-up' – the 'rise to the top' and the 'fall to the bottom' – implies a natural order of the good and the bad university. The talented student, like the talented university, is often seen to be able to choose a path through precariousness, to carve out a new, even more deserving, position. They can cope, the resilient and enterprising worker, the able university – a simple 'scientific fact' of league tables. Being 'good enough', even 'better than', shapes and structures the kinds of politics, performances and investments that are possible.

Educational regimes bring into effect specific institutional practices and procedures, as well as particular identities and materialities. The 'when' of diversity, as timed in heightened policy debates and changing educational marketplaces, also involves a 'where' in locating these shifts in particular international landscapes. This collection places current considerations of diversity within different changing contexts of education from the UK, Ireland, Australia and Taiwan. These perspectives aim to situate discussion of diversity across time and place – including discussion of who is diverse, the feeling of diversity, legislating for diversity and enabling diverse pedagogies – interrogating the sites and subjects of 'difference' as monitored, managed and materialised. In extending the focus to include compulsory and post-compulsory education, there is recognition of the interconnectedness of these realms, from classroom contexts into employment experiences, as echoed in the focus on experiences of staff, students and pupils.

In operating a critical approach to 'diversities', as they become plu-ralised in policy yet divided in everyday realities, this book probes beyond the boundaries of specific territorial-legislative domains in order to develop a more international, intersectional focus. While new urgent contexts are foregrounded in discussing the demands, divisions and desires for 'diversity', the authors aim to historically situate these: varied 'differences' come with different purchase, visibility and recog-nition. In combining an intersectional focus on strands of equality and diversity – often listed as, for example, gender, sexuality, race, religion, age, disability – a fuller recognition of lived experience and multiple axes of inequality is implied (Taylor et al., 2010). Yet contributors show that these strands can be competing and even colliding, (dis)orienting educational users, environments and outcomes as educational hierar-chies are reworked rather than erased. Indeed, discourses about gender, sexuality, race and class inequality have been both mainstreamed and effaced within politics and public policy where debate about the effects of race and class inequalities in particular is seemingly considered to be anachronistic, replaced with words like 'social exclusion', 'inclusion' and 'diversity' (Adkins, 2000).

From varying and critical interdisciplinary perspectives, contributors ask: How is 'diversity' being responded to, managed and perhaps even marketed? Who and what has to change to be included? Can 'diversity' be capitalised upon as a productive difference or a tokenistic dividend; what does it produce and for whom or what? How might divisions be re-inscribed across time and place in the pluralisation of 'diversities'? If diversity is something to be 'added in', involving a change on the part of the educational 'outsider', how might the institutionally included be the subject of 'diversity'? These questions sit beyond legislative provisioning and institutional tick-lists, where white middle-classness, heterosexuality and able-bodiedness are frequently left unproblema-tised, not the subject *of* diversity but simply subject *to* diversity (see Byrne, 2006; Back, 2007; Reay et al., 2011). In addressing these concep-tual and methodological questions, the authors seek to situate journeys and experiences in and beyond education. Our (non)-academic selves, subject matters and senses of education are complicated in retelling the inside in and through a sense of the outside: the proximity and dis-tance of the elite university to the 'local' city; the rhetorical appeal of 'widening participation' and the reality of elitism; the drive of public engagement and the economies of use and impact; and the complex-ities and complicities of power, privilege and (dis)engagement (Taylor and Addison, 2011).

In Section 1, 'Compulsory Education, Compelling Diversity', contributors situate the initiatives, practices and policies in different compulsory education settings. Pupils designated with 'behavioural problems' and 'special needs' are held up as now 'included', as part of a diverse classroom setting. This occurs even as their specific needs are unmet – as they are mainstreamed to 'fit', made to work on transforming their feelings, their senses and even their bodies to fit with schooling practices that welcome the articulate, unemotional, able-bodied and properly gendered pupil. Some pupils are positioned as more excessive and disruptive than others, with schools intervening to enforce a heteronormative order in policing pupils' gender and sexual identities even in the context of diversity legislation. Schools put into force the categories of class and race, entrenching these in expectations of and entitlements in the good and bad pupil.

Val Gillies opens with Chapter 2, ' "Inclusion" through exclusion: a critical account of new behaviour management practices in schools' looking at self-contained onsite units increasingly set up by schools as a method of dealing with challenging behaviour in the classroom. Such initiatives draw heavily on a rhetoric of inclusion despite the fact that attendees are removed from mainstream classrooms and literally put on the outside. It is uncomfortably unsurprising that it is pupils from black and minority ethnic populations who sit in this inside-outside space. Gillies argues that this management of pupils focuses not on structural inequalities as reproduced in educational environments but rather on the troublesome pupil. By virtue of learning how to command their emotions, the school pupil is charged with individually combating institutional racism and socially embedded divisions. This personal change as replacement for social change has the effect of restigmatising groups as disordered and pathological, violently pushed to the margins while signifying an institutional 'diversity'.

In Chapter 3, 'Investigating the value of vignettes in researching disabled students' views of social equality and inclusion in school, Vanita Sundaram and Alison Wilde explore how best, to hear the voices of young people with a range of 'special educational needs' and how to represent the views of these young people, with particular reference to their experiences of equity in school. As with the Chapter 2, the authors assert that educational environments are 'disabling' and fail to provide for the needs of those positioned as 'special'. The category of 'special' places the failure upon the learner rather than on the educational institution. Challenging this, a reconceptualisation of 'unmet educational needs', as against a designation of pupils with 'special educational needs', is proposed. Rather than locating obstacles to achievement in the young people themselves, these are resituated within the policies, organisation, practices and pedagogies deployed in schools. As well as reorientating considerations of difference and need back onto educational practices, this chapter discusses the methodological considerations in capturing and representing young people's voices and accounts of marginalisation.

Elizabeth Mathews in Chapter 4, 'Mainstreaming and the subjectification of deaf and hard-of-hearing children' continues to explore what amount to rather uneasy inclusions based on changing the damaged and/or diseased body, rather than the educational environment itself. As with the Chapter 3, students are made to 'fit in' and are celebrated as 'mainstreamed' when the work of adaptation fits with expectations of leading a 'normal' life. This is explored in relation to provision of deaf education in Ireland, which is now based on deaf pupils' ability to 'perform' as hearing children, linked to their ability to speak and speech-read rather than to sign. Again we witness the role of school as a normalising space: since the goal of education is inclusion, and speech skills are linked to the inclusion of deaf children, the education system disciplines through integration. Mathews explores the spatialisation of integration and segregation, with the emphasis on including deaf students alongside their hearing peers but only if they perform as hearing children. Deaf children without these skills are rarely meaningfully included in mainstream classrooms and continue to be segregated. The very practice of mainstreaming deaf education in Ireland stifles ways of communicating, forcing standard practices against a diversity of needs and ways of communicating. Again we witness the 'unmet needs' of school pupils.

In Chapter 5, 'Shaping young people's gender and sexual identities: can teaching practices produce diverse subjects?' Yu-Chieh Hsieh explores unmet needs in relation to changing legislative provisions which aim to standardise a duty of care and a sense of good practice. This is discussed in relation to the Gender Equity Education Act (GEEA) in Taiwan (2004), which aimed to eliminate discrimination against people's gender identities as well as diverse sexualities in educational spaces. This act, like the raft of European Equalities legislation, offers a space to challenge traditional gender and sexual norms by acknowledging the transformative role of education upon young people's identity formation. Yet this laudable aim is not always followed through in practice, as Hsieh demonstrates via case studies of two senior high schools. Contradictory attitudes to the GEEA are demonstrated among the teachers responsible for implementing it. Teachers still seek to shape young people's gender and sexual identities in the classroom by constructing particular forms of masculinity and femininity, and of gay and lesbian identities. Such reshaping in the context of supposed transformation highlights restricted understandings of gender and sexuality, and the closing down of space through which to produce and support diverse gender and sexual subjects. The spatial dimension of this is accounted for in the very architecture, classrooms and corridors charged with fostering and shaping a diversity of styles, subjects and subjectivities, yet which often fail to deliver as heavily monitored and circumscribed spaces.

Section 2: 'Higher Education, Higher Standards?' attends to post-compulsory educational settings and considers issues of access to higher education, institutional obligations and processes, and the experiences of staff and students as learners and employees. In those different positions, students and staff are again variously placed, recognised and rewarded. Again, classed, gendered and racialised processes intersect with institutional provision and failure; they shape interpersonal accounts and experiences of, for example, seminar interactions, curricular coverage, debt acquisition and choice of university. Contributors in this section convey the ways in which higher education does not necessarily involve higher standards with regard to the recognition of diverse student and staff bodies. Indeed, it is often the working-class, black and minority ethnic body that is positioned as *doing* and highlighting the success of diversity – as a burden which attaches to them, while being celebrated by others in finger-pointing this away from themselves. Elite, white middle-class institutions are also now measured and made to prove their worth. However, any embarrassment of being elite seems not to attach but to travel, while the shame of 'failure' fixes, exposes and becomes your 'choice' and your trajectory.

In Chapter 6 'Unpicking that "something special": student background and the university application process', Sarah Evans examines how young working-class university applicants interpret and perform talent in the University Central Admissions System (UCAS) statements and interviews. At a time when students are encouraged and, perhaps, required to stand out from the crowd, Evans raises questions about how 'talent' is recognised, read and performed in ways which may reproduce – rather than diminish – inequalities in educational access. Her chapter questions the drive to widen access by taking background into account, with admissions officers and broader university administrative structure able to pause on and consider 'talent', 'aptitude' and 'potential' as well as qualifications. For some, this is an opening, a way of looking beyond formal grades. But university applicants are, it seems, being assessed in ways which are still tied to embedded assumptions about class, ethnicity and gender. The 'something special' that elite universities in particular look for is difficult to name and unpick; individual and institutional prejudices are disguised as preferences and even as competencies in the ability to select qualities of a person-in-training ready to become the good graduate. It is also, as we know, difficult for 'non-traditional' cohorts to recognise themselves as possessing 'something special'. Thus the diverse 'mix' advocated in taking account of background and potential becomes a liberal cover which fails to acknowledge the ways in which gender, class and ethnicity shape young people's higher education engagements.

Institutional failures are positioned alongside successes in Chapter 7 'Beyond "Inclusion": mainstreaming equality within the curriculum', by Kath Bridger and Jenny Shaw, who continue to dissect the diversity of the student body. Rather than being embedded in educational practice, 'inclusion' is often positioned as an extra, as a tokenistic nod which is rather grudgingly made and often underfunded. That said, different institutions – from 'elite' Russell group UK universities to post-1992 universities – are very differently placed in negotiating the diversity in and through their institutions (Taylor and Allen, 2011). For some, it can be a marketable deflection and capitalisation upon elitism (a new form of 'diverse elitism'), while for others it can be an uneasy negotiation of different routes into and through university. Issues and negotiations around part-time work, debt and dropping out impact on the 'good' story of diversity which, after all, involves a middle-class individualised trajectory of becoming. More optimistically, the authors highlight the benefits of a diverse student body for staff and students. Fostering a commitment to diversity produces a positive institutional culture: examples of the success of this are important in unpacking structural dynamics across different higher educational institutions and in different disciplines.

In Chapter 8 'Mapping Exclusion in Undergraduate Psychology: Towards a Common Architecture of the Minority Student Experience', Ian Hodges and Sanjay Jobanputra continue to interrogate the 'student experience'. This experience is receiving more attention as universities compete globally to provide the best, most mixed, diverse experience. It often combines immediate social and educational skills with anticipated future employment, as well as curriculum provisions, so that students get the best content and value from their degrees. What happens, then, if you don't appear as part of that content; if you don't recognise yourself in the classroom or curriculum despite all the messages that you, too, are now included? This chapter addresses these questions within the context of the experiences of psychology students with ethnic and sexual minority identifications, such as lesbian/bisexual/gay and asian/black/mixed race, and includes attention to the intersections between these. Hodges and Jobanputra argue that both general departments and overall institutional atmospheres fail to affirm the value of minority identities. Their findings are based on psychology students' reported disillusion with the course content, which was not seen as properly reflecting the diversity of contemporary British society. As psychologists, the authors express concern for positive self-expression and self-esteem, which raises the different disciplinary perspectives on 'dealing with' diversity as an embodied affect as well as an institutionalised structure. The authors identify commonalities in the ways in which students from racialised and sexualised minority groups are positioned and framed within their teaching and learning experiences of psychology: in bringing together an intersectional focus on race and sexuality, they map the common architecture of minority students' experiences. Emotions, places and people are all part of this architecture, which solidifies in the structures of disciplines, in the signs of success and on the surface of bodies.

The pedagogical questions that Hodges and Jobanputra pose about how psychology in particular, and higher education in general, can properly and meaningfully encompass the diversity of its student population are continued in Chapter 9 'Embodying diversity: pedagogies of transformation'. Here, Inkle explores her own and students' accounts of classroom experiences. Pedagogies of progress, she suggests, come not from 'measuring and counting' forms of difference but, rather, through unashamedly embodying non-normativity as a position from which to research, learn and teach. There is a danger in being the embodiment of difference, serving to tick the list as 'one of them'. Yet Kay Inkle seeks to carve out a 'politics of hope' as energising and alternative rather than complicit and defeatist. The burdens of diversity are evidenced in career constraints and glass ceilings within 'decrepit and dysfunctional systems of hierarchy and privilege'. Subverting such dysfunctionality is tied to Inkles' multiply non-normative embodiments (disabled, queer, female, extensively tattooed and pierced) as they are tied also to students' upper middle-class and privileged backgrounds.

The responsibility for – and capitalisation from – 'diversity' is raised in Chapter 10 'Doing Diversity and Evading Equality: the case of student work placements in the creative sector' by Kimberly Allen, Jocey Quinn, Sumi Hollingworth and Anthea Rose. The authors explore work placements as an increasingly important part of the higher education learning experience and as preparation for entry into the creative sector. The highly competitive nature of this work means that students must undertake (often unpaid) work experience as a way of 'getting a foot in the door'; but the undertaking of work placements itself produces profound inequalities in the getting in the door from education to employment – or not. This chapter examines how universities support students from 'equality groups' through education and into work placements which promise to enhance their future employment prospects. These 'equality groups' are defined by the Equality Challenge Unit as disabled students, black and minority ethnic student, and students seeking to enter a labour market sector where there are significant gender imbalances. Importantly, the authors highlight the differences within and between 'equality groups', resisting a tick-box of entry as inclusion and instead investigating the ways in which some diversity can be seen as enhancing, while other points of difference are positioned as excessive and simply wrong. Race and class intersect in this (mis)positioning, and they often remain uncomfortable at the level of individual negotiation and, perhaps, compulsory capitalisation in a marketplace which attaches assets to embodied positions and performances.

The possibilities, obligations and refusals of performing the good learner, good worker and good educator are highlighted in Section 3: 'Boundary Conditions', where the boundaries of institutional change and interpersonal resistance are clarified: What should the diverse subject do, and how should they sustain an occupation of the category 'diversity' beyond individual (mis)placements? In Chapter 11 'Diversity: problems and paradoxes for black feminists', Sara Ahmed argues that we must keep and feel our 'sore points' in banging against institutional brick walls, which contain our 'arrivals' while announcing that we should be happy about our uneasy entries and existences. She specifically examines some of the problems and paradoxes of embodying organisational diversity, drawing on her experience as a black feminist and on interviews with diversity practitioners in higher education institutions. Ahmed describes diversity and difference as emotional matters: in bringing up continued institutional racism, 'bad feeling' is introduced and attached to angry black feminism. Rather than revising angry words through polite requests, she seeks to reclaim the figure of the angry black feminist, to cause trouble and to 'stay as sore as our points'.

There are, of course, real pains in those points, and efforts require resources and recognitions – sometimes we cannot travel through our pain but are immobilised by and stuck in it. We are not seen and 'they' continue to see, to showcase and speculate at us. In Chapter 12, 'Talking about 'diverse genders and sexualities' means talking about more than white middle-class queers' Damien W. Riggs attempts to resist this racist, colonial gaze. Teaching courses on sexuality and gender runs the risk of reinforcing the objectification of marginalised groups when, for example, it fails to include explicit teaching about normative identities. This chapter outlines an approach adopted within one course that encouraged students to recognise the contingency of western categories of gender and sexuality, to understand the cultural specific operations of the objectifying gaze, and to utilise 'intersectionality' as a means to understanding the multiple forces and (dis)advantages across time and place. In doing so, resistance is put up against an easy inclusion which offers coverage of 'them' while continuing to objectify and normalise. Riggs highlights how his course encourages students to adopt a critical relational account of gender and sexuality that places all experiences of embodiment in relation to one another. Nonetheless, there is a vital recognition of different positionalities rather than an equivalence whereby we all become the same 'diverse subjects'.

In Chapter 13 'Knowing your way within and across classed spaces: the (re)making and (un)doing of identities of value within higher education in the UK', Michelle Addison explores employees' emotions in the workplace, in being and doing 'diversity'. Different employees, as cleaners, administrators, managers and academics, are differently positioned in exercising and commanding proper embodied emotion in order to make claims to a valued 'professional identity'. The idea that emotions are erased, worked upon and used in exchange for value has been a key concept of longstanding and more recent feminist interventions. Addison shows how the struggle for a valued workplace identity is a classed and gendered endeavour (her 'cares', his 'professionalism'). Working on emotions in exchange for value has implications for issues of equality and diversity: inequality is translated into an individualised inability to master (her) emotions, to work on herself and 'fit in'. While some employees find themselves in a good position to make claims to a valued identity, others do not and subsequently find themselves pushed to the professional margins, silenced and rendered immobile in relation to employability. The 'sore points' of academics – as differently 'privileged' workers – are retold and resisted. Addison's chapter highlights a need to look beyond ourselves, as we negotiate the tricky issue of researchers' reflexivity in doing research diversity and being diverse. Institutional brick walls do not just surround *us*.

The issue of researchers' reflexivity and responsiveness to institutional (mis)positions is explored in Chapter 14, 'Facts, fictions, identity constrictions: sexuality, gender and class in higher education' by Yvette Taylor. Here, she aims to provide some (personal and professional) insights into the negotiation of higher education, combining classed, gendered and sexual positionings as significant to this experience. Caution is exercised in writing this piece and in negotiating what – or who – constitutes a 'useful addition' and what is seen as a personalised problem. Which versions of ourselves (sexual or classed) get to be and get to speak: who can have voice and legitimacy within this? As with previous chapters, the concern is in making visible varied stories as well as the absence of (legitimate) tales, where the 'ordinariness' of privilege can also be made evident in such articulations and silences. The complexities of 'coming out' in relation to sexuality, gender and class are explored where the constrictions of academia often mean that there is little space to do so: there are disjunctures in diversity rhetorics and realities, in 'coming out' in academia, seeking and even disrupting (un)comfortable spaces. Efforts to challenge heteronormativity within higher educational settings can themselves reveal how identity and space are mutually constituted, reconfigured and re-embedded: I come out and they, perhaps you, don't have to.

This collections hopes to offer and provoke considerations about what it would mean to open up space beyond the numerical appraisal of diversity and beyond 'exclusion through inclusion' (through announcing our arrival, potential, responsibility, choices, if only we could master our emotions, bodies, talents and even unique selling points). Recently, I decided to try to take this question of embodied inhabitation seriously in my own everyday encounters – to try to rethink the space I was in. Taking a tour around a university campus rendered many places suddenly strange: the pictorial cordon around a development site already branded the university, depicting its future and its audiences. In looking at our universities afresh, we may feel rather unfamiliar and unknowing in these architectures and brick walls: for me, the glassy transparent façade of the student services building was countered by not knowing where to go (no signage) and wondering if I was 'allowed' to be there? What happens when we walk through these spaces when we have not been targeted or selected as special, entitled and educated? What are *your* sore points and how might we walk through these spaces and subjects?

This volume offers some critical insights into who is compelled and coerced into making these journeys and who remains on the normative inside, watching diverse others and speculating at what their efforts and presence could add.

Note

1. The raft of equalities legislation includes the Sexual Offences (Amendment) Act (2000); the Adoption Act (2002); the Civil Partnership Act (2004); the Gender Recognition Act (2004); and the Equality Act (2006, 2010). Similarly, the notion of diversity informs policies and practices at a European level; 'diversity' is increasingly employed by the European Court of Human Rights to extend matters pertaining to social justice beyond those 'minority groups' previously enveloped within European equalities and diversity policy and law.

References

Adkins, L. (2000) Mobile desires: Aesthetics, sexuality and the 'lesbian' at work. *Sexualities*, 3: 201–221.

Ahmed, S. (2009) Embodying diversity: problems and paradoxes for black feminists. *Race Ethnicity and Education*, 12(1): 41–52.

Allen, K. and Taylor, Y. (2011) Failed Femininities and Troubled Mothers: Gender and the Riots. http://sociologyandthecuts.wordpress.com [accessed 5 December 2011].

Back, L. (2007) *The Art of Listening*. Oxford and New York: Berg Publishers.

Byrne, B. (2006) *White Lives: The Interplay of 'Race', Class and Gender in Everyday Life*. London and New York: Routledge.

Evans, S. (2010) Becoming 'somebody': examining class and gender through higher education. In Y. Taylor (Ed.), *Classed Intersections: Spaces, Selves, Knowledges* (pp. 53–72). Farnham: Ashgate.

Reay, D., Crozier, G. and James, D. (2011) *White Middle Class Identities and Urban Schooling*. Basingstoke: Palgrave Macmillan.

Taylor, Y. (2008) Good students, bad pupils: Constructions of 'aspiration', 'disadvantage' and social class in undergraduate-led widening participation work. *Educational Review*, 60(2): 155–168.

Taylor, Y. (Ed.) (2010) *Classed Intersections: Spaces, Selves, Knowledges*. Farnham: Ashgate.

Taylor, Y. (2011a) *Fitting into Place? Class and Gender Geographies and Temporalities*. Farnham: Ashgate.

Taylor, Y. (2011b) Accessions: Researching, designing higher education. *Gender and Education*, 23(6): 777–782.

Taylor, Y. and Addison, M. (2011) Placing research: 'City publics' and the 'public sociologist'. *Sociological Research Online*, 16(4).

Taylor, Y. and Allen, K. (2011) Sinking or Swimming? Academic Strokes, Anxious Provokes. http://sociologyandthecuts.wordpress.com/2011/11/22/

sinking-or-swimming-academic-strokes-anxious-provokes-by-yvette-taylor-and-kimberly-allen/ [accessed 5 January 2012].

Taylor, Y., Hines, S. and Casey, M. (Eds) (2010) *Theorizing Intersectionality and Sexuality.* Basingstoke: Palgrave Macmillan.

Taylor, Y. and Scurry, T. (2011) International and widening participation students' experience of higher education, UK. *European Societies,* 13(4): 583–606.

Wakeling, P. (2010) Is there such a thing as a working-class academic? In Y. Taylor (Ed.), *Classed Intersections: Spaces, Selves, Knowledges* (pp. 35–52). Farnham: Ashgate.

Section 1

Compulsory Education, Compelling Diversity

2

'Inclusion' Through Exclusion: A Critical Account of New Behaviour Management Practices in Schools

Val Gillies

Introduction

Discipline in the classroom is a perennially hot topic generating much anxiety and disapprobation. This issue has featured prominently in UK policy making in recent years and reflects a broader contemporary preoccupation with the concept of anti-social behaviour. Despite a national analysis of classroom conduct concluding that pupil behaviour remains satisfactory or better in the majority of schools (Steer, 2008), concerns are regularly stoked by high profile media stories of unruly pupils disrespecting authority, intimidating teachers and undermining the potential for willing students to learn. Anxiety over this perceived decline in classroom standards has been met with a range of high profile interventions from central government designed to strengthen the exercise of discipline in schools, giving teachers greater power to search, detain, physically restrain and exclude challenging pupils (Department for Education (DfE), 2010). Such measures also resonate with parallel concerns to raise academic standards, which have played out through an emphasis on attainment scores, exam results and school league tables.

However, institutional policy and practice frameworks for enforcing good behaviour and demonstrating academic attainment sit uneasily alongside broader commitments to promoting social justice and equality of opportunity. Extensive research conducted over many years demonstrates the extent to which the social structural categories of class, gender, race and ethnicity are implicated in educational trajectories. Children from poorer families are less likely to achieve academically than their better-off counter parts and are more likely to be perceived as disruptive in the classroom (Gillborn and Mirzra, 2000; Parsons, 1999). Official statistics detailing school exclusion rates in England and Wales are a particularly stark reminder of the significance of gender and race, with Black boys disproportionately far more likely to face this sanction (Gillborn, 2008).

Schools have long struggled to embrace diversity while delivering basic equality in learning experiences and outcomes (Clark et al., 1999; Reynolds, 2008, 2010; Vlachou, 2004). Schools have a 'duty to eliminate unlawful racial discrimination and to promote equality of opportunity and good relations between people of different groups' as part of the Race Relations Amendment Act, 2000. Yet cultural difference must be spanned to produce a common outcome of an education for all, reflecting an enduring tension between commonality and difference (Clark et al., 1999). This dilemma is most often articulated and glossed over in terms of 'inclusion', which has been placed at the heart of education policy. 'Inclusion' is a particularly slippery term that despite its origins in a radical agenda for social justice are increasingly used to describe the process by which individuals are made to fit within established institutional frameworks. As I will outline in this chapter, policies and procedures in British classrooms rely heavily on a rhetoric of inclusion to justify inherently exclusionary practices. Drawing on ethnographic research in three inner city secondary schools, I show how the notion of pastoral support has come to rest on a very particular understanding of inclusion as compensating for the personal effects of disadvantage. More specifically, I examine how internal (informal) exclusion has emerged as a solution for containing troublesome difference, with pupils removed from mainstream classrooms with the aim of making them 'includable'.

The research framework

A detailed three-year study[1] of secondary school pupils at risk of school exclusion was designed with the intention of developing a better understanding of young people who were viewed as troubling and troublesome. The research was conducted in collaboration with my colleague, Yvonne Robinson, and was based in three UK inner city comprehensive schools located in markedly disadvantaged catchment areas. Two were co-educational while the other was a single sex girls' school. The study took an ethnographic approach that involved participant observation, regular group work sessions with students as well as interviews with students, their teachers and parents (see Gillies et al., 2010a and b for further details on methods).[2]

While differences were evident across schools in terms of general ethos and specific discipline structures, each had a dedicated on-site unit designed to address persistent and serious conduct issues. The generic term Behaviour Support Unit (BSU) is used throughout this chapter to describe them, although in each school they were differently and quite distinctively named. Significantly, all three BSUs were positioned within the context of a general institutional commitment to inclusion, yet in two of the schools the BSUs were self-contained in that pupils were largely or totally removed from the mainstream school. A more integrated system had been in operation at the third school, until they also moved to a self-contained model towards the end of our research. Additionally, each school also had access to an off-site provision for pupils whose behaviour was viewed as too challenging for the BSUs. Both on-site and off-site interventions enabled the schools to manage troublesome pupils outside of the classroom without recourse to official exclusion channels. Pupils could be referred to BSUs by class teachers and, although this resulted in their effective removal from mainstream education, their status was not visible in any official statistics. Length of stay in the BSUs could vary dramatically between pupils. Some stayed weeks while for others it was years, with some spending extended periods of time moving between on-site and off-site units before they were finally officially excluded. In several cases, pupils with diagnosed special educational needs entered BSUs straight from primary level and remained there without ever troubling the mainstream school.

During our time in the schools we worked with a total of 73 BSU attendees (24 young women and 49 young men). An average of eight BSU pupils were selected by the Unit managers to take part in each group work session, ranging across each half term. These sessions were followed up with individual interviews with pupils, their parents and teachers. Participants were aged between 12 and 15 and came from a range of ethnic backgrounds including Black African and Black Caribbean, Turkish, Eastern European, South East Asian, mixed heritage and White. A majority were Black and minority ethnic and our sample closely reflected the general make up of the units in this respect. Almost all of the students lived in areas characterised by high levels of deprivation. Family incomes were generally low and housing was often extremely poor. Another important social context framing our research relates to the serious problem of teenage knife crime that areas surrounding all three schools were experiencing. Through the course of our fieldwork, three teenagers known to our research participants were fatally stabbed while several of the participants themselves were hospitalised with knife wounds. Unsurprisingly, this situation left pupils frightened and anxious. Those travelling some distance across different boroughs to school were among the most vulnerable with some being actively targeted by elders of criminal gangs offering substantial wages and crucial protection for regular 'errands' (assisting in drug dealing mainly). Moving with large groups of other young people could offer security, but was commonly interpreted as threatening by police and members of the public.

Squaring the circle: supporting, including and disciplining

As we observed, the schools were forced to deal with many competing demands and expectations, particularly with regard to central government missives. Academic attainment and discipline standards were under regular external assessment with poor performance resulting in draconian penalties. Ambitious targets were placed on the schools in relation to examination results, which saw both the co-educational institutions listed as 'failing'. As a consequence they were required to meet the targets within two years or face closure. Inevitably such strictures ensured that resources were disproportionately directed towards the most able pupils, while tolerance of struggling and/or 'difficult' pupils decreased. Yet the schools were simultaneously expected to demonstrate a 'whole school' inclusion policy and a commitment to supporting diversity and equal opportunities. Such contradictory pressures were overlaid by a further tension between providing pastoral care or appropriate punishment in the context of challenging behaviour.

As I will outline, on-site BSUs play a key role in allowing schools to manage these inconsistencies, chiefly by reframing exclusion as a state of mind while approaching inclusion as an active remedial process through which deficit and dysfunctions are corrected. The psychologisation of the essentially social issue of inclusion can be traced back to attempts by liberal educationists to promote a more holistic understanding of pupils as culturally and emotionally embedded individuals. Efforts to recognise the role of affect and embodied identity on learning have since evolved into a very specific and highly regulated approach focusing on emotions in the classroom. More specifically, education policy has sought to inculcate children with 'emotional skills' through the taught curriculum in schools.

Inspired by the work of US psychologist Daniel Goleman (1997, 1999, 2006) claims are made that greater emotional intelligence (or EQ) will improve pupils' conduct, attainment and wellbeing (Department for Education and Skills (DfES), 2005). Anxieties about a perceived deterioration in classroom discipline have been a key factor driving this effort to address the impact of emotionality on learning. Fears have also coalesced around the mental health of particular young people who are viewed as dangerous, disruptive and uncontrollable. According to Goleman, aggression, violence, impulsivity and school disengagement result from an inability to recognise and address emotions. New social pressures and poor parenting have led to an 'emotional malaise' requiring urgent action (Goleman, 1997). Such claims have underpinned a range of school programmes and initiatives designed to teach and nurture emotional literacy as a way of tackling anti-social behaviour and other social problems (Gillies, 2011).

Once viewed as inappropriate in an educational context, emotionality has become a curriculum subject in its own right. A nationwide schools initiative, Social and Emotional Aspects of Learning (SEAL) now operates at primary and secondary level with the aim of providing 'a whole-curriculum framework and resource for teaching social, emotional and behavioural skills to all pupils' (DfES, 2005). Adapted from Goleman's work on emotional intelligence, the SEAL strategy centres on five core domains of self-awareness, managing feelings, empathy, motivation and social skills. The principles of SEAL are intended to inform and guide the day-to-day running of schools, alongside structured lessons designed to equip students with the relevant competencies. Underpinned by the language of developmental psychology, the SEAL initiative has come to foreground the personal determinants of educational exclusion at the expense of broader social and structural relations.

A broad alignment of SEAL initiatives with social inclusion, an anti-bullying stance and a commitment to enhancing child mental health appeals to many professionals and parents, offering an apparently progressive approach to enduring social problems. However, close analysis of the policy literature and the interventions currently operating in schools reveal an altogether more conventional, traditionalist agenda. Conceptually convoluted, often fuzzy ideas frame a common theme of identifying feelings in order to better manage them. In terms of SEAL, this key objective overrides the characteristic liberal reformist language for an emphasis on control and regulation (see Gillies, 2011). Significantly, the SEAL initiative was at its most concentrated in the BSUs. Activities were dominated by 'circle time', which required pupils to sit in groups and discuss personal feelings with teachers, anger management sessions, mentoring and SEAL-themed project work. Key BSU staff across the institutions were highly committed to the SEAL agenda, believing that troublesome behaviour was best tackled by helping young people to better recognise and handle their emotions. However, as our research demonstrates, such practices and pedagogy worked to draw attention away from the enduring gendered, racialised and classed dynamics structuring institutional workings, while denying teachers and other school staff the opportunity to reflect critically on their everyday practices and assumptions.

Personalising inclusion

Analysis of interviews with school staff highlighted the extent to which understandings of inclusive teaching practice are currently built around psychologised assessments of personal competence and well-being. BSUs were viewed, somewhat paradoxically, as sites specifically designed to promote inclusion. In fact, many institutions across the UK have explicitly named their BSUs 'inclusion centres'. In line with this therapeutically orientated approach, meanings of diversity and equality have shifted away from a concern with structural discrimination to focus on individual needs and personal problems as the following quote from a BSU manager demonstrates.

> You've got students who come with a range of public background issues relating to home, so therefore you have students who are 'non-attendants', students who don't like school at all and students who have various home situations which causes them NOT wanting to come into school. Whether because they feel they are going to be intimidated by other students? And those that can't really make friends with ... they can't socialise. Then you've got the students that come in but they've got behavioural issues, which probably is linked to the way the home is run or there's no order or they just speak to their parents anyhow, and so they think they can come into school and conduct themselves in that way. So you have quite a wide range of students coming in.
>
> (Jocyln Reed, BSU Manager at Meedham Girls' School)

All three schools participating in our research were multiracial, ethnically diverse institutions, keen to demonstrate their valuing of difference and multicultural credentials. Walls were decorated with different national flags, minority ethnic music and food were celebrated, festivals and Black history month were marked and culturally specific examples were woven into curriculum subjects. School staff worked hard to encourage feelings of belonging among students, but crucially through a socially disembedded appropriation of culture as a particular component of personal identity. Distinct characteristics (skin tone, religious practices, nationality, etc.) were recognised and valued as sources of self-esteem, with little consideration of the social and political context through which these characteristics are lived as differences (see Gillies and Robinson, 2011). Consequently, certain grounded experiences, values, friendships and family relationships were rarely sanctioned as legitimate expressions of culture within the mainstream school, and were more often overtly viewed as problematic.

As we discovered, a significant number of BSU attendees had not been born in the UK, and many were relatively newly arrived in the country. In the context of broad institutional commitments to inclusivity, the particular challenges faced by these pupils were often obscured by concerns about personal development and social and emotional skills. While the concept of ethnic diversity was celebrated, schools had few mechanisms in place to recognise pupils as migrants unless they arrived during the school year. Given that pupils often transferred from primary school while still in the process of adapting to their new lives in the UK, this lack of recognition could be formative. Migrant pupils could start secondary school with a reputation for being troubled or troublesome to find that they encountered very little understanding of their situation and past experiences from teachers. For example, 12-year-old Max and his family had arrived as economic migrants from Portugal. Max started primary school half way through Year 6, but spoke no English and found the other pupils hostile and mocking.

> The kids, like, because I can't speak English, the kids was, like, taking the mick out of me. So I end up fighting.

> *Wasn't there anyone that you could talk to, within the school, about that?*

> No. Because I didn't have...I couldn't speak...I didn't know how to speak it. I didn't know, I couldn't tell no one, so that's, like, why I was...like, I saw them last, like a month ago, I saw the guy...the guy from the primary school I used to go, and, like, I ask him, 'Why...was it like that? Do you remember me?' He was, like, 'Yeah, you're the kid from the primary school, I was taking the mick.' I was like, 'Yeah', I was like, 'Why you don't take the mick now?' Because I can speak English, and he just walk away. They just take the piss out of you, I hate them.... And I got...I got excluded from it I got excluded from the primary school.... Because no one believed me...I couldn't speak, so they thought I was the one taking the mick

out of them. . . . Not excluded, but I got into loads of trouble. Every time I was, like, in the corner, sitting down with no friends.

(Max, BSU attendee at Hailingbrook School)

In these difficult conditions, Max learned to speak English at great speed and was word perfect by the time he started secondary school a few months later. He retained no trace of an accent and sounded exactly like his London-born counterparts. Nevertheless, his reputation as being difficult followed him to secondary school, where he was quickly referred to a BSU. Newly arrived pupils like Max also lack local knowledge and social connections, making them particularly vulnerable in the playground and on the streets. Gaining peer popularity and earning a tough reputation could assume great importance in this context. A thick skin and the social resources to deal with abuse and incitement were also crucial, but such priorities tended to place pupils from migrant families at the centre of conflict, heightening their visibility in the classroom.

As we discovered, some pupils had experienced considerable disruption, which could undermine established coping mechanisms and magnify confusion and conflict. For example, 12-year-old Rodrigue left his African tribal village and arrived in England with his family when he was nine. After moving around the country, the family settled in London in seriously deprived and overcrowded conditions. Rodrigue was reflexive but matter of fact about the culture shock he had experienced and he explained how he had struggled to make sense of the new rules he found himself bound by. For example, he described how hunger had led him to trap a London pigeon on the way back from school and take it home for a family meal. Catching birds to eat was common practice in his village and he'd been quite proud of his technique, but he had been picked up by the police and brought home in a squad car. Rodrigue struggled to follow teachers' instructions in the classroom and was prone to outbursts of frustration. While he was enthusiastic about school and the importance of education, he loudly challenged decisions he regarded as unfair and broke rules he did not understand. In the pressurised environment of the mainstream school, teachers found him hard to manage, with some interpreting his behaviour as pathologically disturbed. After several months shuttling between the BSU and the off-site provision, Rodrigue was eventually permanently excluded for fighting. His year head concluded that he simply 'did not belong' in the school.

Despite the therapeutic ethos governing BSU activities, teachers participating in our research tended not to explore the wider social and structural context framing conduct. In fact, most teachers carefully policed pedagogic boundaries to ensure that the more disturbing aspect of pupils' lives were kept out of classroom discussion (see Gillies, 2011). In the absence of this awareness, challenging behaviour in the classroom was routinely attributed to personal and developmental causes rooted in poor upbringing. The following excerpt from Rita, a mentor, conveys how BSU staff sought to compensate for perceived parental failings on the basis of little knowledge or understanding.

> When I see poor behaviour I don't necessarily see … well I do see the poor behaviour but I look beyond that … I look behind that and see what might be sparking that poor behaviour off and sometimes when you meet parents you can actually see … you can actually see the reasons why particular things spark particular students off. We can help them with that but, obviously, that is difficult for teachers because teachers aren't privy to all that sort of stuff all the time and there's only a fine line of stuff that you can discuss.
>
> (Rita, BSU Mentor at Meedham Girls' School)

Pupils were regularly described as lacking in self-esteem, aspiration and, most significantly, emotional regulation. The SEAL framework encouraged school staff to evaluate problems by identifying and addressing these perceived individual deficits. The therapeutic principles embodied within SEAL also encouraged staff to make informal diagnoses and tailor support accordingly. Kate Blackman, a BSU manager, described how teaching assistants were allocated to year groups to shadow pupils and take notes on their behaviour and needs. Kate may have been a concerned and committed teacher, but with no formal therapeutic training she relied on an eclectic mix of popular psychology in assessing and supporting pupils.

> I mean, we've had Harry Dunbar this year, who's a very tall lad, a bit chubby, very blond, ADHD, a bit camp, erm, was in cheer leading at primary school! [laughter] … Quite bright, but also (pause) you know, there's social needs there, and emotional needs. He's very (pause) yeah, a bit of (pause) maybe a bit of autism.
>
> (Kate Blackman, BSU Manager at Gravensdale School)

Harry was not involved in our research, but Kate's description and tentative diagnosis of autism highlights the extent to which this individualistic gaze might risk distorting and obscuring the wider social context. Harry's problems are seen as firmly located within his developmentally challenged self, with little consideration given to the pervasive and often vicious culture of homophobia that flourished within the school. Our conversations with the other pupils at the school left us in little doubt about how a 'camp' boy interested in cheerleading would have been received. Yet Harry's problems in relating to others are viewed solely in terms of personal deficit, and he is removed from mainstream classrooms in which sexual bullying is rife, in order to receive help. This example also highlights the normative pull of such therapeutic discourses. As Kate's laughter in the above quote indicates, Harry's manner and interests are viewed as eccentric and socially incongruous. Distinctions between emotional disturbance and lack of social conformity can be complex and inevitably reflect and reinforce a range of gendered, racialised and classed assumptions (Burman, 2009; Gillies et al., 2010c; Gillies, 2011).

Deficit and damage: medicalising boys

Reflecting the current preoccupation with psychological development, the term 'at risk' is commonly used by policy makers and practitioners to describe young people marked out as displaying disruptive or problematic conduct. 'Troubled' and 'troublesome' are readily conflated through a focus on bad behaviour as a manifestation of emotional disorder or deficit. But this generic categorisation overlies the heavily gendered meanings that attach to practices inside and outside the classroom. For young men, narratives of psychological disorder or damage are often drawn on to position them as potentially dangerous. As the reference to Harry in the excerpt above demonstrates, boys were often understood through recourse to a medicalised discourse of dysfunction. Teachers commonly speculated about conditions such as attention deficit hyperactivity disorder (ADHD), conduct disorder and other less specific forms of 'damage'. For example, Beverly is a teacher in a BSU that is almost exclusively attended by boys.

> A lot of them are EBD – sort of Emotional Behavioural Deficiency – which is another type of special need . . . . I mean, it's one of these new ones. I think that, within schools, I've been hearing – since I've been teaching, it's been something that's been bandied around – and it is a specific behavioural deficit kind of syndrome, but my understanding of it, it can, I mean, a lot of the kids are hyperactive in some way, but I think a lot of it. I think the reason they use 'emotional' is that it's possibly come from home in a certain way, so whether it's in parents who haven't done a lot of parenting, or that have had drug

problems, or, or the related other problems, you know, or they're very young, you know, all those various ways that they've been damaged in certain ways.

(Beverly, BSU Teacher at Hailingbrook School)

Many teachers subscribed to this concept of 'damage', most often in relation to boys. The strong gendered element of this discourse was cross-cut and compounded by an unspoken racialised dimension. Working-class and/or minority ethnic parenting stood furthest apart from an ideal of childrearing held many teachers and policy makers. More specifically, the high numbers of Black children living with lone mothers tended to be viewed as a significant factor in conduct issues among boys. Both the co-educational schools employed Black male mentors in an effort to provide role models and address the impact of perceived father absence. As Tracey Reynolds's (2005, 2009) research in this area demonstrates, this 'inclusion' policy works to perpetuate a misunderstanding of Black British family life. She points to the way that fathers are often involved but non-resident, the strong Caribbean tradition of female-headed households and the role that stepfathers, uncles, grandfathers, brothers and male cousins tend to play in caring for and raising Black boys. There was, however, little scope within the schools for viewing lone motherhood as anything other than a significant risk factor for Black boys in particular (Gillies and Robinson, 2011).

Teachers' concerns about dangerous, psychologically damaged boys often revolved around fears that they were involved with criminal gangs. Once again Black boys were most often the focus of this concern, with text messages, slang, clothing and gestures vulnerable to misinterpretation as sinister forms of secret communication. Minor incidents could lead to serious allegations with teachers primed to view behaviour as aggressive (see Gillies et al., 2010c, 2011). This caused great resentment among Black pupils themselves, who could feel unfairly singled out and persecuted, as Marcus a 15-year-old Black Caribbean pupil articulates:

Like he [headteacher] picks on us, constantly, it ain't like a one-off thing, it's constantly, like . . . like hanging round as a group as friends, 'No laughing', 'Move', 'Go away', 'Not to stand here'. Funny stuff. You know, he walks us down to the bus stop for some reason, makes police follows us down [the High street] . . . some kid was spreading rumours that I was hitting him and she [a teacher] phoned my mum saying, 'Marcus and his gang', not like Marcus and his friends or nothing like, 'Marcus and a couple of boys'. It was like 'Marcus and his gang'.

> (Marcus, BSU attendee at Gravensdale School)

Becoming marked out as a potential gang member could have grave consequences, as Marcus found out when he was arrested on suspicion of murder after the headteacher passed his name to the police. Although soon released, he was subsequently regularly followed, stopped and harassed by the police with the effect that he had no one to turn to when he feared for his own safety. In similar contexts, we discovered that boys and young men could become personally invested in presenting themselves as psychologically unstable. Some pupils actively cultivated the image that they were 'mad' or unhinged, with one 13-year-old boy proudly explaining how his wild, volatile behaviour had earned him the nickname 'crazy kid'. A reputation for uncontrolled behaviour inspired fear among other pupils, generating power, status and protection on the streets and in the playground (Gillies, 2011). The psychologisation of behaviour within the BSUs appeared to compound this effect, providing reinforcement and authenticity to self-identified pathologies.

Developmental deficits: challenging girls

While boys attending BSUs were likely to be viewed through a lens of damage and disorder, interpretations of developmental immaturity and 'neediness' tend to shape school encounters for girls. School staff emphasised the developmental struggles that girls were undergoing and described feeling protective towards them. Girls' behaviour was generally viewed as far less threatening to teachers in comparison with boys, with concerns focusing on rudeness, stroppiness and lack of co-operation. Separate groups for girls were established in the co-educational schools to deal with behaviour that was much more likely to be understood from within a normalised framework of adolescent troubles. Girls themselves, in strong contrast to boys, drew readily on the notion that they were needy rather than badly behaved.

> Well, in the beginning, she [mother] wasn't happy, because they... Miss Bridge didn't, like, exactly tell my mum why I was (pause) she just basically told my mum the bad things – why I'm going to BSU. But when she had the meeting, she understood that it's not because I'm bad or whatever, that (pause) just extra support. And she was all right with it.
>
> (Chanelle, attendee at Meedham Girls' School)

School staff implicated hormones, friendships, boys, anxieties over weight and appearance, and general low self-esteem in girls' displays of challenging conduct. Girls were often described (and often described themselves) as 'loud' and 'rude', terms that were rarely applied to boys. While problematised, this behaviour could be viewed, in the words of one teacher, as 'stroppy adolescent girlness'. This tendency to trivialise and downplay the acting out of girls in the classroom ensured that while permanent exclusion was less likely, specific, socially located difficulties and barriers to mainstream inclusion were rarely considered.

For example, 14-year-old Amy attended girls' groups within a co-educational BSU. She was white, small, slim and wore extensive but carefully applied make-up and a 'customised' school uniform. Although generally quiet, calm and withdrawn, she had developed subtle but highly effective methods for disrupting classroom activities. These included non-compliance, goading other pupils and cleverly subverting classroom tasks. During the course of our research we came to know her as complex and troubled, although we sometimes struggled to distinguish the truth from the fictional accounts she often gave us. Amy's immediate concerns revolved around friendships and feuds within her social network. After falling out with her best friend, a substantial number of girls within the school turned on her and she found herself subject to threats, actual violence and cruel tricks. Her mother described how a group of girls befriended Amy to take her shopping, only to surreptitiously fill her bag with unpaid for items and wait for her to trigger the store alarm. She also received abusive Facebook posts, was followed and intimidated when she went to the toilet and was falsely implicated in school misdemeanours. Despite being at the centre of what appeared to be a concerted bullying campaign, the manager of the BSU was dismissive of Amy as a vacuous teenage girl obsessed with boys.

> Amy really wasn't a problem until Year 9 and boys came on the scene, and now the 'Mm-mm', you know, if you've got Luke or Alfie [BSU boys] there, she's okay, because she'll just be listening to them, otherwise there's not much to engage with. [laughter] That's about Amy for you... you know, she's not going to be a beauty queen is she!
>
> Mmm, she's very much into the whole look thing, though.
>
> Oh, it's all they have. So she'll get, she'll have her kids, get married, and, you know, that's what she'll do well.
>
> (Kate Blackman, BSU Manager)

Amy herself was adamant about not wanting children and talked about becoming a writer. However, her place at the school became untenable in the context of the bullying and, after spending time at the off-site provision, she was eventually permanently excluded for fighting. Amy's troubles were both normalised and individualised through a focus on her personal development (or perceived lack of it). Girls were less likely than boys to be seen as lacking in social and emotional skills, but they were commonly infantilised and portrayed as 'spoiled', over-indulged and lacking in potential. The social and relational dynamics shaping and informing the behaviour of both girls and boys were effectively obscured by a preoccupation with a detached, self-regulating ideal.

Issues of class and race also intersect with gender to position girls' behaviour in particular ways. Concerns expressed by school staff about the influence of home life implicitly centred on working-class values and practices. Mainstream teachers articulated a clear vision of appropriate family relations, reflecting a broader policy emphasis on the role of 'good parenting' in mediating inequality. Such discourses portray parenting as a technical exercise that can and should be pursued independently from social, cultural and structural contexts in order for children to be successful (Gillies, 2008). In effect, privilege is claimed as personal entitlement through a valorisation of white middle-class parenting practices in isolation from the lived realities of inequality (Gillies, 2007). From this perspective, working-class culture becomes framed as an impediment to inclusion and a driver of disadvantage, as the following quote from the deputy head at Meedham Girls' School highlights.

> We're exclusively a working class school, and that's fine but that brings with it certain lacks of influences and the impact of these 'special school'–type students is enormous!... you've got the girl in Year 7 whose parents won't really work with us because of their own issues and their own education background. Girls who are inappropriate in terms of their awareness of how [pause] I just sometimes look at these girls open-mouthed at how they have that confidence to say what they do. It's very, very [worrying] I think it's an inner, an inner city problem maybe?
>
> (Sarah Jennings, Deputy Head at Meedham Girls' School)

Working-class culture and home life was directly drawn on by teachers to make sense of conflict in the classroom and was viewed as an influence to be countered and compensated for. Girls were generally subject to 'inclusion' through circle time groups and mentoring to instil more appropriate values and aspirations. But while low-level disruptive behaviour from girls could be normalised and regarded as a trouble-some feature of adolescent development, clear boundaries structured this interpretation. If girls were perceived to transgress the bounds of normality, they could become situated beyond the paternalistic pale. This was particularly evident in the co-educational schools, where if girls were unwilling or unable to take up a subject position as vulnerable they could face harsh consequences. For example, violent or threatening behaviour from girls could result in them being sent to male-dominated behaviour support initiatives, often as the only female. During our time in the schools, the girls placed alongside boys were almost exclusively Black, suggesting that little may have changed since the 1980s when researchers noted how teachers were more likely to view Black girls behaviour as loud, unfeminine and challenging (Fuller, 1980; Wright, 1987). This resonates with Deborah Youdell's (2003) account of how per-formative embodied identities are fashioned through interaction with racialised institutional discourses to produce some undesirable or even impossible learners.

Audrey Osler and colleagues (Osler, 2006; Osler and Vincent, 2003; Osler et al., 2002) have shown how girls are given low priority in school planning for behaviour management, with their needs overshadowed by concerns about boys' anti-social conduct. The unequal resources tar-geted towards boys, driven by a notion that girls' behaviour is naturally less problematic, both obscures the particular needs that girls may have while also ensuring that those receiving referrals are vulnerable to being stigmatised as highly aberrant. As we observed, lone girls in BSU groups could face a barrage of abuse and harassment from the boys, much of it sexualised. The highly charged nature of these interactions and insults reflect a more general dynamic through which normative heterosexu-ality is enforced in the context of institutional silences and exclusions around sanctioned expressions and discussions of sexuality (Mellor and Epstein, 2006; Taylor, 2007).

More specifically, the lone girls in BSUs were subject to constant disparaging assessment of their appearance, questioned about sexual acts they'd engaged in and were the butt of crude jokes. Pornography was accessed on computer screens, or graphic drawings passed around. By the very act of being referred to a BSU, girls were exposed as hav-ing transgressed normative imperatives around gender and sexuality, drawing targeted abuse for failing to produce themselves as 'appropriate' (Mellor and Epstein, 2006). This response from boys was also indicative of a wider ugly, misogynistic and highly sexualised culture within the co-educational schools, with girls commonly falling victim to sexist and sexual bullying, some of it extremely serious. In this hostile and threatening environment, female BSU attendees encountered little support or incentive to moderate their behaviour, placing them at even greater risk of exclusion.

Conclusion

In this chapter, I have explored how current approaches to behaviour management in British secondary schools pursue 'inclusion' through intensive social and emotional support while presiding over de facto exclusion from mainstream classrooms. As part of a broader shift towards therapeutic models that locate problems within individuals and their families, exclusion becomes reinterpreted as a mental state, while inclusion is viewed as a corrective process targeting psychological obstacles to participation. The rise of the BSU as a new school-based solution to challenging behaviour in the classroom highlights the way that understandings of inclusion in education have become increasingly detached from an original concern with dismantling institutional barriers. Social and relational contexts, power dynamics and the practices and responsibilities of schools are commonly overlooked for a focus on the individual psyche of the troublesome pupil. Attention and resources are directed towards personal change, while the backdrop of socially embedded disadvantage, discrimination, violence and institutional racism are ignored.

With the term 'inclusion' now commonly used to describe an expulsion of troublesome or troubling difference to the margins of school life, institutional responsibilities to promote equality and social justice are similarly deflected.

BSUs do not just contain difficult pupils, they also work to obscure and neutralise difficult questions around patterns of discrimination.

Very little information is collated centrally about how many BSUs exist, who gets sent to them, why and for how long. Ethnic monitoring is carried out by individual schools but, as this information is retained as confidential, there is no way of knowing how or even whether that data are being interrogated. Certainly, school staff who participated in our research were unclear about who took responsibility for collecting and entering ethnic monitoring data. It was similarly not possible to find out how many BSU attendees in total were considered to have special educational needs. A number of the pupils participating in our research were on medication for ADHD, while others had been diagnosed with dyslexia and dyspraxia.

As I have outlined, dimensions of class, gender and race remain firmly implicated within school exclusion/inclusion practices, ensuring that ingrained patterns of inequality remain unchanged. Working-class culture is associated with personal, family and cultural deficit, while gender frames and guides classroom interventions. Boys' behaviour is most often interpreted in terms of damage and disorder, placing them at higher risk of school exclusion, while girls are more likely to be viewed as developmentally vulnerable, unless they breach the gendered and racialised codes structuring classroom interactions. Our research has also revealed the extent to which BSUs operate within an enduring context of institutional intolerance, with unprocessed racialised narratives informing policies, procedures and exclusions.

The effect of this current drive to 'inclusion' is the individualisation and continued pathologisation of difference that is socially, culturally and structurally embedded. By seeking to make students 'includable' within a broadly unchanged framework, BSUs compound existing problems of structural discrimination and institutional racism. As a result, 'includability' is reserved for those best able to reproduce white, middle-class ideals.

Notes

1. The project, Disruptive Behaviour in the Classroom: Exploring the Social Subjectivity of Disaffection, was funded by the Economic and Social Research Council under grant numbers RES-061-23-0073.
2. All names and locations have been changed to preserve anonymity and confidentiality.

References

Burman, E. (2009) Beyond emotional literacy in feminist and educational research. *British Educational Research Journal*, 35(1): 137–155.

Clark, C., Dyson, A., Millward, A. and Robson, S. (1999) Theories of inclusion, theories of schools: Deconstructing and reconstructing the 'inclusive school'. *British Educational Research Journal*, 25(2): 157–177.

Department for Education (DfE). (2010) *The Importance of Teaching. The Education White Paper*. London: HMSO.

Department for Education and Skills (DfES). (2005) *Excellence and Enjoyment: Social and Emotional Aspects of Learning: Guidance*. London: HMSO.

Fuller, M. (1980) Black girls in a London comprehensive school. In R. Deem (Ed.), *Schooling for Women's Work* (pp. 52–56). London: Routledge.

Gillborn, D. (2008) *Racism and Education Coincidence or Conspiracy?* Abingdon: Routledge.

Gillborn, D. and Mirzra, H. (2000) *Educational Inequality: Mapping Race, Class and Gender. A Synthesis of Research Evidence.* London: Ofsted.

Gillies, V. (2007) *Marginalised Mothers: Exploring Working Class Parenting.* London: Routledge.

Gillies, V. (2008) Childrearing, class and the new politics of parenting. *Sociology Compass*, 2/3: 1079–1095.

Gillies, V. (2011) Social and emotional pedagogies: Critiquing the new orthodoxy of emotion in classroom behaviour management. *British Journal of Sociology of Education*, 32(2): 185–202.

Gillies, V. and Robinson, Y. (2010a) Managing emotions in research with challenging pupils. *Ethnography and Education*, 5(1): 97–110.

Gillies, V. and Robinson, Y. (2010b) Shifting the goalposts: Researching pupils at risk of school exclusion. In M. Rob and R. Thomson (Eds), *Critical Practice with Children and Young People* (pp. 281–295). Bristol: Policy Press.

Gillies, V. and Robinson, Y. (2010c) Including and excluding: Exploring gendered and racialised constructions of risk and vulnerability in the classroom. *Race Equality Teaching*, 29(1): 9–13.

Gillies, V. and Robinson, Y. (2012) 'Including' while excluding: Race, class and behaviour support units. *Race, Ethnicity and Education*, 15(2): 157–174

Goleman, D. (1997) *Emotional Intelligence: Why It Can Matter More than IQ.* New York: Bantum.

Goleman, D. (1999) *Working with Emotional Intelligence.* London: Bloomsbury.

Goleman, D. (2006) Emotional intelligence: What does the research really indicate. *Educational Psychologist*, 41(4): 239–245.

Mellor, J. and Epstein, D. (2006) Appropriate behaviour? Sexualities, schooling and hetero-gender. In C. Skelton, B. Francis and L. Smulyan (Eds), *Sage Handbook of Gender & Education* (pp. 378–392). London: Sage.

Osler, A. (2006) Excluded girls: Interpersonal, institutional and structural violence in schooling. *Gender and Education*, 18(6): 571–589.

Osler, A., Street, C., Lall, M. and Vincent, K. (2002) *Reasons for Exclusion from School.* London: Department for Education and Employment.

Osler, A. and Vincent, K. (2003) *Girls and Exclusion: Rethinking the Agenda.* London: Routledge.

Parsons, C. (1999) *Education, Exclusion and Citizenship.* London: Routledge.

Reynolds, G. (2008) *The Impacts and Experiences of Migrant Children in UK Secondary Schools.* Working Paper No. 47, Sussex Centre for Migration Research, University of Sussex.

Reynolds, T. (2005) *Caribbean Mothers: Identity and Experience in the U.K.* London: Tufnell Press.

Reynolds, T. (2009) Exploring the absent/present dilemma: Black fathers, family relationships, and social capital in Britain. *American Annals*, 624(1): 12–28.

Reynolds, T. (2010) *Single Mothers Not the Cause of Black Boys' Underachievement.* Runnymeade Trust eConference. http://www.runnymedetrust.org/events-conferences/econferences/econference/alias-3.html [accessed 20 July 2010].

Steer, A. (2008) *Learning Behaviour. The Report of the Practitioners Group on School Behaviour and Discipline.* London: Department for Education and Skills.

Taylor, Y. (2007) Brushed behind the bike shed: Working class lesbians' experiences of school. *British Journal of Sociology of Education*, 28(3): 349–362.

Vlachou, A. (2004) Education and inclusive policy-making: Implications for research and practice. *International Journal of Inclusive Education*, 8(1): 3–21.

Wright, C. (1987) The relations between teaches and Afro-Caribbean pupils: Observing multiracial classrooms. In G. Weiner and M. Arno (Eds), *Gender under Scrutiny* (pp. 173–186). London: Hutchinson.

Youdell, D. (2003) Identity traps or how black students fail: The interactions between biographical, sub-culture and learner identities. *British Journal of Sociology of Education*, 24(1): 3–20.

3

Investigating the Value of Vignettes in Researching Disabled Students' Views of Social Equality and Inclusion in School

Vanita Sundaram and Alison Wilde

Introduction

This chapter is based on a small-scale, longitudinal research project with young people who have been designated as having 'special educational needs' (SEN). The project had two overarching aims: first, to contribute to knowledge about how best to hear the voices of young people with a range of 'special educational needs'; and second, to represent the views of these young people, with particular reference to their experiences of fairness in school. The chapter will discuss the methodological complexities in capturing and representing voice with this group of young people. In particular, we will examine significant themes of identity and voice and contradictions inherent in institutional 'celebration' of diversity and young people's accounts of marginalisation, exclusion and management of disabling environments.

Background

There is increasing concern to draw on pupil voice in educational research, as the positive outcomes for policy and practice have been recognised. The British Educational Research Association has called for more research to be conducted with young people, in order to inform child-led educational initiatives and interventions. It can be argued that for schools to foster democratic and inclusive cultures and practices, the voices of the children for whom these are developed must be sought out and used as a basis for action. Accordingly, there has been an increase in the number of studies that draw on pupil voice to investigate wide-ranging educational issues, including curriculum design and assessment (Rudduck, 2004), civic engagement (Fielding, 2001), school violence (Sellman, 2011) and inclusion (Rudduck and Flutter, 2000). Much research has been conducted to investigate the barriers to learning of particular pupil groups, for example, children from socio-economically disadvantaged backgrounds and children designated as having SEN. These studies have drawn on pupils' voices to illuminate school or classroom-level factors that shape positive and negative learning experiences.

Typically, however, research in this field has been done with pupils who are identified as being 'at-risk' of exclusion, or indeed, when they have already been excluded (e.g. Hamill and Boyd, 2002). Few studies have been conducted to illuminate the experiences of young people who are still engaged in education and, of these, hardly any have been conducted with pupils who have severe, or even moderate, learning, emotional and/or physical impairments. Even in research concerned with disadvantaged and marginalised pupil populations, the voices of pupils designated as having SEN are relatively underrepresented. Further, the experiences of pupils who experience learning, physical or emotional impairments and/or stigma associated with these (Rose and Shevlin, 2004) have rarely been compared with those of pupils defined as 'successful'.

There has been much attention given to the strategies, policies and practices for inclusion that schools can adopt. Schools that have been considered to be 'inclusive' have explicitly talked about their celebration of 'diversity' and 'difference'. However, research with young people who have been labelled as 'diverse' or 'different' reveals that difference is often conceptualised as 'difficulty' (Rogers, 2007), reflecting a tendency of education professionals to conceptualise particular impairments or learning needs as obstructive to the 'normal' learning environment. In the UK, the marginalisation of pupils labelled as 'different' is particularly true for the large number of pupils who are positioned in transitional or less formalised stages of SEN, especially those with fewer categorical impairments or unmet needs who are placed in the categories of School Action and School Action Plus.[1] These learners are often given fewer formal entitlements to adjustments for their 'unique' difference to mainstream pupils and the associated educational needs. It is expected that 'extra or different help' (Department for Children, Families and Schools (DCFS), 2009, p. 7) will be given at School Action and that a Special Educational Needs Coordinator (SENCO) or other professionals will be consulted and offer support at School Action Plus. Effectively, where there has been insufficient attention to pedagogies that prioritise unique learning needs, young people with moderate learning difficulties or internalised emotional and behavioural difficulties are less likely to be considered as an eligible locus of concern. As potential subjects of inclusion policies, young people with moderate learning difficulties are more likely to be viewed in terms of 'general difference' (ibid.), working to separate them from their classmates. Thus, school policies and practices towards particular pupils have been developed around an understanding of the need to 'deal with' or manage young people's problematic difference as an extra task rather than conceptualising their unmet needs as a failing of educational provision. The focus is placed firmly on inherent difficulties of individual learners, signifying a deficit of individual pupils or pupil groups.

The views of pupils designated as having these less obvious 'learning difficulties' or SEN are under-represented in the emerging body of work that does draw on pupil views. Further, there has been little research done to examine the optimal techniques for eliciting the views of young people with communication difficulties and those who perceive themselves as outside the schools' cultural and academic norms. As such, discussion of methodology and research techniques tends to support the individualistic emphasis invariably placed on the study of SEN, tending to neglect the ways in which research replicates a deficit or difference-based model of students' needs. Instead, this study is innovative in its conceptualisation of SEN in terms of unmet need. It aims to explore new methodologies for gaining the views of young people designated as having SEN, yet simultaneously marginalised from this identity as 'difficult' students, by placing the emphasis upon how these students understand relatively abstract concepts of fairness, inclusion, social equality and marginalisation. This chapter will thus explore the need to examine school-based marginalisation and exclusion from the pupils' perspectives, before discussing the development and use of alternative methodologies to explore exclusion with pupils for whom traditional research methods are not meaningful or productive.

Why pupil voice?

There is an increasing recognition of the value of pupil voice in educational research, and particularly in relation to understanding the specific barriers to pupils' learning and engagement with school. The United Nations Convention on the Rights of the Child (1989) asserts that children and young people have the right to express their opinions on all matters affecting them. The convention calls upon governments and agencies working with young people to listen to and act upon the views they express on matters that directly affect their lives. As education concerns its pupils, they should therefore be consulted seriously about its conduct and reform (Fielding and Bragg, 2003), and treated with respect in its implementation (Osler, 2000). Further, the introduction of citizenship education into the National Curriculum in 2002 highlighted the potential of pupil voice in contributing to learning processes, and also emphasised the links between young people's experiences of fairness, participation and inclusion in school and their expectations as citizens in society.

However, the views of pupils are still surprisingly scarce in educational research, despite their clear competence as commentators (Wood, 2003). This absence is perhaps particularly marked for pupils in already marginalised groups (Hamill and Boyd, 2002; Rose and Shevlin, 2004). As Reay (2006) among others has pointed out, the use of pupil voice may perpetuate existing hierarchies and peer relations that disadvantage particular groups or individuals. First, the views of the most able, articulate and resourceful students are usually represented in pupil voice research and this is particularly the case when teachers select the pupils who will participate in the research. Further, the concerns and interests of the most successful pupils may be taken uncritically to represent those of the pupil group as a whole and experiences of marginalisation and exclusion can be written out of the pupil experience in this way. Thus, it is important in understanding more about equity to seek out the views of all pupils, including the most disadvantaged and least likely to speak out.

Among pupil groups thought to be disadvantaged by current, conventional schooling arrangements, the views of pupils designated as having 'SEN' are particularly under-represented in educational research. The experiences of pupils who experience learning, physical or emotional impairments, impairment effects or stigma (Hunt, 1966; Rose and Shevlin, 2004) have rarely been compared with those defined as 'successful'. One consequence of this is that the experiences of young people who could be marginalised in school, for a range of social, medical and academic reasons, may be overlooked. Various explanations have been put forward for the relative exclusion of these pupils from pupil voice research. First, this group has been thought not to have strong views on their schooling experiences due to their supposed cognitive and emotional deficiency (e.g. Hamill and Boyd, 2002). Incomplete or insubstantial responses to researcher questions have thus been viewed as a reflection of their lacking comprehension, rather than poor research design. Second, and directly related to this, research that has been conducted *on* pupils designated as having 'SEN' has historically used conventional and restrictive methods that presuppose language and standard communication methods as the sole basis for eliciting pupils' views.

The use of alternative methodologies

So, while an emerging body of research has sought to document the schooling experiences of pupils with unmet educational needs, less research has been conducted on appropriate alternative methodologies for working with young people who have communication barriers, and even less has been done to evaluate the utility of alternative methodologies. For example, does the use of facilitators hinder the expression of views or affect the validity of views being expressed (Lewis and Porter, 2004); does the use of symbols and pictures simplify the level of response that respondents can give; do subjects that researchers consider important have any meaning to respondents? In other words, how can we elicit the experiences of students in a meaningful way that is faithful to their lived experiences, and allows them to disclose concerns in a safe way?

Lumby and Morrison (2009) have argued that there is a need to move from rhetoric of human rights-based approaches to education (including discourses of social justice and inclusion) to seeking out ways in which young people can be facilitated to realise these rights. Rogers (2007, p. 30), too, has argued that inclusive education (and educational research) in its current form is 'rhetoric based on ideals about promoting the tolerance of difference', rather than actually destabilising and adjusting power relations between marginalised young people and their teachers and peers. So, while there is an increasing emphasis on eliciting the views of children and young people who may be alienated in/from school, there tends to be greater importance given to the production of 'opportunities' and less on the complexities involved in accessing these young people, collecting data on their views and interpreting their narratives (Lewis, 2001).

It has also been noted that the subjects about which participants are being questioned or the context in which the questions are located must be consequential to participants in order to generate meaningful responses about that topic (Lewis and Porter, 2004), as well as to have potential for impact on their schooling experiences. Thus, some studies have found that what students are interested in is not what takes place in the classroom itself, but the social contexts within the educational setting, such as the canteen or the playground and/or the toilets (Wilde and Avramidis, 2011). So, not only do 'researchers have to establish the best medium through which communication takes place,[they] also have to conceptualise the message in a way that is meaningful to the recipient' (Lewis and Porter, 2004, pp. 194–195).

Research conducted with children and young people is often scrutinised in terms of the reliability and validity of views elicited. The contradiction between the rhetoric of inclusion and rights, and a culture of mistrusting young people as competent commentators, is evident in much educational research. This wariness may be heightened in work with young people labelled as having learning 'difficulties' (Lewis, 2001). Bryman (2008) has pointed out that alternative criteria for reliability and validity need to be used for qualitative work, including that conducted with young people. Principles of trustworthiness, transparency and authenticity are prioritised, as is the wider political impact of research. There is thus a concern not only to fairly represent the views of participants, but also to be transparent about the ways in which these views are elicited and the ways in which the research itself has acted as an impetus for participants themselves or members of their context to engage in action to change their circumstances (Bryman, 2008, p. 379).

Methods

Using vignettes

There is a dearth of literature on the specialised skills necessary for conducting research with pupils who have communication needs not designated as the 'norm', in terms of fluency in English, literacy, sensory, physical or cognitive impairments. The use of traditional questionnaire methodology among students with SEN and behavioural or physical impairments poses an undeniable ethical problem. Lengthy, and often abstracted, sections of prose may place a number of pupils, for example, those with reading or concentration difficulties, at a disadvantage. Furthermore, this method usually requires of pupils that they can write at length and complete the questionnaire independently, thereby also placing some pupils with physical and communication/cognitive impairments at a relative disadvantage. Using semi-structured interviewing can similarly demand particular forms of answer from participants, rather than freely exploring underlying perceptions and views held. As Lewis (2001: 03) has noted, 'A range of work with children has shown the value of making statements that prompt a response, rather than a direct question, to elicit views. The tendency for adults, particularly teachers, to use question-answer feedback routines has been described by some writers as reflecting power relationships.' Our substantive focus on equity necessitates the development of tools and settings that ensure the equal participation of pupils across a wide range of abilities and backgrounds.

Using statements as a prompt, rather than demanding a response through questioning has been argued to reflect a more equal relationship in which the young person can retain some control over the direction of the discussion, as well as a useful technique for triggering responses with young people. Barter and Renold (2002) have argued that vignettes can allow participants to retain control over the research process. While a growing body of interdisciplinary work has used vignettes to explore a range of social issues, including violence among adolescents (Barter and Renold, 2002), young people in care (Moules, 2009) and gender norms (Felmlee and Muraco, 2009), there has been less work conducted to examine the methodological utility of vignettes, particularly in work with young people. A vignette is a short story or scenario that provides 'concrete examples of people and their behaviours on which participants can comment. The researcher can facilitate a discussion around the opinions expressed' (Hazel, 1995, p. 2).

Vignette is a useful method for exploring subjective belief systems and can help to identify group norms, shed light on social processes occurring inside and out of school, and stimulate discussion on potentially sensitive subjects by removing these from the level of the individual pupil (O'Kane, 2008, p. 140). Vignettes could also be argued to provide an avenue for 'conscientisation' (Freire, 1970) by exposing oppressive elements in the lives of students and thereby enabling them to express and name their experiences of oppression (including marginalisation and exclusion) in a safe way.

In the present study, vignettes were constructed on the basis of previous research on sensitive topics with young people (e.g. Barter and Renold, 2000; O'Kane, 2008). The vignettes comprised short scenarios of no more than three lines about a young person with an impairment. The example below was used in the present study:

> Veronica is deaf and she communicates mostly using sign language. The other pupils in her class sometimes leave Veronica out of games at break time because it is a lot of effort to communicate with her.

The scenarios were based on examples of social and academic exclusion that young people in previous research studies had named (Hamill and

Boyd, 2002). The vignette was read out to the pupils and presented to them on card. This was followed up with probes asking pupils whether this was a familiar situation, what their reactions to the scenario were and whether they thought this was a fair outcome for the pupil featured in the vignette. The vignettes were written in accessible language and were printed onto cards in large font so that these could be picked up and read by the pupils in our study. Pupils talked about one vignette for as long as it held their interest and they had opinions they wanted to share about the specific scenario presented to them.

Context

The study was conducted in a mainstream school in North Yorkshire in 2008–2009. The school is located in a relatively affluent catchment area and it has an integrated 'resource centre' to provide additional learning support for pupils designated as having SEN. The school has won numerous inclusion awards and it badges itself as a model of good inclusive practice in its mission statement, school behavioural policy and other documentation. The school adopts a capabilities approach (Sen, 1999) to inclusion and wellbeing in terms of encouraging young people to 'be what they can be in school'. The school mission statement thus states that the school 'aims to be a successful learning community that gives learners the confidence and capability to develop as far as their imagination can take them'. The discourse of celebrating diversity and promoting inclusion is prevalent at official as well as informal levels. The school was thus opportunistically and purposively selected as a model of good practice on the basis of resources, accolades and policies committed to inclusion.

Sampling

Small-group, mixed-gender interviews were conducted with four pupils, aged 14–15 years, who were designated by the school as having SEN. The pupils were selected for participation in the study by the school's SENCO, who stated that they experienced a range of impairments to their learning and that they needed differing levels of support. The pupils were interviewed on four occasions over the school year. Although we had asked to speak with pupils with a range of impairments, all the pupils we met with were fluent communicators and defined themselves as relatively well-integrated and functioning (at least in terms of the school's definition of these terms). We did wonder whether the school had selected these particular pupils in order to demonstrate their competence at 'including' young people. We were not advised of the pupils' impairments ahead of conducting the small-group interviews and we deliberately refrained from asking what they were (to avoid stigmatisation and disengagement). Despite their frequent references to their own experiences as 'different' from other pupils, only one participant made specific reference to having an (officially unrecognised) SEN[2]:

> *Sam:* You know mum has been trying and trying and trying again to get me a statement of education but they won't give me one because they say it doesn't make any difference...well, if I do my exams, if I don't get through all of the questions because I haven't got a statement of education, their fault they didn't give me a statement of education [...] Well, I really...well, it was really mum who made my autism...at a normal level, because she sort of took me out to places like the cinema, when I was very young, so my autism could improve on itself, and I could get more into society.

From the small-group interviews and subsequent data analysis, we can estimate that the remaining three students had specific and/or moderate learning difficulties. As such, given the comments in their accounts, they can all be seen (retrospectively) as students whose impairments frame them as difficult rather than disabled.

Lewis (2001) has written about the problematic nature of sampling in work with young people. The most obvious problem is the power of gatekeepers who allow (or disallow) access to the young people, and frequently, give consent on their behalf by opting them in. Where the gatekeeper is a headteacher or SENCO, a young person may quite clearly feel dissuaded from refusing to participate due to the hierarchical relationship between teacher and pupil, as well as between adult researcher and pupil. Where young people have communication difficulties, the provision of informed consent may be further problematised (as may that of informed dissent) (Lewis, 2001). At every meeting, we reiterated to our participants their right to withdraw participation and to remain silent on issues they did not wish to comment on, as well as assuring them of confidentiality and anonymity. We also offered them opportunities to retract any statements they had made.

The value of vignettes – our findings

The vignettes offered depersonalised accounts of labelling, marginalisation and exclusion, which allowed students a safe mode of expression about these accounts, especially as the interviews were conducted in relatively close proximity to teachers. The SENCO was in an adjacent room and could, possibly, have heard what they were saying. Not only did the vignettes provide the young people with a greater freedom to comment on scenarios that were not specific to their school, but the vignettes also seemed to minimise the young people's fears of talking openly about processes of exclusion and discrimination. Their propensity to move between literal and referential statements (Liebes and Katz, 1993) increased over time, resulting in stronger criticisms of the school at every small-group interview. Students used the vignettes as a means by which to disclose their own experiences of marginalisation and other aspects of everyday school experience, leading them to criticise their own teachers' practices. Thus, the method worked on multiple levels to facilitate expression by our participants. Using Barter and Renold's (1999) assessments of the vignette method, their value will be explored in the following sections, discussed in terms of their suitability to this specific group and to explore contexts of social marginalisation.

Barter and Renold propose that '. . . vignettes allow for a less threatening discussion of sensitive experiences' (1999, p. 2). This was crucial in this school context, a location that would normally restrict disclosures due to the lack of privacy and consequent fears of exposure. Opening conversations on sensitive issues through the use of fictional characters facing exclusion and discrimination in vignette-based scenarios allowed for a sense of detachment, where issues could be addressed dispassionately, in both abstract and referential terms, judging school experiences in 'comparison with the "normality" of the vignette' (Barter and Renold, 1999, p. 2).

Also, in terms of these participants, vignettes offered a way to clarify 'individual judgements, often in relation to moral dilemmas' (ibid.). In particular, the fictional scenarios offered to participants were particularly useful in allowing them to see several viewpoints. It was common for them to position statements of how things 'should be' alongside alternative considerations drawn from their own and other students' lives. These processes of clarification often led the young people towards 'blue sky' visualisations of how things could be more inclusive. While these discussions often highlighted ambivalent and contradictory opinions, they also offered us a number of useful insights into the school habitus, contributing to our understanding of young people's experiences as a result of disabling school cultures. This was particularly useful in their reframing of school discourses of individual deficit as processes of exclusion. These individual judgements also illustrated sharp contrasts of opinion between the students, highlighting a heterogeneity that is often lost in more individualistic accounts of disabled students' experience.

As such, this diverse range of experience enhanced the growing criticisms made of school culture, policies and academic processes providing us with an 'interpretation of actions and occurrences that allows situational context to be explored and influential variables to be elucidated' (ibid.). Often through comparison with the vignettes, the fictional scenarios led the students to introduce their own interpretations of exclusionary processes and social marginalisation, demonstrating how this differed according to influential variables (such as teacher's attitudes), and tacit, or sometimes explicit, expectations of the 'normal' student in each learning context. Further, these accounts revealed some of the ways in which processes of exclusion and judgements made about academic competency were inherently gendered (see Gillies, this volume). These particular strengths of the vignettes will be examined further in the following sections, evaluating their particular potential for investigating disabled students' experiences.

Sensitivity, disability and the 'normality' of the vignette

By presenting a range of fictional scenarios for the students to discuss, they were able to talk about distressing and exclusionary events from a detached point of view, leaving the decision about whether to make personal disclosures firmly in their control. The vignettes also offered a number of recognisable stories, which allowed them to form identifications in a less stigmatising fashion. Over time, as the stories of exclusion and impairment-related dilemmas were approached as a more common form of experience, and feelings of stigmatisation were more openly confronted in less individualised ways, this resulted in more direct reference between the vignettes and their own experiences of marginalisation. Consequently, the students were well placed to introduce their own sensitive disability-related topics solely on their own terms. It was notable that one member of the group did this from an early stage; a young man, Sam, whose family had experienced great difficulty in getting his social and educational needs recognised, and therefore met, for many years. As such, his more politicised views on disability were apparent from the start, allowing him to confront sensitive issues on a referential basis with a considerable degree of anger, as well as humour. Chief among the issues he raised were the substantial degrees of segregation and isolation he had faced in his school life and the anger he expressed about his mother's futile struggle to get a statement of educational[3] need for him. Referring to himself as unfairly treated in comparison to other disabled students in the school, who had statements and were seen as having more legitmate needs, Sam said:

> When I do something similar I get really punished. They only get a warning but I get a negative in my planner and I know why I am the only pupil in the [SEN resource centre] with no statement of education.

Although his assertive manner created a little dissonance in the group, Sam's eagerness to talk about disabling educational processes enhanced the gradual movement of the other group members from the general (of the vignette) to the particular (of their own experiences).

Individual judgements and moral (would/should) dilemmas

In composing the vignettes, we made up believable scenarios, which blended the mundane with unusual or controversial behaviour, placing an individual disabled pupil at the centre of each story. The students were able to respond with confidence as Barter and Renold (1999) suggest, enabling them to give more detailed comments on the educational needs and rights of the disabled young person in the vignette. The more abstract nature of the conversation and the shifting of the locus of disability onto the young person in the vignette enabled our participants to speak more openly and to make comparisons with the practices of the school, as well as their own views on how disability should be accommodated (or not).

> *AW:* How would you feel about it if there was a kid in the class who was always with the TA [teaching assistant]?
> *Jenny:* I think that it's up to them whether they want a TA or not but if they don't want one they don't have to have one do they?
> *Sam:* or maybe she needs a TA.
> *AW:* But say you were in that position, and it was like you, think say like I've got to choose between my friends or flunking everything cos I need the help.
> *Sarah:* then you would have the TA wouldn't you? . . . They are just a person, they need extra help it's not their fault it's just a person.
> *VS:* So you wouldn't see the TA as a barrier in any way.
> *Jenny:* No.
> *AW:* Do you think there is ways round it in the classroom if that happened that somebody could do something to make sure that

Jenny: Involve them even if they've got a TA you can still talk to them and involve them in the conversation.

VS: Even if that is going through the TA so for example even if it's someone who couldn't speak very well.

Sarah: Yeah you can still involve them or use hand gestures.

Sam: Or maybe someone who doesn't understand things well.

Sarah: Then you will make it so they understood you; you will try to make them understand.

Sam: Well what if she needed a TA for certain lessons like English say if she had trouble understanding punctuation and stuff she would need a Teaching Assistant for that but maybe for something like science she didn't need a TA.

The provision of sufficient but 'fuzzy' context (ibid.) allowed the students to engage with depictions on their own terms, especially where aspects of the vignettes could be found in their own experiences. Prompt questions (such as the role of the teacher towards the disabled pupil and responsibilities towards the wider class) were often supplied by the researchers after initial comments were given. These follow-up questions from the researchers and the conflicting views of the students created a multi-perspectival platform, producing data that gave clear evidence of the would/should dilemmas they faced on a daily basis. This served to highlight the differences in their own actions towards inequity and their beliefs about how they and other people should be educated. In turn, this highlighted the conditions of possibility for their inclusion, allowing us many insights into disabling aspects of the school culture, particularly in illustrating how narrowly defined discourses on academic competency were linked to ideas of deservingness and personal value. Disabling practices included the physical segregation of pupils accredited with SEN, the simultaneous labelling of pupils with SEN and non-recognition of their educational needs, and the negative attitudes of some teachers towards pupils accredited with SEN, numerous examples of which were provided by the young people in this study. As such, the vignettes provided a valuable tool for these students to question the 'doxa' (see, for example, Bourdieu and Eagleton, 1992; Throop and Murphy, 2002) of the school. Doxa is conceptualised here as the field of opinion, or common belief, which is 'beyond question and which each agent tacitly accords by the mere fact of acting in accord with social convention' (Bourdieu, 1977, p. 169). Opening up everyday understandings of teachers' and students' roles to scrutiny helped the students to defamiliarise themselves with the common-sense beliefs in the 'taken for granted' stuctures and processes of school life, and to unravel the ways that this has constituted them as 'difficult' subjects of education. This was made possible by the removal of themselves from the fictional scenarios, helping them to denaturalise everyday situations as a 'neutral' onlooker, which simultaneously resonated with their own experiences.

The elucidation of situational contexts and influential variables

Where appropriate, our follow-up questions allowed pupils to take a more complex view of inclusion, and their own agency in facing disabling structures, leading to more dialogue on what 'should' be done as well as what *can* be done. This challenged them to discuss how the competing needs of different pupils may sometimes be hard to reconcile, extending their multi-faceted consideration of inclusion, while allowing them also to consider the teachers' points of view alongside their own and other students' unmet needs. In turn, this often led them back to more forceful statements on the limited possibilities of their own agency, especially in meeting academic standards at the school's fast and (ostensibly) undifferentiated pace:

> *Sarah:* She doesn't see everybody as equal she is you know 'I like her better so I am going to go with her'.
>
> *VS:* So someone she thinks might do better at the subject she treats them better?
>
> *Sarah:* Yeah, you know she will help the A stars but you know the Bs and Cs she is like yeah I am not helping them.
>
> *Luke:* Yeah, they're always picking on us, and they think like you're rubbish but all you're trying to do is do your best, but they don't see it like that sometimes. 'Cause I mean, like when you're playing football, and say, you passed the ball to the wrong person, sometimes they can have a real go at you, but you're just trying to do your best.

Although their identification as disabled students was never directly addressed, their willingness to move from vignettes about disability to their own experiences of marginalisation was indicative of the liminal place they occupied within the school. They knew they were being treated as 'abnormal' but all of these students were treated as 'difficult' in the classroom, as well as in the SEN resource base, rather than as disabled or as having unmet educational needs. As young people with unmet needs, but with no obvious physical or sensory impairments or statements of SEN, they illuminated how the disavowal of their value was two-fold, being neither identified as 'normal students' nor as disabled ones.

It is notable that the vignettes we created tended to be about students who had more obvious physical or sensory impairments, situations that were substantially different from those encountered by the young people in our study, who were deemed as slower learners or as students with inappropriate social and behavioural needs. This distancing or non-recognition of themselves as 'really' disabled was clear in their accounts of unfair (perceived favouritism) treatment of pupils with more obvious impairments or statements of educational need.

The excerpt below revolves around a young person in the school who was also designated as having SEN. The young people who we interviewed demonstrated intolerance and impatience with teachers' attitudes towards this pupil, who they felt received 'special treatment' and was not punished equally to other students.

> *Sarah:* I think she [the teacher] feels sorry for him cos she knows he is a bit special, not special but you know what I mean so she feels sorry for him so she doesn't want to make him feel bad but he is still a person he is in Year 9, he should remember ingredients.
>
> *Jenny:* Yeah she doesn't want to punish him cos she doesn't know how he will react. Well she is going to have to punish him sometime cos he has done something wrong he needs to be punished she shouldn't treat us differently to how she treats him.

However, their tacit recognition of commonalities of disablement was there from the start, demonstrating the importance of exclusion on the basis of difficulty as a major point of identification. We were also able to gain a sense of significant variations in experience according to differentiated pedagogical strategies. For example, one of the students explained how the 'protective' intent of a segregated resource base failed in respect of this central purpose:

> *Sam:* [The resource base] is supposed to protect students in [it] from bullying but it doesn't say anything about stopping people annoying me and there is this student called Walter and he is annoying me all the time.

Here, and elsewhere, the students were able to reveal how strategies the school had adopted to accommodate disabled students were built on simplistic assumptions of potential dynamics between students and expectations of homogeneity between disabled students. Sam's statement indicated that although his exclusion from mainstream classes was supposed to protect him from other students, he clearly expressed that his needs remained unmet (and on other occasions stated that he did not like being segregated within the context of the school).

The development of new topics for the vignettes and the subsequent discussion over time also allowed us to gain deeper insights into the way that expectations of gender fed into processes and experiences of inclusion. This was perhaps most apparent in the ways that the young women in the study felt ignored and disregarded as less able students compared to the higher achieving 'teacher's pets' and in the reports from the young men in the study of being more likely to get into trouble for inappropriate behaviour.

The vignettes were especially valuable in elucidating these kinds of situational contexts of school culture as Barton and Renold suggest (1999), particularly as they challenged the individualism inherent within discourses of SEN and the foregrounding of specific impairment-related needs (Lewis and Norwich, 2005). They were also useful in exploring the influential variables of school, wider administrative/policy structures and the pedagogies of individual teachers from the perspectives of those who were affected by them, illustrated clearly by the students' comments about statementing and teachers' attitudes. Hence the data gathered lend weight to arguments for inclusion and a capabilities approach (Lumby and Morrison, 2009), putting the students voices at the centre.

Strengths, caveats and considerations

The findings of this study indicate that the young people in this sample were keenly aware of the homogenising discourse used around disability, SEN and inclusion by the school. Assumptions of similarity were made clear in teachers' treatment of pupils deemed as having SEN and the school's expectations of 'disabled' pupils. The data suggests, further, that these young people occupied a liminal place within the school, demonstrating awareness of their positioning as 'difficult' by the school, but simultaneously distancing themselves from identification as disabled. However, recognition of communality with other pupils deemed to be problematic within the school context did emerge; exclusion within the classroom context on the basis of difficulty was particularly evident as a primary point of identification.

On a methodological level, the data gathered from this research demonstrated that the vignette method had particular value for this group of disabled students. Vignettes were particularly suitable for this group of students who are doubly marginalised by liminal positioning, as people with 'invisible' impairments and without statements of educational need, and as people who did not identify as disabled but narrated experiences of social and academic exclusion on the basis of their 'difficulty'. We did not want to make direct references to their impairments as the main focus of our interest, given that the pupils did not identify explicitly with a disabled status; questions asking them directly about their own impairments and experiences of disability would have fed the discourses that emphasised their sense of difference and marginalisation. The naming of their difference and the purpose of our visits are likely to have affected levels of trust in the researchers, particularly if we emphasised their value in the more partial terms of *their* special educational needs. This highlights another important issue of 'voice'; rather than a more partial personalised perspective, the use of vignettes provides a very flexible structure and has considerable potential for participants to present a more multi-voiced perspective on their own lives. Participants retain control over when and where they interact, they have a choice of points of identification with the vignette and choice regarding whether they discuss personal experiences and/or offer more abstract comments.

This freedom in the ways that the young people approached and used the vignettes certainly allowed them to move from stories to their own experiences and to focus a growing amount of attention on the conditions of their own learning and exploration of the ways they had been treated within the school (on an everyday basis and over time). It is difficult to assess whether this exploration of disabling structures and processes contributed to a greater 'conscientisation' (Freire, 1970), particularly as we would like to think that they fully understand and express the conditions of their oppression away from the prying ears of adults. It did, however, allow for a fuller expression of their voice, on their own terms.

Analysis of the transcripts reveals a steady rise in confidence in speaking over time. It is improbable that one visit would have produced valuable or valid data on their experiences. Numerous visits allowed trust to build and for the reserved members of the group to take a more active role. While criticisms of the school were apparent in the first transcript, these were usually made by the most 'political' member of the group and these criticisms were more evenly spread between the participants as time went on. It is also possible that the students reflected on the vignette discussions between visits as some of the comments in the latter groups built on earlier discussions, providing a more nuanced picture. This was apparent in the growing number of comparisons between their own experiences of fairness and the treatment of the 'preferred' students.

Although the increasing enthusiasm of these students to reveal more of themselves over time provided us with useful data on the culture of the school, these disclosures can be seen as a potentially oppressive aspect of the research, especially as there was a comparative degree of reluctance to talk about the school in the first visit and the ever-present risk of their teachers overhearing them. This was anticipated and minimised in two main ways. In addition to assurances of confidentiality and anonymity, we encouraged primary school pupils to ask us questions and offered them information on ourselves (on their terms) to lessen the inequitable relationship between us. They were also given regular opportunities to check and retract data, as Oakley (1981, pp. 30–61) suggests. Further, we encouraged the participants to write vignettes of their own in between our visits, so that they could have some control over what was spoken about and ensure that the issues discussed were meaningful to them.

Drawing on Finch (1987), Barter and Renold (1999, Summer) argue that 'the indeterminate relationship between beliefs and actions is the biggest danger in using this technique in isolation' (not paginated). This was a strength in our project in that their discussions illuminated the dissonance between beliefs in equity and actions taken or deemed possible, highlighting major barriers to inclusion within school culture. As such, vignette methods are likely to be of more general use in investigating other disabled students' experiences of exclusion in school. Used sensitively and creatively, they have great potential as an inclusive and anti-oppressive methodology, where care is taken to present vignettes in an accessible manner, providing students with a wide number of points of identification over time. They are a particularly valuable method for eliciting the views and accounts of those who feel themselves to have 'inbetweener' identities, where more direct methods of investigation might add to feelings of liminality and exclusion.

Overall, then, we found that vignettes were a method that was very well suited to the study of these young people's experiences and opinions of equity. For a number of reasons, the vignettes allowed us to gain clearer insights into disabled young people's opinions of their school environment and wider pedagogical issues, while minimising the oppressive dimensions manifested in many educational studies of disability, particularly those that take an individualistic or deficit model of children or young people accredited with SEN (see Wilde and Avramidis (2011) for a more detailed discussion).

At the same time, these students' accounts illuminated the disabling effects of school doxa, demonstrating how (unstatemented) students attributed as having SEN are positioned as difficult and 'abnormal' subjects of education. Perceiving themselves as not competent, not 'special', not disabled, these students struggled to find an identity within the school's culture, distanced from both disabled students and their non-disabled peers. Their accounts of exclusion suggest that SEN are seen as a polarity rather than a continuum, providing a compelling case for inclusion based on the recognition of a continuum of needs, abilities, competencies and different ways of participating in learning environments and school cultures.

Notes

1. The UK 2001 SEN Code of Practice School introduced School Action and School Action Plus, designed to provide graduated programmes of help. These are interventions provided to children who have been identified as needing 'extra' or 'different' help with learning. If School Action is insufficient, School Action Plus increases the resources available and includes direct help from external professionals.
2. In this study, multiple levels of designation of SEN were identified: 'self-perceived', 'official' and 'resourced'. While all pupils selected for participation in the study were officially designated, that is, by the school, as having SEN, none of the pupils in the sample had a statement of educational needs, that is, no resources were specifically attached to meeting their additional learning needs. All of the pupils in the sample appeared aware that they were designated as having SEN by the school, but only one of them explicitly referred to their SEN during the course of the interviews.
3. A statement of educational need is given to students who are recognised as having needs for additional resources that the school cannot meet. A statement is a lengthy, detailed document provided by the local education authority, which describes all the child's 'additional needs' and the support they should be given.

References

Barter, C. and Renold, E. (1999) The use of vignettes in qualitative research, *Social Research Update*, Issue 25, Department of Sociology, University of Surrey. http://sru.soc.surrey.ac.uk/SRU25.html [accessed 1 March 2011].

Barter, C. and Renold, E. (2002) 'Dilemmas in control: Methodological implications and reflections of foregrounding children's perspectives on violence'.

In E. Stanko and R. Lee (Eds), *Researching Violence.* (pp. 88–107) London: Routledge.

Bourdieu, P. (1977[1972]) *Outline of a Theory of Practice.* R. Nice, transl. Volume 16. Cambridge: Cambridge University Press.

Bourdieu, P. and Eagleton, T. (January/February, 1992) Doxa and common life. *New Left Review*, 191(1).

British Educational Research Association. (2009) BERA Insights Tender Specification. http://www.bera.ac.uk/files/2009/03/bera-insights-tender.pdf [accessed 1 March 2011].

Bryman, A. (2008) *Social Research Methods.* Oxford: Oxford University Press.

DCFS. (2009) Children with Special Educational Needs: An Analysis, 8th October. http://www.education.gov.uk/rsgateway/DB/STA/t000851/index.shtml [accessed 1 March 2011].

Felmlee, D. and Muraco, A. (2009) Gender and friendship norms among older adults. *Research on Aging*, 31(3): 318–344.

Fielding, M. (2001) Students as radical agents of change. *Journal of Educational Change*, 2(3): 123–141.

Fielding, M. and Bragg, S. (2003) *Students as Researchers: Making a Difference. Consulting Pupils about Teaching and Learning.* Cambridge: Pearson Publishing.

Finch, J. (1987) The vignette technique in survey research. *Sociology*, 21: 105–114.

Freire, P. (1970) *Pedagogy of the Oppressed.* New York and London: Continuum Books.

Hamill, P. and Boyd, B. (2002) Equality, fairness and rights – The young person's voice. *British Journal of Special Education*, 29(3): 111–117.

Hazel, N. (1995) Elicitation techniques with young people, *Social Research Update*, Issue 12, Department of Sociology, University of Surrey. http://www.soc.surrey.ac.uk/sru/SRU12.html [accessed 1 March 2011].

Lewis, A. (2001) Reflections on interviewing children and young people as a method of inquiry in exploring their perspectives on integration/inclusion. *Journal of Research in Special Educational Needs*, 1(3). doi: 10.1111/j.1471-3802.2001.00146.x.

Lewis, A. and Porter, J. (2004) Interviewing children and young people with learning disabilities: Guidelines for researchers and multi-professional practice. *British Journal of Learning Disabilities*, 32: 191–197.

Liebes, T. and Katz, E. (1993) *The Export of Meaning: Cross-Cultural Readings of Dallas.* Oxford: Oxford University Press.

Lumby, J. and Morrison, M. (2009) Youth perspectives: Schooling, capabilities frameworks and human rights. *International Journal of Inclusive Education*, 13(6): 581–596.

Moules, T. (2009) 'They wouldn't know how it feels...': Characteristics of quality care from young people's perspectives: A participatory research project. *Journal of Child Health Care*, 13(4): 322–332.

Oakley, A. (1981) 'Interviewing women: A contradiction in terms'. In R. Helen (Ed), *Doing Feminist Research.* London: Routledge and Kegan Paul.

O'Kane, C. (2008) 'The development of participatory techniques: Facilitating children's views about decisions which affect them'. In P. M. Christensen and A. James (Eds), *Research with Children: Perspectives and Practices* (2nd ed). Oxon and New York: Routledge.

Osler, A. (2000) Children's rights, responsibilities and understandings of school discipline. *Research Papers in Education*, 15(1): 49–67.

Reay, D. (2006) 'I'm not seen as one of the clever children': Consulting primary school pupils about the social conditions of learning. *Educational Review*, 58(2): 171–181.

Rogers, C. (2007) *Parenting and Inclusive Education: Discovering Difference, Experiencing Difficulty*. Basingstoke: Palgrave Macmillan.

Rose, R. and Shevlin, M. (2004) Encouraging voices: Listening to young people who have been marginalised. *Support for Learning*, 19(4): 155–161.

Rudduck, J. (2004) Consulting students about teaching and learning. In A. Pollard and M. James (Eds), *Personalised Learning: A Commentary by the Teaching and Learning Research Programme*. Cambridge: ESRC TLRP.

Rudduck, J. and Flutter, J. (2000) Pupil participation and pupil perspective: 'carving a new order of experience'. *Cambridge Journal of Education*, 30(1): 75–89.

Sellman, E. (2011) Peer mediation services for conflict resolution in schools: What transformations in activity characterise successful implementation? *British Educational Research Journal*, 31(1): 45–60.

Sen, A. (1999) *Development as Freedom*. Oxford: Oxford University Press.

Throop, C. J. and Murphy, K. M. (2002) Bourdieu and phenomenology: A critical assessment. *Anthopological Theory*, 2(2): 185–207.

Wilde, A. and Avramidis, E. (2011) Mixed feelings: Towards a continuum of inclusive pedagogies, in Education, 3–13, 38(4): 1–19.

Wood, E. (2003) The power of pupil perspectives in evidence-based practice: The case of gender and underachievement. *Research Papers in Education*, 18(4): 365–383.

4
Mainstreaming and the Subjectification of Deaf and Hard-of-Hearing Children

Elizabeth S. Mathews

Systematic education organised via institutional spaces for deaf and hard-of-hearing (D/HH) children began in the late eighteenth century and flourished through the nineteenth century. While these schools predominantly used Sign Language in instruction, by the beginning of the twentieth-century Sign Language had almost completely disappeared in the instruction of D/HH students in schools across Europe and the USA. Teachers who were themselves D/HH and had been working alongside their hearing colleagues for over a century became redundant in the deaf education system.

This chapter presents a Foucauldian analysis on the history of deaf education and the implications this has for contemporary movements in deaf education. In particular, it examines the historic subjectification of D/HH children through the education system. This process of subjectification (in the Foucauldian sense) takes place in three stages: dividing practices, scientific classification, and subjectification (Rabinow, 1984). Using the example of deaf education (paying particular attention to the case of the Republic of Ireland), this chapter traces the chronological development through the three stages. In particular, it is argued that while dividing practices and scientific classification have long been part of the deaf education landscape, the subjectification of D/HH children is much more a feature of recent educational trends marking a move towards bio-power. The historicist analysis will focus on two international events to illustrate this phenomenon: the entry of the physician into the system of deaf education,[1] and the subsequent change from a manual education system to one focusing on aural rehabilitation and speech training. The recent trend examined is the mainstreaming of deaf education. Mainstreaming identifies the local public school as the preferred environment for the education of children with special educational needs (SEN) (including D/HH children) and has become almost hegemonic as an educational philosophy in recent decades (Holt, 2003).

While the historical context surrounding these events was addressed by Branson and Miller (2002) in relation to the British system, and the French and American systems have also been well documented (Baynton, 1996; Lane, 1989; van Cleve and Crouch, 1989; Winefield, 1987), such theoretical positioning has been rare in the Irish context,[2] where instead histories of deaf education are largely biographical or descriptive in nature (Crean, 1997; Griffey, 1994; Pollard, 2006). Furthermore, while Branson and Miller (2002) take Foucault as their inspiration in conducting their 'sociological imagination' of deaf education, and his writings are echoed through the book particularly in their examination of 'the great confinement' and 'clinical gaze' of D/HH people, they refrain from making explicit connections between the specific techniques outlined by Foucault in the creation of subjects and how these might apply to D/HH people. As a result of this gap in the literature, this chapter hopes to explicitly and critically connect the techniques of discipline and modes of creating a subject outlined by Foucault to examine the development of deaf education.

In particular, this chapter focuses on changes that took place during the eighteenth and nineteenth centuries, giving rise to a systematic discipline of deaf education that created subjects out of D/HH children. Due to the influence of the US and European school systems on the situation in Ireland, the international focus of this chapter will limit itself to those jurisdictions, in particular France, the USA and the UK. By taking Foucault's 'Birth of the Asylum' as an example, the history of deaf education will be traced from its anatamo-politic history to its bio-politic present. As deaf education developed (much like psychiatry as analysed by Foucault), the element of control moved from the body of the D/HH person in its entirety controlled through segregation practices, to an internalised control of the mind by constructing a discourse of deafness to be rejected by D/HH people themselves. In carrying out this analysis, instead of concentrating on changing social conditions as others have done, the focus here is on the rise of a medicalised deaf education system by examining the rise of the social authority of the doctor in educational matters and the subsequent development of a negative discourse of Sign Language. Such a negative discourse of Sign Language came about as the medical process of 'curing' hearing loss concentrated its efforts on the production of speech as a signifier of overcoming this impairment. Sign Language, in contrast, was viewed as the linguistic 'back up' for those children who failed to acquire speech successfully.

Foucault and the creation of subjects

The theoretical framework used throughout this chapter comes from Foucault's writing on the creation of subjects. Foucault examines how the change from a feudal to a state system of governance during the sixteenth century created an opportunity for the state to become involved in all forms of human activity, with the goal of establishing how each activity could be best (most economically) accomplished (Foucault, 1978). This change culminated in the development of bio-power, a new range of power dedicated to the life, growth and care of the population. This development was epitomised by the emergence of statistics in the seventeenth century, a discipline devoted to the knowledge, categorisation and normalisation of individual human beings. Using examples from psychiatry, education, the military and sexual practices/behaviours, Foucault illustrates how, from the eighteenth century on, a great body of knowledge was generated around human beings through the sciences of life, extending the level of control available over individual subjects and promoting what would eventually become a self-administered discipline constructed through the establishment of norms (Rabinow, 1984).

While a great deal of Foucault's writings focused on these processes of discipline, Foucault himself saw his work not as a study of power, but more as a study of 'creat[ing] a history of the different modes by which, in our culture, human beings are made subjects' (in Rabinow, 1984, p. 7). Rabinow (1984) reflects on Foucault's work to identify three stages in this 'objectification of the subject': dividing practices, scientific classification and subjectification. Dividing practices refer to how the subject is objectified by a process of division either within himself/herself or from others (Rabinow, 1984). Scientific classification describes methods of enquiry 'which try to give themselves the status of sciences [...] the objectivizing of the sheer fact of being alive in natural history or biology' (Rabinow, 1984, p. 9). Finally, subjectification refers to 'the way a human being turns him- or herself into a subject' (Rabinow, 1984, p. 11).

These stages are not independent of each other, but rather swap characteristics and flow into each other. Nonetheless, there is a general chronological development from dividing practices starting in the eighteenth century, through scientific classification of the nineteenth century, to more recent processes of subjectification (see Figure 4.1).

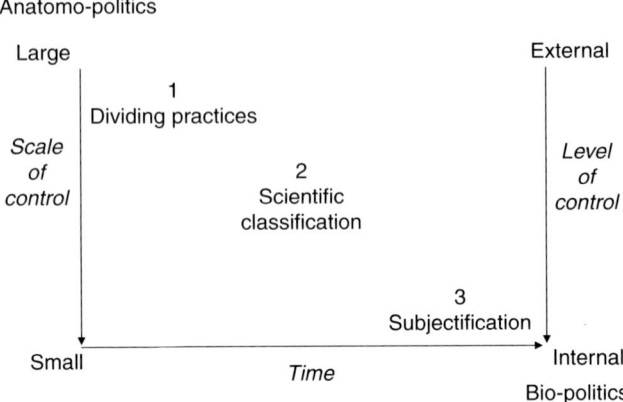

Figure 4.1   Foucauldian processes in the creation of a subject.

Furthermore, there is a refinement in the scale at which these forces take effect upon the body, moving from large-scale control (confining the entire body in dividing practices) to small-scale control (containing and training thoughts in the mind in subjectification). This is mirrored in the location at which control is exerted, moving from external control (again focusing on the exterior of the body or space the body occupies) to internal control (controlling the mind, how the body functions and behaves in space in quite minute detail).

Foucault categorised these different forms of power into two distinct eras: the period of anatamo-politics, where power was concerned with the physical body (body as machine), and the period of bio-politics, where power focused on the body as a species (Foucault, 1978, pp. 261–262). The former relied on more explicit forms of punishment, as a warning and thus incentive to comply among the populace. This developed into a more sophisticated form of control, involving an element of spatial organisation through the development of centralised institutions. Developing beyond this, bio-politics and bio-power (governmentality) disperse power to such an extent that it becomes internalised, encouraging self-regulation and self-governance without the need of a particular spatial institution of domination.

While this internalisation of discipline began on a concrete spatial environment, represented by Bentham's Panopticon, the Panopticon has now become more metaphorical in nature, and though its architecture may be increasingly dismantled in an age of deinstitutionalisation, the ideology remains. Thus, the chronology of Foucault's analysis on power moves from spatially specific sites of control such as the hospital (Foucault, 1965) or the prison (Foucault, 1977) to spatially dispersed forms of governmentality through bio-power in the modern state (Foucault, 1982). This chronological progress therefore mirrors the progress of deaf education from spatially specific sites to dispersed forms of education, with children traditionally segregated and confined in particular enclosed spaces (work houses, asylums, and later, schools for the deaf), now moving towards integration in their local community.

The suitability of Foucault's theories for analysing deaf education has been noted by other authors, for example, analyses on the history of deaf education in the USA (Baynton, 1996), the UK and Australia (Branson and Miller, 2002) and France (Lane, 1976, 1989). My intention here is not to repeat these analyses but to extend them by focusing on specific aspects. The focus on Ireland is useful (not simply because it was the field for my doctoral research) but because it is unusual in its trend of deaf education. Where the development from dividing practices, through scientific classification and onto subjectification took several centuries to witness in most other countries, because Ireland was late to adopt an oralist or speech-centred system of education (approximately a century after much of the USA, the UK and continental Europe), the progress through the three stages mentioned above are more easily witnessed in quick succession. The remainder of this chapter will deal with this issue, beginning with an examination on how these three stages manifest in the history of the deaf education system before progressing to the impact this has on contemporary trends.

Deaf education and the development of D/HH subjects

Dividing practices were a significant feature in the early establishment of education for D/HH children, with the large-scale segregation (or congregation) of D/HH children. McDonnell (2007) highlights the important role the establishment of poor houses and, following that, early modern hospitals had in paving the way for charitable institutions, such as schools for D/HH children catering for the needs of the 'unfit' of society. As a result, schools for the deaf were opened in abundance throughout Europe and the USA from the eighteenth century onwards. With this widespread delivery of deaf education, student demographics changed substantially. Originally limited to the children of nobility and upper-class families, and conducted in small one-to-one settings, education became accessible to the D/HH children of poor families. While private entrepreneurs remained significant players in deaf education, the clergy took on a leading role in the establishment of schools across Europe and the USA.

The world's first state-sponsored school for the Deaf opened in Paris circa 1760, established by a Catholic clergyman Charles Michel Abée de l'Epée. This was soon followed by a school in Britain established by Thomas Braidwood, an entrepreneur rather than a clergyman, which was funded by the King from 1783 onwards (Branson and Miller, 2002). Systematic education would not be established in the USA and Ireland until the beginning of the nineteenth century, but again the clergy was to play a significant role in its development. The religious undertones of this movement were highlighted during the inaugural speech at the first commencement ceremony at the National College of Deaf Mutes (later to become Gallaudet College) in Washington, DC:

> From moral darkness, deeper even than that of heathen ignorance, wherein no proper idea of God or religion could germinate, to the full light of comprehended and accepted Christianity, stimulating the soul to the highest development possible in our world of many clouds, and revealing the glorious hope of ripened fruitage under the rays of the Sun of Righteousness in the land of eternal day.
>
> (Gallaudet, 1983: 252)

During this period, Sign Language was the dominant method of instruction, itself symptomatic of the goals of mass education. While teaching D/HH children to speak and lip-read had been pursued by entrepreneurs in deaf education, the goal of 'opening the minds' of D/HH children to the gospel was best achieved through the use of Sign Language. Speech training required intensive one-to-one tutoring, and was at the time a haphazard and often unsuccessful pursuit. Sign Language, on the contrary, allowed for the education of large groups by a single teacher and had greater success in terms of overall comprehension of pupils. Much of this movement was rooted in the first state school for the deaf in Paris, where a system of Sign language based on those signs used by his pupils and was devised and standardised by its superintendent – L'Abée de l'Epée. This system was brought to the USA by Laurent Clerc, a pupil of the Institute in Paris who accompanied an American clergyman (Gallaudet) and spread rapidly across the continent through their efforts.

While a degree of debate ensued over the use of Sign Language for speech, the period was largely characterised by schools for the deaf following a manual communication system. This did not last long, however, and while education through Sign language was flourishing in the USA, the home of the manual method – the Institute in Paris – was undergoing dramatic changes that would soon shift the emphasis away from manual instruction to a pure oral system. These changes largely came about due to the presence of a new figure in the deaf education field – the physician – and the coinciding rise in the authority of medicine during this period. This rise in the authority of medicine marks the second method of objectification, scientific classification. Foucault had noted that 'starting in the 18th century human existence, human behaviour, and the human body were brought into an increasingly dense and important network of medicalization that allowed fewer and fewer things to escape' (Foucault, 2002, p. 135).

Under this movement, deafness became pathologised and medicalised in finely measured deviations from what was established as a hearing norm. Foucault observes that in the eighteenth century the field of medicine emerged as a strong force in the identification and treatment of deviant bodies and notes that '[t]he doctor becomes a great adviser and expert, if not in the art of governing at least in that of observing, correcting, and improving the social "body" and maintaining it in a permanent state of health' (Foucault in Faubion, 2002, p. 100). The medicalisation of D/HH bodies, and its subsequent entry into 'a machinery of power' began a little later, at the turn of the nineteenth century in France. Branson and Miller (2002) highlight that the ready availability of guillotined heads following the French Revolution at the end of the eighteenth century provided cadavers for medical research, giving rise to a more rapid development of knowledge in audiology in France than was happening elsewhere. These developments were accompanied by the entry of a physician into the Institute in Paris, which was to dramatically influence the direction of deaf education for the coming centuries.

On 31 December 1800, Jean-Marc-Gaspard Itard began his post as resident physician at Epée's Institute in Paris. Ironically, Itard had been hired, not as a physician for D/HH children generally, but to take over the care and education of Victor, the *enfant sauvage* who had been found one year earlier in the forests of Aveyron and entrusted to the care of the Institute. During and after his five years of training with Victor, Itard transferred his attention to the D/HH students at the institute, making a number of discoveries about deafness that led significantly to the establishment of a systematic approach of assessment, classification and oral instruction of D/HH children, a realm that had been largely haphazard until this time. As Lane summarises, 'To Itard must go to credit for developing, largely independently, a systematic, principled program of oral training which would later be instituted in France and elaborated and modified by other teachers of the deaf throughout Europe and America' (1976, p. 185).

The 'success' of Itard's work with D/HH children rested on a number of factors, which were later to become characteristic of the rise of the authority of the medical professional in the field of deaf education and the period of scientific classification. Firstly, Itard reduced the scale at which treatment of the D/HH child was targeted from the child en masse to the individual components of their hearing and speech. Secondly, they selected 'appropriate' candidates and provided intensive individual tutoring in speech, establishing speech instead of language as the goal of deaf education. Thirdly, he established a meticulous and standardised medical approach to documenting and disseminating his findings. Finally, he mobilised the support of medical authorities who could lend weight to his method. In 1808, when he presented his most successful articulation student to the Society of the Faculty of Medicine, they concurred with his recommendation stating that 'the development of speech will be more prompt and more complete the less the subject is able to use manual sign language' (Lane, 1976, p. 204). Thus, the medical pursuit of speech for D/HH children began in earnest.

Deaf education in Ireland, established as it was during a time when great debate was taking place in both the UK and on mainland Europe regarding educational methodology, saw a complex mix of dividing practices and scientific classification come into play. The methods employed at the various schools in Ireland at the time seemed to represent the complexity and fluidity of the contemporary situation. The first school for the deaf, the Claremont Institute, was opened in 1816 by the medical doctor Charles Edward Herbert Orpen. Typical of scientific rationality of the time, and following in Itard's footsteps, Orpen's progress utilised his social authority as a physician and focused on the complete study of one individual. One Thomas Collins was selected from a group of children chosen from the Foundling Hospital and the Bedford Asylum for Orphans and used as a case study to garner public support for the need for an education system for the deaf across Ireland. Thomas spent three months under Dr Orpen's care and featured in Dr Orpen's lectures at the Rotunda Assembly Rooms in Dublin. These lectures in Dublin and a later series across the country brought a great deal of interest, and funds were gathered by the Protestant Archbishops to open a school in Dublin, which would eventually be housed in Claremont, Glasnevin.

The religious sponsorship of the school was typical of education in Ireland at the time, and although Orpen was a medical doctor, he approached deaf education from the salvation model. In 1827, he published a book on his findings entitled *The Contrast, between Atheism, Paganism and Christianity, illustrated; or the Uneducated Deaf and Dumb, as Heathens, compared with those, Who Have Been Instructed in Language and Revelation, and taught by the Holy Spirit, as Christians*. The title underlines the significance that religion had to play in the Irish context even within this medical setting. With this religious goal in mind, however, and considering the divisive nature of religious politics in Ireland at the time, it would not be long before a Catholic counterpart to the Protestant school in Claremont would be opened. Indeed, religious segregation in schools for D/HH children was to become a characteristic feature of deaf education in Ireland over the coming century.

The Very Reverend Thomas McNamara, C. M. instigated the search for funds to open a Catholic school for D/HH children in Dublin. As a result, in 1845 the Catholic Institute for the Deaf and Dumb (CIDD) was founded and St Mary's School for Deaf Girls (1846) and St Joseph's School for Deaf Boys (1857) were opened in Cabra, Dublin. The enrolment figures for the Claremont school went into significant decline after the establishment of the Cabra schools (Pollard, 2006). Like much of the education system in Ireland of the era, the CIDD operated with the voluntary service of Catholic Clergy. As Catholic-run schools, the Cabra institutions took their methods, not from the nearby Claremont School, who were beginning to introduce aspects of Oralism, nor from the renowned Protestant Braidwood family in England, but from French Catholic schools in Le Bon Sauveur, Caen (Crean, 1997). As a result, Cabra was like much of Europe in that the early development of systematic deaf education was largely manual and not oral. However, when the vast majority of schools for the deaf across the UK, the USA and continental Europe had changed to an oral system of education by the end of the nineteenth century, the Cabra schools remained true to the manual methods onto the middle of the twentieth century.

It was the Dominican Sisters teaching in St Mary's School for Deaf Girls (hereafter referred to as St Mary's) in Cabra, Dublin who paved the way for the change to oralism in the Irish deaf education system during the 1950s. Because St Mary's made the move before the Christian Brother's school for the boys, and because the documentation on that move is more plentiful than that in the boys' school, the situation in the girls' school will be recounted here at the expense of the other. Indeed, the Dominican Sisters had established their leadership status in deaf education 100 years previously when it was they, and not the Christian brothers, who established the first school for D/HH children under the CIDD. As the Christian Brother's frequently sought the advice of the Dominican Sisters in their educational endeavours (Crean, 1997), we can assume that their path into oralism was somewhat similar.

The change to Oralism at St Mary's during the 1950s was particularly significant, considering that it was a school that had, for over 100 years and with great international acclaim, promoted the education of D/HH girls through Sign Language. The concept of dividing practices and scientific classification as it occurred in the international development of deaf education has been covered above. However, a number of changes to these methods were implemented in the oral context. D/HH children were segregated from their hearing peers throughout the eighteenth and nineteenth centuries for education, but the oral system saw more minute practices of segregation of deaf students from their *deaf* peers, with those using Sign Language separated from new students entering the school who had not been exposed to Sign Language. This segregation happened in stages in St Mary's progressing in severity with time, and reflects the convergence of methods of turning D/HH children into subjects.

In 1946, segregating those students who were partially deaf from those who were profoundly deaf became a priority in St Mary's (Griffey, 1994). This form of categorisation introduced an overt medicalisation of the students enrolled there, which had hitherto been absent. This segregation process began with testing all students' hearing levels to facilitate appropriate placement. However, this form of scientific classification was new to the school in Cabra and funding was necessary to purchase the audiology equipment necessary to test and categorise students, so an audiology clinic was opened in the school in 1947.

During this initial phase of oralism, pupils already enrolled in the school were taught using a mixture of signs, speech and lip-reading, while those newly admitted students were taught with an oral method only (Griffey, 1994). However, after a number of years, the principal at the time concluded that the school was still a manual one. In particular, she observed that students in the oral programme mixed with those taught manually during their free time and that it was 'obvious that all pupils were more interested in manual communication than in speech' (1994: 43). Their segregation strategies were not, it appeared, stringent enough. Following a visit to Le Bon Sauveur school in Caens in 1951 (where the Dominican Sisters had first travelled 100 years previous), they concluded that complete separation of those students who used

Sign Language from those on the oral programme was necessary. The advice of the Caen Sisters was:

> [y]ou are wasting your time, you must separate the oral and the manual pupils. Find a building where the oral pupils will have no contact with those who are using signs. Separate! Separate! This is how we developed an oral atmosphere in the school.
>
> (Griffey, 1994, p. 47)

As a result, students continuing to use Sign Language were housed separately from those on the oral programme in a new wing on the top floor of St Mary's, which was called St Pius' School (Grehan, 2008). Later in the 1960s, plans were made so that the oral programme would be further divided into two: a programme for partially deaf students (Rosary School) and one for profoundly deaf students (St Mary's). The students were to be housed in separate sections of the school building, with different uniforms for each programme. While planning permission was sought to build a completely separate school for partially deaf students, this was not established until the 1970s. As a result, students attending Rosary School and St Pius were both located on the same floor, though separated by a long corridor. To ensure that these students did not mix, spatial segregation was accompanied by temporal segregation, which meant that common areas such as the playground or corridors were only inhabited by a particular group at each time, thus preventing students from seeing or communicating with each other (Grehan, 2008).

The use of different uniforms helped teachers in monitoring this segregation as it distinguished between categories of students, enabling teachers to quickly identify individual students and the communication stream within which they were placed, as well as their age group. Grehan (2008) describes the six different uniforms she wore as a profoundly deaf student going through St Mary's, showing the use of small changes in uniform between age groups as a means of identifying students. Furthermore, those students in St Pius wing had their hair cropped short. Another important feature, both supporting and being supported by the segregation of students was a number of restrictions around the use of Sign Language, which would become increasingly significant in the future of deaf education in Ireland. The use of spatial segregation, timetabling and uniforms shows the micro level of governance these D/HH girls were subject to, echoing again Foucault's concept of docile bodies.

It is evident that, similar to developments in Europe and the USA in the century before, Sign Language became devalued during the change to oralism in Ireland, a factor that applied not only to students but also to teachers. There is evidence that D/HH teachers, as well as hearing teachers who were able to sign, were let go during this period (Grehan, 2008). In examining the devaluing of Sign Language, McDonnell and Saunders (1993) refer to internal and external strategies used to enforce speech over signing. Internal strategies were focused on activities within the school and were directed at pupils. They consisted of controlling and disciplining strategies to try to minimise the use of Sign Language within the school through surveillance and punishment. For example, older students were encouraged to report on younger students who used signing, and students were instructed to be vigilant with their movements, with strategies such as holding their hands behind their back or sitting on their hands to discourage them from signing (McDonnell and Saunders, 1993).

Not content that these strategies would deter students from using manual communication if left to their own devices, a second set of strategies creating a negative discourse of Sign Language was implemented. McDonnell and Saunders (1993) highlight that this tackled the values and belief systems of the students, instilling a sense of shame and inferiority in those who used Sign Language. It extended control over student behaviour to those spaces and times where they were not supervised directly. This negative discourse of Sign Language represents the move to subjectification. It represents the move away from an anatamo-political control of D/HH bodies to a bio-political control by moving the focus of attention from the external control of an exterior body (through surveillance and punishment) to an internalised control of the mind (through the creation of a negative discourse of deafness that D/HH people will themselves come to reject). By internalising discipline, power over D/HH people becomes self-perpetuating, or in Allen's (2003) terms, imminent.

The very existence of a separate school for those students incapable of learning speech was the first step in establishing this negative discourse, by both socially and spatially isolating those students using Sign Language. Those students who failed within the oral system were socially isolated by being categorised as 'oral failures' and labelled 'deaf and dumb' (in spite of the fact that the term 'dumb' had been removed from the school name), and spatially isolated in the St Pius wing. Furthermore, students were explicitly told that Sign Language was aligned with 'being stupid' and that it would prevent them from learning speech specifically, as well as from learning in general (McDonnell and Saunders, 1993). Symbolically, the girls in the manual school had their hair cut short and wore it with a large bow, while those in the oral programme were allowed long hair (Woolfe, 2007), marking the manual students as different, inferior and childish. Indeed, the associations drawn between Sign Language and moral failure are highlighted by the fact that students from the oral programme have recounted that they were on occasion sent to St Pius as a punishment for misbehaviour. Grehan stresses:

> [i]t is important to emphasise that the threat of being sent to the 'Deaf and Dumb' school was held constantly over the girls in the oral programme. The 'Deaf and Dumb' school for them became synonymous with lack of intelligence, ostracisation and academic failure.
>
> (2008, p. 19)

Religion also played a part in the creation of a negative discourse of Sign Language and those who used it. Signing was seen as a sin to be confessed to a priest and students were encouraged to give up signing for Lent.

As well as strategies at play within the school, McDonnell and Saunders (1993) cite external strategies that were used to target the general public in obtaining recognition for the oral successes of the school. Students succeeding in the oral programme were rewarded by having access to public exams, access not granted to students in the Sign Language section of the school (McDonnell and Saunders, 1993). In public performances, signing students did not feature. Furthermore, the negative discourse of Sign Language used within the school was extended outside of school grounds and beyond the school life of children. McDonnell and Saunders' participants (1993) recounted that their employer was contacted by the principal of the school telling them not to allow D/HH staff to work together or to use Sign Language in the workplace, thus controlling the behaviour of students into their adult lives. As well as employers, parents were instructed not to sign with their children, creating communication difficulties in the home.

The continuity of the oral programme was ensured by establishing a teacher training programme, beginning in the 1970s, that was built around an oral methodology, and Sign Language did not appear on the curriculum until later. Therefore, through these internal and external strategies at play on the students and staff within the school, as well as future staff in training and the general public, a hegemonic medical model was established in the Irish system and simultaneously a negative discourse of Sign Language was promoted, the effects of which are still felt today. While it is beyond the scope of this discussion, it is important to note that these strategies were not implemented without resistance from pupils (for further discussion see Mathews, 2011; Saunders, 2004).

Overall, the changes that took place at the middle of the last century created an educational environment saturated with both material and discursive techniques of discipline and domination, with the aim of classifying, segregating, surveying, disciplining and subjectifying D/HH children through a pathological-medical model in pursuit of speech. As such, instead of the role it once held as a valid and valued language among the student population, the use of Sign Language became relegated as a threat to children's educational and moral wellbeing. It is difficult to measure the extent to which this belief was internalised by the students, though the negative attitudes that some D/HH people still express towards Sign Language, as well as the divisions felt within the deaf community between those students labelled as 'successes' and 'failures' to this day, suggest that this subjectifying process had some degree of success. A further measure of the success of subjectification is the extent to which this hegemonic medical mindset is still visible in the contemporary setting.

Contemporary educational endeavours

The deaf education system described above has undergone dramatic changes in the last 20 years in Ireland, and for somewhat longer on the international scene. Since the late 1990s in Ireland, the mainstream classroom has been identified in policy as the preferred environment for the education of most children with SEN (Government of Ireland, 1998). This development is in line with international practice, which has seen an increase in integrative and inclusive placements since the instigation of mainstreaming in the USA in the 1970s, culminating in the recommendations of the Salamanca Statement in 1994 (UNESCO, 1994). In terms of D/HH children, there has been an almost complete reversal in placement patterns as a result, with the vast majority of Irish D/HH children now attending mainstream placements.[3]

While mainstreaming is often held in positive regard as a symbol of the social model of disability, with ideals of inclusion and integration at its core, the situation for D/HH children is somewhat different owing to their particular language needs, highlighted by their exceptional mention in the Salamanca Statement. Furthermore, the placement of D/HH children in mainstream schools where they are often one of few, if not the only D/HH child in that school has thus been met with concern over the potential isolation they face. Indeed, it has been argued that this isolation in the mainstream system is 'destroying the embryo of the Deaf Community' (Crean, 1997, p. 28). The oral method instigated in Cabra in the 1950s was consolidated in 1972 by a report (Department of Education (DfE), 1972) examining deaf education in Ireland, which paved the way for mainstreaming. The mainstream environment, under this philosophy, would provide an ideal opportunity for the ultimate dividing practice. By removing D/HH children from their D/HH peers altogether, and immersing them in a full oral/aural environment, Sign Language could be replaced with speech indefinitely. This report was followed by the establishment of the visiting teacher service, as well as the teacher training programme in University College Dublin, both of which were populated by those who had worked in the Cabra schools during the changeover to oralism. While a number of teachers who were trained in those programs have retired, many others continue to work in deaf education today. Thus, the legacy of this period cannot be underestimated in the context of the current system of mainstreaming.

Indeed the current system is one that views the advantage of mainstreaming as the potential it gives for normalising D/HH children through spoken language acquisition (Mathews, 2010). Psychologists' reports identify the mainstream classroom as the optimum environment for spoken language acquisition and favour it over placements specifically for D/HH children; Sign Language interpreters are not provided and teachers rarely have any experience with D/HH children; children who use Irish Sign Language for their communication are still marginalised through enrolment in schools and units for the deaf; parents still receive the misinformed direction that they should not use Sign Language with their child as it may prevent speech development (Mathews, 2011). While new staff members and subsequently a change in attitude towards deaf education may push for progress, the system at present is still one that is rooted in a negative discourse of Sign Language (Mathews, 2010) and the stigmatisation of those who use it and become members of the Deaf Community. The legacy of this process, which began with dividing practices and scientific classification in the eighteenth and nineteenth centuries, transforming eventually to subjectification has been carried into the current mainstream system, arguably strengthening the subjectification of D/HH children rather than improving their situation through a so-called inclusive system.

Conclusion

Foucault's writings on the creation of subjects show a general chronological development from dividing practices through scientific classification and on to subjectification. This chapter followed this chronology
in an examination of the deaf education system, in particular looking
at the rise of the medical authority on deafness and the subsequent
development of oral deaf education and a negative discourse of Sign
Language. It shows how, since the establishment of systematic education for D/HH children in France in the eighteenth century, there has
been an increase in the medicalisation and subsequent subjectification
of D/HH children. The significance of the employment of a physician
in a school for the deaf cannot be underestimated. The work of Itard
during the early nineteenth century in Paris paved the way for a change
in methodology that crossed almost the entire Western world. Ireland
was an exception in that it remained predominantly manual until the
1950s.

While the progress of deaf education from its establishment in Ireland
in 1816 mirrors, to a great extent, what happened across the rest of
Europe and the USA, this similarity ends when it comes to the situation of oralism. While Claremont school (a comparatively small, private,
Protestant establishment in Dublin) did make the change to oralism in
line with the rest of Europe, the major stakeholders in deaf education in
Ireland, the Catholic institutes of Cabra, remained true to the manual
system some 70 years after it had been abandoned almost everywhere
else. Because the changeover to oralism was so late, the period of time
when it was instigated allows for the three stages of subjectification to
be viewed in quick succession.

Oralism in Cabra brought with it a strict mode of assessment, segregation and instruction. Dividing practices, in the first instance, had
separated D/HH children from their hearing peers for educational purposes. Scientific classification was used to distinguish between those
children deemed capable of using speech from those who were not with
finely measured audiological assessments. A further level of dividing
practices then came into play with segregation of D/HH children from
their D/HH peers, through the use of spatial control, timetabling and
demarcation through school-uniform strata. This allowed staff to easily
identify, and thus keep apart students in different streams within the
school. The result was the stigmatisation of those using Sign Language,
and the subsequent alignment of speech with success for D/HH children
of the era. This stigma followed children into the community and into

their adult lives, and the effects of the system are still felt on community relations to this day.

The oral method instigated in Cabra in the 1950s was consolidated in the 1972 report (DfE, 1972) examining deaf education in Ireland, which paved the way for mainstreaming. The mainstream environment, under this philosophy, would provide an ideal opportunity for the ultimate subjectification of D/HH children through a continuation and intensification of the oralist movement. The almost complete separation of D/HH children from their D/HH peers under the mainstream system and the absence of sign language in that system, coupled with a reinforcement of speech, saw mainstreaming as a final step in the subjectification movement. As such, rather than represent social progress for children who are D/HH in terms of inclusion with hearing peers, this educational process can be read as one of further, and perhaps final, subjectification.

Notes

1. I am indebted to Dr H. Dirksen L. Bauman, Deaf Studies Professor at Gallaudet University for his class on Enforced Normalcy in 2005 which first introduced me to Foucault's theories and their relevance to deaf studies and, in particular, the significance of the entry of a physician into the deaf education system.
2. For a notable exception, see McDonnell (2007). Though this work focuses on disability in general, there is some reference to schools for the deaf.
3. This trend is repeated across much of the 'developed' world, although the percentage of mainstreaming in the Irish context is likely to be higher owing to the severe shortage of alternatives.

References

Allen, J. (2003) *Lost Geographies of Power*. Oxford: Blackwell.

Baynton, D. C. (1996) *Forbidden Signs: American Culture and the Campaign against Sign Language*. Chicago, IL: The University of Chicago Press.

Branson, J. and Miller, D. (2002) *Damned for Their Difference: The Cultural Construction of Deaf People as Disabled*. Washington, DC: Gallaudet University Press.

Crean, E. J. (1997) *Breaking the Silence: The Education of the Deaf in Ireland 1816–1996*. Dublin: Irish Deaf Society.

Department of Education (DfE) (Ed.). (1972) *The Education of Children Who Are Handicapped by Impaired Hearing [Report of the Committee on the Education of the Hearing-Impaired]*. Dublin: Stationery Office.

Faubion, J. D. (Ed.) (2002) *Michel Foucault: Power*. London: Penguin Books.

Foucault, M. (1965) 'Madness and civilization'. In P. Rabinow (Ed.), *The Foucault Reader* (pp. 124–140). New York: Pantheon Books.

Foucault, M. (1977) 'Discipline and punish'. In P. Rabinow (Ed.), *The Foucault Reader* (pp. 169–213). New York: Pantheon Books.

Foucault, M. (1978) ' "Right of death and power over life" history of sexuality', Volume 1. In P. Rabinow (Ed.), *The Foucault Reader* (pp. 258–272). New York: Pantheon Books.

Foucault, M. (1982) 'The subject and power'. In J. D. Faubion (Ed.), *Michel Foucault Power: Essential Works of Foucault 1954–1984* (pp. 326–348). London: Penguin Books.

Foucault, M. (2002) 'The birth of social medicine'. In J. D. Faubion (Ed.), *Michel Foucault: Power* (pp. 134–156). London: Penguin Books.

Gallaudet, E. M. (1983) *History of the College for the Deaf 1857–1907*, Washington DC: Gallaudet University Press.

Government of Ireland. (1998) Education Act. Republic of Ireland.

Grehan, C. (2008) *Communication Islands: The Impact of Segregation and Attitudes to ISL among a Sample of Graduates of St Mary's School for Deaf Girls.* Applied Linguistics, Unpublished MPhil Dissertation, Trinity College, Dublin.

Griffey, S. N. (1994) *From Silence to Speech: Fifty Years with the Deaf.* Dublin: Dominican Publications.

Holt, L. (2003) (Dis)abling children in primary school micro-spaces: Geographies of inclusion and exclusion. *Health & Place*, 9: 119–128.

Lane, H. (1976) *The Wild Boy of Aveyron.* Cambridge, MA: Harvard University Press.

Lane, H. (1989) *When the Mind Hears: A History of the Deaf.* New York: Random House.

Mathews, E. S. (2010) 'No sign language if you want to get him talking': Power, transgression/resistance, and discourses of d/Deafness in the Republic of Ireland. *Population, Space and Place*, n/a–n/a.

Mathews, E. S. (2011) *Mainstreaming of Deaf Education in the Republic of Ireland: Language, Power, and Resistance.* Geography, PhD Thesis, National University of Ireland, Maynooth.

McDonnell, P. (2007) *Disability and Society: Ideological and Historical Dimensions.* Dublin: Blackhall Publishing.

McDonnell, P. and Saunders, H. (1993) 'Sit on your hands: Strategies to prevent signing'. In R. Fischer and H. Lane (Eds), *Looking Back: A Reader on the History of Deaf Communities and their Sign languages* (pp. 255–260). Hamburg: Signum.

Pollard, R. (2006) *The Avenue: A History of the Claremont Institute.* Dublin: Denzille Press.

Rabinow, P. (1984) 'Introduction'. In P. Rabinow (Ed.), *The Foucault Reader* (pp. 3–29). New York: Pantheon Books.

Saunders, H. (2004) 'Growing up deaf in Ireland'. In P. McDonnell (Ed.), *Deaf Studies in Ireland: An Introduction* (pp. 29–49). Gloustershire: Douglas McLean.

UNESCO. (1994) *The Salamanca Statement and Framework for Action on Special Educational Needs.* Spain: Salamanca.

van Cleve, J. V. and Crouch, B. A. (1989) *A Place of Their Own: Creating the Deaf Community in America.* Washington, DC: Gallaudet University Press.

Winefield, R. (1987) *Never the Twain Shall Meet: The Communications Debate.* Washington, DC: Gallaudet University Press.

Woolfe, R. (2007) 'Hands on 2 part special on ISL: Part 1'. In R. Woolfe (Ed.), *Hands On.* Ireland: Radio Teilifís Éireann.

5
Shaping Young People's Gender and Sexual Identities: Can Teaching Practices Produce Diverse Subjects?

Yu-Chieh Hsieh

Introduction

Two social incidents have been deeply intertwined with the establishment of the Gender Equity Education Act (GEEA, 2004) in Taiwan. A long-term activist for women's rights, Mrs Peng Wan-Ru was raped and murdered in 1996. This incident shocked Taiwanese society and triggered angry demands that the state tackled the issue of women's safety and equality by implementing gender equity education in schools. In 2000, a mysterious death of a *feminine boy* in school again attracted attention of feminists; teachers; lesbian, gay, bisexual and transgender (LGBT); and human rights organisations. These incidents then inspired activists to expand the scope of the GEEA from primarily focusing on equity between men and women to equity between all gender and sexual subjects.

The objective of the Act is stated as being to '...promote substantive gender equality, eliminate gender discrimination, uphold human dignity, and improve and establish education resources and environment of gender equality' (Article 1, GEEA, 2004). The Enforcement Rules for the GEEA (ERGEEA, 2005) later defines 'substantive equality of gender status' as 'no one shall be discriminated [against] based on his or her *sex, sexual orientation, gender temperament or gender identity*' (Rule 1, ERGEEA, 2005 [emphasis added]). This definition indicates the ethos of the GEEA, which is to validate diverse gender and sexual subjects and ensure equality between them. The Act is important because it aims at transforming gender and sexual ideology in Taiwanese society by focusing on educational environments, where younger generations are supposed to be enlightened as well as protected.

Constant news reports in Taiwan suggest that there has been a gap between the implementation of the GEEA and the accomplishment of its objectives in schools. For example, in December 2010, a young lesbian couple committed suicide in southern Taiwan, where teachers in their school did not know they were couple and so had not been able to provide any assistance in advance. This example highlights that focusing on the production of an educational policy is insufficient to understand its actual impacts. Policy analysis needs to examine the ways in which policies are enacted in the social arena, in this case, schools. Thus, this chapter examines how the GEEA was implemented in two Taiwanese schools by focusing on teaching practices as shaping young people's gender and sexual identities. The research argues that teachers and teaching practices matter in (not) successfully implementing the legislation. This chapter also highlights the importance of paying attention to teaching practices and their influences on young people's identity formation and experiences in school. With regard to the structure, this chapter is divided into four parts. After the first section on reviewing geographical literature on education, the methodology of the research is illustrated in second section. Discussions on teachers' attitudes to and practices of shaping pupils' masculinities, femininities and sexual identities then constitute the third section, and are followed by the conclusion.

Geographies of education

Over the past decade, there has been a notable growing interest from geographers towards educational issues, with a wide range of studies carried out at various scales and in different contexts (Holloway et al., 2010). In her recent article, Thiem (2009) proposes an agenda for developing outward-looking literature on geographies of education. The outward-looking geography of education is defined as 'one that deliberately situates its object(s) of analysis relative to broader research programs (that is, beyond the sector)', exploring the implications of educational institutions and practices in disclosing cultural, social, political and economic processes in society (Thiem, 2009, p. 115). In contrast to the outward-looking research, the inward-looking approach is defined as focusing on spatial processes within the education sector. Thiem (2009) seems to suggest that geographical studies of education can only adopt either an inward- or outward-looking approach. However, children's geographers have attempted to complicate this inward- and outward-looking dichotomy in understanding young people's experiences in school. For example, Holloway et al. (2000) demonstrate different ways to understand the spatiality of school space in a study of discussing young people's gender and sexual identities. They suggest that the school is embedded within wider places and affected by them, is an important site for identity formation, and that its spatial meanings can be (re)shaped by contextualised notions of gender/sexual identities. Therefore, it is argued that geographers of education need to think beyond the binary framework of inward- and outward-looking approaches in order to fully understand the role of education in our society (Holloway et al., 2010).

Moreover, it is suggested that experiences of different social actors in schools are overlooked in the current geographical research on education (Holloway et al., 2010). However, geographical work on children and young people in educational spaces contributes to this lacuna by exploring young people's subjective experiences and their interactions with different groups of social actors. These studies of children's geographies are insightful and remind geographers of education to pay attention to the impact of unequal power relations and social interaction among different actors in shaping educational environments and teaching/learning experiences. Undoubtedly, the education system cannot exist without people's participation. As the discussion shows, in order to further understand the role and impact of education in society by exploring subjective experiences in schools, geographical studies of education need to further engage with research on children's geographies, to which the following discussion now turns.

The influence of the New Social Studies of Childhood (NSSC) is significant on the development of children's geographies. Holloway and Valentine (2000) identify two challenges raised by the NSSC, suggesting different agendas for social scientific research on children. First, studies of diverse childhoods become crucial in understanding childhood as a social construct according to different times and places. Thus, the production of childhood is inevitably intertwined with other social differences such as class, gender, ethnicity, (dis)ability and so on (Holt, 2007; Taylor, 2009; Thomas, 2005). Second, children's own rights as human beings here and now as well as being social actors able to speak for themselves are highlighted. Being inspired by the NSSC, geographers have argued that social constructions of childhood vary between places but the majority of existing geographic studies focus on the global North and the Western urban areas. Thus, one of the aims of this chapter is to address this imbalance by exploring experiences of young people in East Asia. Current research mainly explores how children and young people's experiences are shaped in and through unbounded everyday places, including public spaces, the home and the school. The fluid and penetrative nature of everyday places was suggested by Holloway et al. (2000) in conceptualising the school space to be re(constructed) through a series of different geographies (such as wider society and beyond). In terms of academic debates, the reproduction of social differences is one of the key themes discussed by children's geographers. Lately, some research has attempted to further analyse the intersection between different social identities such as gender, religion, race and age that affect young people's lives (Hopkins, 2006). Nevertheless, the majority of work still focuses on a particular axis of social differences to reveal how children and young people's experiences are shaped.

Among studies exploring the reproduction of social differences in school space, there is a sizable body of work illustrating the significance of school space in affecting young people's gender and, less explicitly, sexual identity formation (Ansell, 2002; Hyams, 2000; Taylor, 2007a, 2009). These studies have suggested important connections between the notions of gender and sexuality when young people construct their identities in school. However, more thorough investigation of how exactly educational practices affect the mutual construction between gender and sexual identities needs to be further explored (although see Taylor, 2007a, b). In addition, highlighting young people's voices in order to explore their experiences is emphasised by children's geographers. Yet, paying attention to other groups of social actors (for example, parents, teachers, siblings, grandparents and so on) who play important roles in shaping young people's experiences is also crucial, as young people's lives are produced through interacting and negotiating with others (Holloway et al., 2000; Taylor, 2007b). However, there is limited research exploring how teachers' understandings of gender and sexual identities and their educational practices shape young people's experiences, especially when they are compelled by particular legislation to promote gender and sexual equity. This informs and locates the position of this chapter's interrogation of educational policy.

Thus, this chapter engages with current geographical research on education and young people by expanding the *space* of geographical interest. By focusing on East Asia, the discussion of this chapter highlights the significance of exploring experiences beyond the *West*. Specifically, this chapter explores how teachers in Taiwanese schools shaped young people's gender and sexual identities in the context of policy intervention. An essential question that needs to be answered in this chapter is: when schools are required by the Taiwanese government to implement the GEEA, can teaching practices produce, validate and support equal gender and sexual subjects? In order to answer this question, this study focuses on teachers' understandings of young people's masculinities, femininities and sexual identities. The ways in which teachers reproduce particular notions of gender and sexualities in the classroom will also be explored. Ultimately, this chapter examines to what extent these gender and sexual constructions correspond to the objective of the GEEA in producing diverse and equal subjects.

Methodology: researching the GEEA and education in Taiwan

This chapter is based upon postgraduate research that explores the production of the 2004 GEEA and its subsequent implementation in two senior high schools in Taipei City from both teachers' and young people's perspectives. The discussion in this chapter specifically focuses on teaching practices in implementing the GEEA. Two themes are included in this section. First, a brief introduction to the GEEA is provided. Second, research methods adopted in this study are explained.

With regard to the emergence of the GEEA, it can be attributed to three crucial social contexts in Taiwan: the development of women's movements since the 1970s, educational reform movements during 1990s, and a significant social incident, *the Peng Wan-Ru incident*,[1] which happened in 1997. This incident was particularly important, as it precipitated the passing of the Sexual Assault Crime Prevention Law (1997), where two sexes equity education initially gained the legitimacy to be implemented in schools.[2] Because of these social contexts, the issues of gender and education were gradually brought together in Taiwan. The Act was officially passed and came into effect in 2004. This piece of legislation applies to all formal educational institutions such as schools, colleges and universities.[3] The production of the GEEA was seen as a milestone especially for feminists and gay and lesbian activists, as equality between different gender and sexual subjects was finally recognised and appeared on the educational agenda.

In terms of research methods, the data used in this chapter was collected from interviewing 28 teachers in two senior high schools, Azalea and Banyanin, Taipei City.[4] Being public and co-educational environments were the criteria for selecting case study schools, reflecting representative experiences of teachers (and young people) in Taiwanese senior high schools. A snowballing strategy was used to recruit schools.

Apart from two exceptions, the qualitative interviews with most teachers in two schools were audio-recorded with consent, fully transcribed, coded and analysed thematically.[5] Among the 28 teachers who were interviewed, 12 were in Azalea and 16 were in Banyan. Fifteen interviewees were female teachers and the other 13 were male teachers. Those who were interviewed were school managers, class teachers who were also members of the Gender Equity Education Committee (GEEC),[6] and other class teachers.

Individual interviews with teachers were conducted between April and June 2008. Interviews were carried out in a variety of spaces according to teachers' preference such as teachers' offices, the library and the classroom. All interviews were conducted during teachers' spare time in schools in consideration of teachers' heavy workload and long working time. Most interviews lasted around two hours. All interviews focused on three key themes: teachers' roles and experiences of implementing the GEEA, their opinions about key issues of schools' implementation of the GEEA, and the influences of the GEEA on their role as schoolteachers in senior high schools. These issues were formulated to understand how teaching practices affect the implementation of the GEEA, in terms of producing diverse gender and sexual subjects within schools. The following sections focus on teacher's understandings and constructions of masculinities, femininities and sexualities and the ways in which they shaped young people's identities.

Teachers' understandings and practices of shaping young people's gender and sexual identities

Numerous academic studies have explored schools as important sites for (re)producing young people's gender and sexual identities (Holloway et al., 2000; Hyams, 2000; Jackson, 2006; Renold, 2005; Taylor, 2007b). The existing discussion on how schools construct, normalise or police young people's gender and sexual identities has focused on the role of the formal or informal curriculum. In terms of the implementation of the GEEA, there has not been a formal curriculum developed specifically for senior high school education in Taiwan. Therefore, in order to promote gender equity education in high schools, the idea of *integration* into the existing curriculum is highlighted in the GEEA (Article 17, GEEA, 2004). In this context, it is crucial to note that teachers' individual efforts and interpretations of their own subjects are relied upon and their pedagogical practices come to play an important part in implementing the GEEA.

Before revealing the research findings, it is important to explore how the notion of gender and sexual identities is conceptualised in the GEEA. This serves as the foundation to understand whether teachers' attempts to shape young people's gender and sexual identities correspond to the objective of the GEEA. In drafting reports to the GEEA, it was clearly stated that gender equity education has to be informed by understanding gender and sexual identities as *social constructs*. This understanding challenges essentialism for claiming that gender and sexual identities are pre-existing, fixed and rooted in biology. Based on the understanding of identities being socially constructed, the GEEA therefore aims to enable diverse gender and sexual identities and ensure no discrimination against subjects with difference (or subjects considered to be *different*).

Masculinities: *active learners, messing about* and *non-feminine*

In both the GEEA and ERGEEA, there are explicit statements that people's different gender temperaments should be respected rather than discriminated against. Therefore, in implementing gender equity education, recognising diverse forms of masculinity (and femininity) is one of the significant tasks for schools. However, three primary constructions of masculinity were found from interviews: *active, messing about and non-feminine*. These findings suggest that, to a great extent, teachers in two case study schools still tended to conform to fixed ideas in relation to masculine identities. Essentialist understandings, which were in contrast to the GEEA, were often articulated by teachers.

The first construction of masculine identities relates to teachers' perception of boys being better or more active learners than girls. This construction in fact related to the idea that boys and girls had *naturally distinct aptitudes*. However, teachers' narratives often focused on how well boys perform in certain subjects. For example, a history teacher in Azalea explained why boys did better in her class: 'Boys are good at logical thinking and boys are *naturally* interested in politics, wars and debates' [emphasis added]. Similarly, in Banyan High School, the Head of the Academic Affairs Office also indicated that physics teachers in their school resisted integrating gender equity education into teaching by insisting that '*girls cannot do physics!*' [emphasis added]. Despite the legislation, it is clear that essential understandings of gender differences were invoked in both schools. Furthermore, Western research (Mac an Ghaill, 1994; Renold, 2005) suggests that boys who are devoted to academic achievement are often considered as less masculine than boys who enjoy exercise, highlighting physical competence. However, in

Azalea and Banyan High Schools, the importance of academic achievement was the most valued idea. Therefore, boys who did well in
their studies were not considered less manly in the Taiwanese context.
This can be attributed to an extreme academic-oriented value in the
Taiwanese education system.

My findings also reveal that teachers interacted with boys more than
girls during class. This is due to teachers' understanding boys as active
and girls as passive in learning processes. Some teachers pointed out that
they intentionally picked boys more than girls when asking questions,
because they were worried about girls being embarrassed if they did not
know the answer. This had the effect of making boys the focus in class.
Simultaneously, boys were (re)constructed as more intelligent, emotionally controlled and ready to be challenged through teachers' pedagogical
practices in class. During the process, teachers constructed young people's masculinity by repetitively expecting boys to be active and socially
confident learners while this expectation did not equally apply to girls,
who were collectively understood as passive, emotional and vulnerable
in nature.

A second construction of masculinity in both Azalea and Banyan High
Schools is that boys liked to *mess about*. Teachers suggested that *making fun* was an important part of peer culture among boys. Examples
such as not answering teachers' questions seriously, or clapping and
cheering loudly when other boys answered questions correctly during the class, were usually considered as harmless by teachers. Some
teachers even considered that boys could create a more relaxed atmosphere in class because of their 'funny behaviours or jokes'. However,
the understanding of boys being clown-like as a part of masculine
identities did not necessarily facilitate the implementation of gender equity education. It depended on individual teachers' awareness
of the implications of boys' behaviours, where research demonstrates
that young men's humorous performance can have oppressive effects
on other pupils (Kehily and Nayak, 1997). As a positive response to
the GEEA, some teachers indicated that they would intervene to stop
boys' behaviours, which involved physical contact that might constitute sexual harassment. For example, a counselling teacher in Azalea
High School disapproved of the idea that some of boys' behaviours were
understood as *only jokes*. She gave the example of the game *taking off others' trousers* (to see 'if he is a man or not') played by boys as an example
of sexual harassment and gender-based bullying (discrimination against
non-normative performances) among pupils.

The third construction of masculine identities relates to schools being unfriendly spaces to non-normative masculinities, which counters the goal of the GEEA. During the interviews with teachers about the requirement of the GEEA to respect different gender temperaments, *feminine boys* often first came to their minds. Teachers' understandings of *feminine boys* were based on their clear contrast to normative masculine identities. Terms such as *Niang Niang Qiang* and *Niang Pao*[7] were common expressions to name those feminine boys among pupils in Taiwanese schools. Sometimes, *Niang Pao* can also mean being gay, with the adjectives of *Niang* and *gay* being interchangeable. This implies the interrelated construction between normative gender identities and heterosexuality. Teachers in both schools pointed out that the main features of feminine boys were related to their appearance (delicate looks), behaviours (feminine gestures) and voice (higher pitch). Teachers also indicated that other pupils often made fun of feminine boys. A history teacher in Azalea stated that when a boy with a *nice voice* was reading a poem with cadence in her class, other pupils were sniggering.

In Banyan High School, some teachers suggested that feminine boys were not discriminated against in their school. The Head of the Counselling Office pointed out that they had a boy with a very high-pitched voice, but '*no one* did anything bad to him' [emphasis added]. An English teacher said she had met two boys being called 'sissy' by their classmates. '*One of them said he was fine with it*, because he was who he was. *Another boy denied it*, but he still played with others' [emphasis added], according to the English teacher. However, the Head of the Pupil Affairs Office in Banyan High School depicted a different picture indicating that a boy could not stand being called *Niang* or made fun of by other pupils anymore. The boy was described by the Head of the Pupil Affairs Office as *quiet, shy, having less interaction with other classmates, and always wearing the uniform properly* (for example, shirt tucked into trousers and wearing a tie). This example shows that there were boys suffering from discrimination towards their non-normative gender performances in Banyan High School. Nevertheless, some teachers overlooked the issue because they were unaware of or insensitive to these *feminine boys*' negative experiences and often took a 'sit-back' approach. Thus, the GEEA was understood *in theory* but when it came to the implementation, teachers seemed to lack training as well as enthusiasm to put the legislation into practice.

In summary, teachers in both schools were mostly sympathetic to what feminine boys experienced in the school, but they did not demonstrate any proactive strategies that they had tried to prevent further discriminatory practices happening. As a result, young people were left to deal with discriminations in schools as their own *personal issues*, while teachers shed their responsibility to protect vulnerable pupils. This finding suggests that teachers failed to achieve the aim of the GEEA in terms of enabling diverse and equal gender subjects by not recognising the more active role they could play in eliminating prejudice and discrimination against non-normative gender identities. The discussion in this section demonstrates that teachers in both schools have not yet achieved the objective of the GEEA of producing equal subjects of difference, because particular masculine identities were favoured and essentialised understandings of gender identity were articulated. Also, teachers' reactive attitudes to reduce discriminations against *feminine boys* suggested that they were unaware of the possible traumas that these boys had to experience everyday in school. However, teachers did intervene in some of the boys' messing-about behaviours when these were viewed as constituting sexual harassment. This exception is an example of positive response to the GEEA.

Femininities: *passive learners, professional women* and *well-dressed/behaved*

Diverse femininities were also differently positioned by teachers in Azalea and Banyan High Schools. Some were encouraged while others were policed through teachers' different practices. Three different constructions of feminine identities were suggested by teachers. First, girls were conceptualised as passive learners compared with boys. Second, teachers emphasised young women's capability of pursuing successful careers in the future. Third, non-femininities in relation to the exposure of bodies and the use of bad language were particularly noted by teachers. The first and third constructions conformed to normative notions of femininity, which were related to essential understandings of gender identities. However, by highlighting women's potential career success, the second construction challenged the understanding of normative femininities that often constrain women's life choices beyond being wives or mothers at home, as women are traditionally portrayed as being dependent on men economically.

With regard to constructing young women as passive learners, teachers in both schools indicated that girls were shy, polite and more likely to feel embarrassed in class, especially when they were asked questions. Therefore, teachers were not keen on motivating girls in class, as they did not want to 'embarrass or frustrate' girls. Teachers prioritised their responsibility to *protect* girls based on ideas related to gender stereotypes rather than to help girls become better learners. For example, a history teacher in Azalea pointed out that she often picked boys for difficult questions because she did not want to upset young women. However, this meant that less was expected of girls and that they were given fewer opportunities to develop their ability to become active learners. The research findings suggest that passivity in girls was first assumed and then reinforced by teachers' pedagogical practices in both schools.

Becoming *professional women* in the future was the second feminine construction that teachers encouraged female pupils to aspire to. This shows that teachers positively responded to Article 19 of the GEEA, which states that 'teachers shall *encourage* pupils to take courses in fields that are *not traditionally affiliated with their gender*' [emphasis added]. This chapter challenges essential ideas of gender difference in aptitudes, fixed gender roles and distinct employment options for men and women. In both Azalea and Banyan High Schools, some teachers tried to disseminate the idea that women can achieve excellence in different areas. By doing this, teachers intended to enlighten and broaden young women's future career decision. In Azalea High School, in organising lectures/workshops for pupils to attend, the Head of Library invited more women speakers to visit their school to balance the fact that more male guests had been invited in the past. The Head of Library also deliberately invited successful women in a variety of professional fields, for example, female athletes and scientists: 'I want them [pupils] to know that *girls can do very well in some areas which are generally considered as difficult for girls*' [emphasis added]. A military training instructor (MTI) in Banyan High School also challenged an idea that women were not suitable for joining the army or police force by encouraging female pupils to apply for military or police academies. In particular, the MTI tried to encourage girls through sharing her own experiences and highlighted that women can achieve what is required during the training process. It is evident that teachers in Azalea and Banyan High Schools shared a similar idea of encouraging female pupils to pursue different career choices. It might just be a coincidence but female teachers seemed keener on delivering this message into their educational practices than male teachers.

As for the third construction of feminine identities, schools tended to produce a particular type of appropriate femininity by regulating female pupils' appearance and behaviours. The controversy of whether girls should be forced to wear skirts has raised constant debate in Taiwan. Nevertheless, in Azalea and Banyan High Schools girls were still requested to wear skirts as summer uniform according to their school regulations.[8] This regulation can be understood as a way that schools encourage girls to be acceptably attractive, but avoid being overly sexualised. This also suggests that girls must manage their bodies to stay on the right side of the slippery boundary between these two judgements (Valentine, 2001). Covering to avoid so-called *unnecessary exposure of female bodies* was the focus of the enforcement of dress code in schools (Hyams, 2000). Apart from school regulations and commentaries on dress and appearance, a growing number of girls using bad language seemed to be a recent concern for teachers as a behaviour that challenged prior, accepted understandings of femininity. The Head of the Pupil Affairs Office in Banyan High School pointed out: 'I cannot understand girls nowadays. They are different from girls we knew in the past. In the past, girls could only use bad language in private with their best friends. *Now it is different. Girls do it directly in public*' [emphasis added]. Although teachers seemed to be concerned with *changing femininity* in terms of using bad language, they had not developed further understandings or strategies to deal with the issue. However, it is interesting to note teachers' different attitudes to boys' and girls' usage of bad language. In general, boys' usage of bad language was considered *normal* by teachers and therefore did not raise the same concern as girls did, who were then scrutinised more strictly for the same behaviour.

This section has demonstrated that although one of the objectives of the GEEA is to promote equality between boys and girls, it was evident that girls were given fewer opportunities as learners in class. Moreover, female pupils were also under more pressure in terms of regulating their dress and appearance. These findings also suggest that teachers in both schools had restricted understanding of feminine identities and thus normative femininities were profoundly reproduced through school regulations and teachers' gender-biased attitudes in disciplining female pupils' behaviours and shaping their learning experiences. Nevertheless, there was an exception for teachers in both schools to promote new identities relating to women being successful in future careers and having the ability to exercise different employment choices. This challenged fixed gender roles and improved gender equality, in the realm of employment, in the way that the GEEA aims to achieve.

Sexual identities

When teachers were asked about which issues they had addressed in terms of implementing gender equity education, the management of intimate heterosexual relationships among pupils was often the first topic to be raised. This response was attributed to the fact that gender equity was still profoundly understood in relation to intimacy between men and women: teachers seemed to understand equity as encouraging pupils to develop equal gender relations, including heterosexual relationships. However, this research finds that teachers were more concerned with the appropriate boundary than the equality of pupils' heterosexual relationships. In addition, although teachers were aware of the GEEA requiring the creation of equal subjects with different sexualities, very few teachers addressed non-heterosexual (for example gay, lesbian or bisexual) relationships. Rather, they predominantly focused on heterosexual relationships among pupils. The following section explores how schools policed boys' and girls' sexual identities in terms of issues of heterosexual relationships and gay and lesbian identities.

Heterosexual intimate relationships

Teachers in Azalea as well as Banyan High School had contradictory attitudes towards pupils developing intimate relationships. On the one hand, some teachers thought it was understandable, even *natural*. Teachers' tolerant attitudes to pupils developing intimate relationship were closely related to the way that heterosexuality was conceptualised as ubiquitous and normal. However, on the other hand, there were also some teachers who tried to persuade pupils that it would be better to wait until they get to university to engage is such relationships. Teachers were worried about the negative effects of pupils' having intimate relationships (distraction from studying, emotional instability, teenage pregnancy and so on) as well as on the school's reputation. However, whether teachers approved or disapproved of pupils developing relationships, they all agreed that disciplinary strategies were necessary. Thus, ensuring pupils' behaviours within the acceptable boundary for developing intimate relationships became one of the crucial issues for schools.

The most significant strategy adopted by teachers in both schools for maintaining the appropriate boundary of intimacy was to discipline pupils' public displays of affection. Nevertheless, the definition of those so-called *inappropriate behaviours in public* varied among teachers. The Head of the Pupil Affairs Office in Banyan High School pointed out that he would tackle any form of physical contact between boys and girls. However, other interviewed teachers in the two schools considered pupils holding hands as acceptable, but would intervene to stop behaviours further than that such as putting hands on each other's waists (or even shoulders), embracing, kissing, stroking hair and sitting on laps. Teachers' actions to discipline pupils' public displays of affection involved utilising a discourse of school as a *public space*, where other people might feel uncomfortable about intimate behaviours. Teachers also considered pupils' intimate behaviours in schools as intimidating. A Military Training Instructor in Banyan High School pointed out: 'Young people nowadays really ... those behaviours [intimate behaviours] seem to be *direct and fearless*' [emphasis added]. Therefore, schools had developed different strategies to prohibit pupils behaving intimately. For example, in Banyan High School, pupils who stayed for self-learning hours in the evening were congregated in particular classrooms, which was convenient for the school to manage. The electricity supply to other classrooms was cut off. Teachers on duty also patrolled the school and paid extra attention to some private corners or toilets for preventing pupils carrying out intimate behaviours. Teachers in both schools indicated that the development of sexual relationships between pupils was what they were actually worried about. Therefore, behaviours beyond holding hands drew teachers' attention because more intimate physical contact suggested a greater likelihood that pupils would develop sexual relationships in the future, which was what teachers did not want to confront at this stage. Teachers' control of pupils' intimate relationships focused on making physical contact among pupils as limited as possible.

In terms of implementing the GEEA, schools' control of pupils' intimate relationships was against the aim of the GEEA to create equal subjects in the sense that girls were under more pressure than boys to maintain the appropriate intimate relationships, that is, not to develop sexual relationships. Girls were constructed as vulnerable and more emotionally sensitive than boys. For example, a biology teacher in Banyan High School called for a special meeting for girls only, during the school field trip to highlight the importance of *self-protection* by not developing sexual relationships in school. The Head of the Pupil Affairs Office in Banyan High School also pointed out that he had told girls about the importance of protecting themselves and avoiding the loss of a new life, which appeared to assume that there was an inevitable causal relationship starting from having sex, to getting pregnant and having an abortion. This suggests that to a great extent teachers constructed the idea of young people having sex as dangerous and unavoidably linked to negative outcomes.

Moreover, these educational practices illustrated that girls were positioned in a *spatiality of protection* (Hyams, 2000). These teaching practices delivered gender-differentiated messages that girls needed to consider the consequence of developing sexual relationships and the possibility of becoming young parents, while boys' were taught less about the need to consider these issues. In both schools, most teachers had a strong tendency to construct girls as powerless, especially in sexual relationships, although a few teachers presented different stories. Yet, a counselling teacher in Azalea High School pointed out that girls' attitudes to sexual relationships had changed. She pointed out that five or six years ago, girls did not know how to say no when they did not want to develop sexual relationships with their boyfriends. However, nowadays, she claimed that girls seem to take more control about this issue. This finding counters a common discourse that girls engage in sexual practices because they do not know how to say *no* to their boyfriends. In terms of young people developing sexual practices, dominant discourses often consider that the situation is *out* of girls' control. This construction is partly based on the understanding that women are passive in sexual matters. Therefore, girls must be victims of early sexual relationships. However, my research suggests that, in some cases, girls were actually *in* control of their sexual lives. Therefore, it is evident that there is the contradiction in discourses about *in* and *out* of control in considering young people' sexual autonomy.

Rule 13 of the Enforcement Regulations of the Gender Equity Education Act (ERGEEA), 2005, states that the curriculum related to gender equity education shall cover courses on relationships and sex education. However, as the research findings suggest, one of schools' main strategies to carry out *affective education* (that is, how to deal with the issue of intimate relationships) was to avoid pupils developing sexual relationships. As high school pupils had passed the age of consent (16 years in Taiwan), these young people ought to have the right to decide whether they would like to develop sexual relationships or not. Schools should provide necessary information and assistance to young people on this matter. However, this research found that pupils' expressions of sexual autonomy were clearly restrained by the schools' favoured approach of abstinence. Completely disapproving of young people's sexual relationships meant that schools had no way to assist pupils when real problems and inequalities arose in these relationships.

Gay and lesbian identities

It has been argued that acknowledging gay and lesbian identities in schools can draw attention to the issue of sexuality in the school space and is helpful to explore the heterosexist structure of school relations. As aforementioned, the GEEA requests that people should not be discriminated against not only because of their gender, but also because of their sexuality. Nevertheless, the dualistic conception of heterosexuality versus homosexuality was so strong that teachers in both Azalea and Banyan High Schools equated the issue of non-heterosexual identity with the issue of gay and lesbian identity. Both Azalea and Banyan High Schools paid less attention to gay and lesbian identities, which had never been a major theme for schools in terms of providing relevant activities (for example, lectures) or as a key element of any teaching practices. Nevertheless, the attitudes and reactions of teachers in Azalea and Banyan High Schools were different in the sense that those in Banyan were more tolerant and open-minded than their counterparts in Azalea in terms of implementing the GEEA by engaging with the issue of gay and lesbian identities.

In Azalea High School, some teachers indicated that they did not pay specific attention to the issue of gay and lesbian identities, because they did not have many gay and lesbian pupils and they considered that it was not the proper time to discuss this issue:

I think it is about *demographic composition* of each school ... so it is not a key issue for our school as we have *very very very few gay and lesbian pupils.*

(The Head of the Counselling Office, Azalea High School [emphasis added])

Even for a psychiatrist, when he/she would like to confirm if someone is gay or lesbian, he/she might also want to wait for the person *getting old enough,* for example, *after eighteen years old.*

(Head of the Library, Azalea High School [emphasis added])

These two quotes suggest that the heterosexual presumption and heterosexism were prevalent in Azalea High School. The claim of only having a small number of gay and lesbian pupils was based on a presumption, as the school had not carried out any form of sensitive investigation, which itself highlights another flaw, of course, that sexual identities are *out and measurable.* Also, being gay or lesbian was continuously understood as a medical/psychic issues that needed to be diagnosed by a doctor. These understandings further affected teachers' practices: most teachers in Azalea High School indicated that they would encourage pupils to *respect* each other, but they would not be keen to approach the issue of gay or lesbian identities. Teachers' attitudes to gay and lesbian relationships among pupils also suggest a rather reactive approach:

> *It is a neglected territory*...for pupils developing same sex relationships, if their behaviours go too far, instead of being picked up, teachers are more tolerant to them.
>
> (Counselling Teacher, Azalea High School [emphasis added])

> Because boys grab or hug each other or girls do so, *we would usually leave it.*
>
> (Counselling Teacher, Azalea High School [emphasis added])

As the quotes suggest, teachers held a tolerant attitude to *possible* gay and lesbian pupils because they could not tell whether these pupils were 'really' gays or lesbians or they were just very close friends. Even if teachers knew that particular pupils were gay or lesbian, they would not intervene either, as they tended to 'desexualise' relationships between pupils of the same sex. This again reflects how teachers were deeply invested in the heterosexual perspective even as a 'neutral' non-response. It is somewhat ironic that the control of gay and lesbian couples was less strict than heterosexual couples, because teachers deliberately overlooked their relationships. Thus, this practice excluded not only the issue of gay and lesbian identities, but failed also to offer official support to gay and lesbian pupils, as they were virtually invisible in teachers' eyes.

In Banyan High School, teachers had a more proactive attitude and reaction to gay and lesbian identities. The Head of the Academic Affairs Office indicated that the biggest achievement in implementing gender equity education had been that 'more gay and lesbian pupils can express themselves in our school'. This interviewee also mentioned that in the past teachers may have felt frightened by or gossiped about pupils' sexualities, but now most teachers seemed to accept them and without much gossip. Also, some individual teachers had carried out different strategies to develop pupils' understandings and a neutral attitude to gay and lesbian identities. A history teacher pointed out that she integrated the issue of gay and lesbian identities into her teaching by introducing histories and cultures of gay and lesbian people. A geography teacher took the chance in class when some boys were teasing another boy about being *Niang*. She then revealed her positive attitude to gay and lesbian people by expressing her willingness to be invited to a gay wedding in the future, if any of her pupils were gay or lesbian. Some pupils challenged her claim at that time by asking whether she would mind her own son being gay, and she retained a positive attitude. These teachers were all positive about the possible effect of their practices in having some influence on changing pupils' perception about respecting people's different sexual identities.

To summarise, in Azalea High School the issue of creating equal subjects with different sexualities was deliberately overlooked, whereas teachers in Banyan were more attentive to engaging with the issue of gay and lesbian identities. Nevertheless, because of teachers' predominantly dualistic understanding of sexualities, bisexuality was completely absent from their narratives and agenda of implementing the GEEA in both schools. This suggests that teachers' understanding of sexual identities beyond heterosexuality need to be improved, if the aim of the GEEA to produce diverse and equal sexual subjects in schools is to be successfully achieved in the future.

Conclusion

During the research process, all teacher interviewees in Azalea and Banyan High Schools indicated that they were aware of the GEEA and the importance of respecting diverse gender and sexual identities. However, the research shows that not all their teaching practices reflected the landscape and practice of equality. Teachers had not fully fulfilled their responsibilities to implement the GEEA successfully. One of the main reasons for this was that teachers lacked understanding of diverse gender and sexualities. Therefore, rather than taking gender and sexual identities as social constructs as the GEEA promotes, essential understandings were articulated and reinforced in different ways and in a variety of contexts. Thus, instead of merely expecting teachers to actively engage with the policy, the state needs to adopt more progressive strategies for teachers to learn the ethos and content of the GEEA in order to enable diverse gender and sexual subjects in educational spaces. Without this measure, teachers and educational practices can in fact work against equality legislation and further suppress the emergence of diverse identities and performances, as opposed to validating equal gender and sexual subjects in schools.

This chapter shows that young people's gender identities are ever-shaped in ways that are closely related to teaching practices in Taiwanese schools. For example, teachers' perceptions of different learning attitudes between male and female pupils affected their constructions of young people's gender identities and further reinforced gender norms.

Interestingly, while much current Western literature focuses on boys' 'underachievement' in schools, teachers in Taiwan considered boys as better learners than girls. This understanding is attributed to teachers' constructions of masculinity as being active and interactive, as the preferred characteristics of pupils in class. This chapter has challenged the binary imagination of the global North versus the global South by exploring young people's experiences in East Asia, highlighting the importance for geographers to expand their spatial scopes in exploring young people's experiences in different geographical contexts. To understand the intersection of young people, education, gender and sexuality in other parts of the world brings meaningful insights for researchers to further explore legislative change, social-spatial processes and their profound institutional and individual impacts.

This research has illustrated that the binary understanding of heterosexual versus gay and lesbian identities was still prevalent among teachers in Taiwanese schools. In contrast to claiming that they were aware of their responsibility to enable diverse sexual identities, some teachers were virtually gay/lesbian blind because they were still heavily invested in the heterosexual presumption. There were also some teachers who 'asexualised' gay and lesbian identities and saw such pupils as 'just friends'. Consequently, gay and lesbian identities were repressed to a great extent in school. In this sense, schools were unable to provide necessary resources and support for the students involved. In addition, although the GEEA promotes more diverse understandings of sexualities, the acknowledgement of bisexuality was totally absent in teachers' narratives. Another elision is the re-inscription of heterosexuality as profoundly age-dependent. While developing sexual relationships with the other sex is generally considered a normal or natural heterosexual practice for adults, the norm of appropriate heterosexual identity for young people in Taiwanese schools was 'asexual'. This particular form of deferred (hetero)sexuality was constructed by teachers' regulations of pupil's public displays of affection, whereby affection becomes a sign for undertaking further sexual practices.

In conclusion, the chapter has demonstrated the possibility of engaging inward- and outward-looking approaches by examining how the state's agenda to transform gender and sexual notions in Taiwanese society was related to educational practices in schools, where teaching practices as well as school spaces were crucial to shape young people's gender and sexual identity formation. More importantly, by exploring teachers' constructions of young people's gender and sexual identities in the East Asian context of Taiwan, this chapter reveals age-differentiated and spatially (re)produced (hetero)normativities, even in – and against – a context of legislative change.

Notes

1. In 1996, on 30 November, Mrs Peng Wan-Ru, a long-term activist of the women's movement, was found raped and dead with 35 stab wounds all over her body. The news shocked Taiwanese society and the long-hidden issue of women's safety was raised. Feminist campaigners considered that school implementation of a gender equity education would be the foundation for eliminating future discrimination, harassment and assaults on women.
2. The term, 'two sexes equity' highlights a restricted understanding of equity only between men and women. However, 'gender equity' might mean equity between men and women in some cases, but now is often understood to emphasis both gender and sexual equity after the passing of the GEEA in 2004.
3. The current education system in Taiwan consists of elementary schools (six years), junior high schools (three years), senior high schools/vocational high schools/colleges (three/three/five years), and university (four years). Currently, the period of compulsory education in Taiwan includes elementary and junior high school education, nine years in total from age 6 to 15.
4. These are pseudonyms schools used in the case study to maintain their anonymity.
5. All interviews were carried out in Chinese (Mandarin). They were also transcribed in Chinese to maintain the language specificity, which helped the researcher to analyse the interviews appropriately. Only quotes used in this chapter were translated into English.
6. According to the GEEA, the central government, local governments and educational institutions are all required to set up their own Gender Equity Education Committee for implementing the legislation.
7. Niang Niang Qiang and Niang Pao are negatively used to name males with feminine features (for example, appearance or behaviours).
8. In Azalea and Banyan High School, girls are still requested to wear formal uniform (skirts) on a particular date for school investigation. The length of skirts was also regulated. Behaviours considered as hyper-feminine were also prohibited such as wearing make-up and earrings.

References

Ansell, N. (2002) 'Of course we must be equal but…': Imagining gendered futures in two rural southern African secondary schools. *Geoforum*, 33(2), 179–194.

Holloway, S., Hubbard, P., Jöns, H. and Pimlott-Wilson, H. (2010) Geographies of education and the significance of children, youth and families. *Progress in Human Geography*, 34(5), 583–600.

Holloway, S. and Valentine, G. (2000) 'Children's geographies and the new social studies of childhood'. In S. Holloway and G. Valentine (Eds), *Children's Geographies: Playing, Living, Learning*. London: Routledge.

Holloway, S., Valentine, G. and Bingham, N. (2000) Institutionalising technologies: Masculinities, femininities, and the heterosexual economy of the IT classroom. *Environment and Planning A*, 32(4), 617–633.

Holt, L. (2007) Children's sociospatial (re)production of disability within primary school playgrounds. *Environment and Planning D*, 25(5), 783–802.

Hopkins, P. E. (2006) Youthful Muslim masculinities: Gender and generational relations. *Transactions of the Institute of British Geographers*, 31(3), 337–352.

Hyams, M. S. (2000) 'Pay attention in class … [and] don't get pregnant': A discourse of academic success among adolescent Latinas. *Environment and Planning A*, 32(4), 635–654.

Jackson, C. (2006) 'Wild' girls? An exploration of 'ladette' cultures in secondary schools. *Gender and Education*, 18(4), 339–360.

Kehily, M. J. and Nayak, A. (1997) 'Lads and Laughter': Humour and the production of heterosexual hierarchies. *Gender and Education*, 9(1), 69–87.

Mac an Ghaill, M. (1994) *The Making of Men: Masculinities, Sexualities, and Schooling*. Buckingham: Open University Press.

Renold, E. (2005) *Girls, Boys, and Junior Sexualities: Expiring Children's Gender and Sexual Relations in the Primary School*. London: RoutledgeFalmer.

Taylor, Y. (2007a) Brushed behind the bike shed: Class and sexuality in school. *British Journal of the Sociology of Education*, 28(3), 349–362.

Taylor, Y. (2007b) *Working-Class Lesbian Life: Classed Outsiders*. Basingstoke: Palgrave Macmillan.

Taylor, Y. (2009) *Lesbian and Gay Parenting: Securing Social and Educational Capital*. Basingstoke: Palgrave Macmillan.

Thiem, C. H. (2009) Thinking through education: The geographies of contemporary educational restructuring. *Progress in Human Geography*, 33(2), 154–173.

Thomas, M. E. (2005) 'I think it's just natural': The spatiality of racial segregation at a US high school. *Environment and Planning A*, 37(7), 1233–1248.

Valentine, G. (2001) *Social Geographies: Space and Society*. Harlow: Prentice Hall.

Section 2

Higher Education, Higher Standards?

6
Unpicking that 'Something Special': Student Background and the University Application Process

Sarah Evans

> [...] universities and colleges have a responsibility to identify the talent and the potential of applicants and to treat all applicants fairly and transparently. Institutions should also recognise that talent and potential may not be fully demonstrated by examination results [...] institutions should explicitly consider the background and context of applicants' achievements.
>
> (Schwartz, 2004, p. 23)

Introduction

The notion of 'getting it right' has been written about in terms of the strategies adopted by working-class people in order to 'pass' in middle-class social fields (Hughes, 2004; Lawler, 1999). Producing oneself as 'passable' within a field for which the 'rules of the game' must be learned afresh can result in the need for social actors to reflect upon the kinds of strategies that might aid their passing. What can be important in these circumstances is that the individual possesses a socially astute reading of the kind of knowledge and performances that are accorded value in the field in which they wish to 'pass'; supported by circumstances that enable the use of this knowledge as a means of acquiring capitals. This was an issue for the respondents in my PhD study, upon whose words and experiences this chapter is based. The ideas presented here emerged during qualitative research with a group of 21 girls from working-class backgrounds in inner South-East London during 2005–2006. All of the girls were in their final year of A-level study, were aged 17–18 and were in the process of applying to enter higher education (HE). Of the 21 girls I interviewed, 7 (one third) were from minority ethnic backgrounds

(Somalia, China, Vietnam, India and Bangladesh). These girls had 'succeeded' thus far in their education, and hoped to go onto professional careers.

Terry Lovell has written about how women can be 'subjects with capital accumulating strategies of their own' (2000, p. 38) and has highlighted the need for further research into the strategies that women may use to accumulate social and cultural capital. The kinds of strategies to accumulate capital that this group were able to make were limited in many cases by other commitments and by a sense of the social world that was a product of particular material conditions and gendered expectations. Attempts at accumulating capital through the vehicle of higher education were also affected by the knowledge that the respondents had of the system (as written about by Diane Reay and Stephen Ball, among others), and of their expectations about the transferability of 'value' to the investments that they had already made in their lives. Using two vignettes, this chapter will examine the issues that facilitated and restricted the respondents' experiences in accessing HE and will explore how these issues were structured by class, gender and race.[1]

Since the beginning of 2010, the UK has had a change of government and we are in the midst of assessing how the new government's HE policies will affect the educational opportunities and outcomes of young people from minority backgrounds. At the time of writing (December 2010), less than one month has passed since the government voted to raise the tuition fee cap for universities in England and Wales to £9,000 per year, about which there has been considerable anger by students and educationalists (among others). Indeed, there was significant dismay from many at the introduction of tuition fees by the New Labour government in 1998, which were raised again in 2006. It was this context of fees for HE and their impact on women, working-class people and minority ethnic groups that was one of the factors that influenced my focus on young working-class women's relationship to higher education. At the time during which I undertook my research with working-class women seeking to enter HE, fees for undergraduate study were roughly £3,000 per year. For the young women whom I got to know, £3,000 per year would be a considerable percentage of their household income. The section below will outline the context in HE during the time at which I undertook this research and will also outline some of the changes to HE policy that will impact on how and when working-class and minority ethnic women will enter HE. These issues will be returned to in the concluding section.

HE in a post-1997 context

The context in which this research took place was the recent expansion and supposed 'democratisation' of the HE system in England and Wales. As outlined by Reay et al. (2005), the expansion of HE has been an observable trend throughout the twentieth century. In the last 50 years (and particularly since the Robbins Report of 1963), we have seen considerable changes to the demography of university students. Throughout much of the twentieth century, it was the sons and (eventually) the daughters of the middle-class who were the students at universities; the gradual post-Robbins expansion of the universities recruited to the 'new' universities, established in the 1960s, greater numbers of the professional and managerial middle-class, and in particular young women from these backgrounds (Tapper and Palfreyman, 2005). The Further and Higher Education Act of 1992 has supposedly 'opened up' and democratised the HE system, and while the extent of this 'democratisation' is arguable (Hodgson and Spours, 1999; Reay, 2001), this change, combined with the rhetoric of the previous New Labour government, saw a large increase in the numbers of HE participants. For instance, the HE Statistics Agency reported an increase of 4.3 per cent in HE enrolments between the academic years 2001–2002 and 2002–2003.[2]

Part of the education policy of New Labour was to extend the normalisation of HE to those sections of the population that HE had so far significantly failed to reach: young people from working-class backgrounds and those from certain ethnic backgrounds. Policies were developed to provide additional resources for the recruitment of students from 'non-traditional' backgrounds.[3] At the same time, New Labour supported the increasing commercialisation of the HE sector, producing a university system that during their time in government became increasingly subject to commercial pressures. In September 1998, tuition fees were introduced and, from September 2006, universities in England and Wales were given the freedom to set their own tuition fees at a rate of between £0 and £3,000 per year (Department for Education and Skills (DfES), 2003, p. 76): fees referred to as 'top-up' fees. The addition of top-up fees was justified as part of an expanding HE system, which had so far 'not yet extended to the talented and best from all backgrounds' (Charles Clarke in DfES, 2003) and therefore as part of a strategic move that sought to 'make the system of supporting systems fairer' (ibid.) as these fees could be paid retrospectively through the student loans borrowing system. The fairness of this system was heavily criticised by journalists[4] and academics alike and there is significant evidence to suggest that the introduction of tuition fees, in 1998, and then top-up fees, in 2006, has had the effect of deterring students from non-traditional backgrounds. For example, in the summer of 2006, before the majority of the respondents in this study were intending to enter university, it was estimated by the National Westminster bank that those starting university in the academic year 2006–2007 can expect to pay £33,512 to complete a three-year degree course (Leach, 2006) – a significant sum to those from low-income families. In addition, Galindo-Rueda et al. (2004) found that the difference between proportions of middle-class and working-class children going to university almost doubled between 1994–1995 and 2001–2002 and have demonstrated that almost 80 per cent of students from professional backgrounds study for a degree, compared to just 15 per cent of those from unskilled backgrounds (Reay et al., 2005, p. 6).

In May 2010 a new UK coalition government, comprising of the Conservative and the Liberal Democrat parties, was formed following an election in which no party won an overall majority. Prior to the election, these two parties had espoused considerably different views on the future of HE funding in the UK. The leader of the Liberal Democrats, Nick Clegg, had pledged that his party (when in government) would work to abolish the tuition fee system. Nevertheless, in December 2010, both the House of Commons and the House of Lords voted to implement an amended version of one of the recommendations made by Lord Browne (2010) in his report on the future of HE funding. Lord Browne's report recommended the removal of the cap to tuition fees, alongside an amended student loan system, which would ensure that 'No one has to pay back the loan unless they are earning above £21,000 per year. Payments are linked to income' (Browne, 2010, p. 37). Rather, the government voted to raise the basic threshold for fees to £6,000 per annum with a cap at £9,000 to be implemented from the academic year 2012–2013. For the purposes of this chapter, it is worth considering that one of the central principles advocated in the report was thus:

> Principle 3: Everyone who has the potential should have the opportunity to benefit from higher education.
>
> (Browne, 2010, p. 26)

It is notable that the nebulous notion of 'potential' is also used here as a central determinant as to whom should have access to HE. These issues of HE funding, and the specific nature of access to HE by 'non-traditional' applicants are relevant context to this chapter, which focuses on some of the less visible barriers to access to HE for young White working-class and minority ethnic working-class women. It is important to highlight that the context of inequity in access to HE for non-traditional applicants when this research took place is only likely to worsen under the policies of the present government.

Background

The methodology used in undertaking this research has been written about elsewhere (Evans, 2008, 2009, 2010) and will be considered below in brief. Rather than replicating a full explanation of the methodologies used, it relevant to focus here on the theoretical background that informed this research and to point towards contemporary sociological and philosophical discussions around the issue of misrecognition.

Since the late 1990s, the work of Pierre Bourdieu has helped fuel this resurgence of interest in class through providing conceptual tools that bring together structural and cultural accounts of the way in which class operates. Bourdieu's work has facilitated an analysis of class that moves beyond stratification theories based on employment structure: the concepts of cultural capital, *habitus* and field provide the means by which the embodied nature of social inequalities can be integrated with theories of the cumulative effects of economic dis/advantage. For many contemporary sociologists, there is convincing evidence about the ways in which social inequalities operate that drive the need for a more cohesive account of the relationship between class and culture (Savage, 2000, p. 31). The work of Bourdieu and, more specifically, feminist reworkings of Bourdieu's theory, provided the key conceptual tools within the broader research project from which this work is drawn.

The issues of *misrecognition* and *performativity* will be engaged within this chapter. These concepts connect the work of Bourdieu and Judith Butler, and have been interrogated in the work of Nancy Fraser (2007). In Bourdieu's work, misrecognition is one of the processes through which cultural domination and symbolic violence occur. As Terry Lovell puts it:

> Misrecognition of the dominated by the dominant takes the form of a (legitimated) refusal to grant any but inferior standing to the dominated or to recognize them other than on the terms of the

dominant culture on which their own claims to distinction are based.

(Lovell, 2007, p. 71)

Performativity, for Butler, contests the very notion of a subject (1994, p. 33). It is the unthinking process of 'doing' through which the subject comes into being. For Butler, distinctions are made and remade through sequences of social actions that embed and inscribe power differentials. Thus performativity and misrecognition are both processes that reproduce cultural domination in ways that are not necessarily conscious or thought out. Misrecognition is one way though which the dominant refuse the claims and identities of the dominated; the enactment of this can be performative insofar as both the dominant and the dominated are themselves constructed through social action and language.

Both Valerie Hey (2008, 2009) and Caroline Pelletier (2009) have used these notions as a means through which to examine social class and inequality in education, particularly with respect to the acts of misrecognition that exclude working-class students from the discourse of intelligence. Before introducing the respondents whose words are central to this chapter, I want to briefly turn to a particularly relevant paper by Caroline Pelletier, which articulated a central quandary in Bourdieu's thesis, and which has been taken up by Hey (2009). Pelletier posits the work of Jacques Ranciere – and in particular his book *The Ignorant Schoolmaster* – as an account that brings Bourdieu's work into question. Pelletier (via Ranciere) queries Bourdieu's account of domination. She suggests that it can be seen to miss the extent to which working-class students understand the acts of symbolic violence that refuse them parity within education, and does not adequately respond to how the working-class are positioned vis-à-vis dominant versions of 'intelligence' and knowledge. In Bourdieu's model, she suggests, the working-class must reflexively take on the dominant version of knowledge in order to contest their domination. Thus 'the dominated' are 'posited as unable of themselves to emerge from their own modes of thinking and being which the system of domination has assigned to them' (Pelletier, 2009, p. 139). Her work therefore questions what Bourdieu's thesis offers in terms of how the voices of the dominated can be heard without their having first to engage in the discourses of intelligence which already mark them as 'Other'. This opens up a set of questions about how working-class and minority groups can achieve parity and recognition within the dominant pedagogical system. For instance, how can these groups achieve equity within this system without a loss of authenticity? What suppositions within education must be deconstructed to avoid reproducing hierarchical versions of knowledge in which working-class and minority groups will always be constructed as 'Other'? This chapter offers two case studies to be read with both Bourdieu and Butler's work in mind, but also to be considered alongside Pelletier's alternative problematic.

That 'something special'

This chapter focuses in particular on the experiences of Mai and Beth, 2 of the 21 respondents whom I followed during their final year of A-level study. Mai was from a working-class Vietnamese family and hoped to study dentistry at a university in London. Beth was from a White working-class family and hoped to study drama and theatre studies at a university outside London. Both had carefully considered Oxbridge, but for some of the reasons outlined below, had decided not to apply.

As described above, the young women with whom I spoke were Year 13 students at a sixth form attached to a mixed comprehensive school in South-East London. All of the young women intended to go to university and the majority would be the first in their family to attend. The school at which they studied had not long normalised university study as a prospect for its students. I had been a student at the school myself and was one of only a handful of people in my cohort who had attended university. In the year during which I interviewed these young women (the academic year 2005–2006), I was 26–27 and was 8–9 years older than the young women I interviewed, who were all 17–18.

I interviewed Mai and Beth, along with the other respondents on two occasions during their final year in the sixth form. As well as this, I was often present at the school as a participant observer and was also there on the day during which they received their A-level results. Each semi-structured interview lasted between 45 minutes and 2 hours and was supplemented with many informal conversations as I bumped into the girls and their friends during that year.

Many of the young women with whom I spoke recognised that A-level results alone may not be sufficient to secure entry to the most prestigious universities. They spoke variously as having to have 'talent' to secure entry to universities such as Oxford and Cambridge, although unpicking what 'talent' meant was difficult to do and often entailed a recognition of how they – as working-class and minority ethnic women – might be subjectified during the application process. This issue is made clear in the words of Jo, a White working-class girl who had grappled with strong feelings about the University of Cambridge.

> *Interviewer:* What did you think of Cambridge?
>
> *Jo:* I thought it was lovely! It was really nice. [...] The thing that scares me is that it's so competitive and I feel like it's a different class – completely different to...anything round here and anything I've experienced, so I'd feel *so* odd. [Interviewer: *A different class of people?*] Yeah. I know, I know it's very difficult to like think that only upper-class or middle-class or rich people can go there but it's got a certain reputation...and I know, I know I would be – I dunno – because I know you've got to have something special – well, I think you should have *something special* to go there and I dunno...

Jo recognised that should she apply to Cambridge, or indeed be offered a place, there was considerable potential for her to be subjectified by those who were in the majority. This recognition led to her feeling 'odd' about Cambridge, which she then reinterpreted as connected to her own 'deficiency' in not being 'special' enough to go there (Evans, 2009).

Like Jo, many of the respondents to whom I spoke did not pursue an Oxbridge application despite having the credentials to apply. The sense of opportunity that these young women described elsewhere in the interviews was opportunity confined to particular social spaces. Thus, while Oxbridge colleges and other elite institutions might suppose that the academic ability of candidates can be assessed in 'class-free' ways, working-class students often have a sense of the lack fit between their class habitus and the field of the elite university, and of how this might be enacted during the application process. These perceptions may cause some working-class and minority ethnic students to become highly organised with regards to the choices they make during the HE application process (Reay et al., 2005).

Misrecognition and Mai

The extent to which universities use the University Central Admission System (UCAS) personal statement in assessing the 'aptitude' of university applicants remains subject to rumour. At the time of writing the first draft of this chapter, the Cambridge admissions process was the subject of a number of broadsheet newspaper articles (for instance, Shephard, 2009; Frean, 2009), which indicated that Cambridge did not at that time use the personal statement to assess 'potential'. This would clearly render pointless the immense time and effort spent on these statements by schools aiming to help their students achieve an offer from Cambridge. The current advice from UCAS suggests that the personal statement remains an important part of the application process, because it:

> ... is your opportunity to tell universities and colleges about your suitability for the course(s) that you hope to study. You need to demonstrate your enthusiasm and commitment, and above all, ensure that you *stand out from the crowd*.
>
> (UCAS, 2011 [emphasis added])[5]

Indeed, the young women I spoke to had been advised by teachers that *getting the personal statement right* was crucial, particularly in applications to the most prestigious institutions. Those young women who were expected to achieve the highest results were given significant assistance in preparing these statements to reflect their successes and show their 'talent' and 'potential'. However, what 'getting it right' meant was elusive and difficult to untangle for both students and, often, teachers too. Indeed, the young women frequently received conflicting advice about how best to demonstrate their capacity, which they sometimes imagined should be obvious from their predicted grades and academic credentials. (In fact, the difficulty facing students in knowing how they will be assessed had at this point already been recognised in the review into Fair Admissions (Schwartz, 2004, p. 21).)

A significant example of how 'getting it right' can be problematic for those with little knowledge of the social field in which they are attempting to access became apparent when Mai received feedback for the reasons behind the rejection of her application to study dentistry at a well-considered London university. Her personal statement and out-of-school activities were considered by admission tutors to fail to meet the expectations of a potential dentistry student at this institution.

Mai's personal statement revealed that her 'extra-curricular' hobbies included studying a part-time nail and beauty course, working with refugees and taking classes at weekends to improve her English. The reason for her rejection was perplexing for Mai, for while she did not hold any particular expectations of achieving a place at the London university,[6] she did not expect to be rejected because of the activities that she took part in during her spare time; particularly given the sincerity with which she had made investments in her particular hobbies.

It is also worth considering here that the activities that Mai had invested in played a crucial role in maintaining her sense of self and Vietnamese identity. In fact, Mai and another respondent, Kim-Ly, who were of Vietnamese origin, both had fathers who had opened nail and beauty salons in the local area. The training that Mai had done in nail and beauty therapy was not only something that she enjoyed, but also had the potential to bring future benefits to her father's enterprise while allowing her a shared interest with her mother (who was undertaking beauty training), and her older sister who had also completed training in beauty therapy. In addition to this, it arguably enabled her broader connections and networking with people of Vietnamese origin because nail shops were around that time the fastest-growing UK Vietnamese business sector – making up over half of all Vietnamese owned businesses in London (Bagwell et al., 2003).

There are a number of points that are worth further consideration here. The first regards the issue of getting the UCAS personal statement 'right'. The guidance that the respondents received about how to fill in their UCAS application forms and personal statements was particularly varied and ranged from minimal to fairly intensive.[7] Mai, along with those other respondents who were applying for dentistry and medicine (which had earlier deadlines than the other UCAS applications) were in the privileged position of receiving one-to-one assistance from a teacher who had significant experience with the UCAS system. This particular teacher had invested considerable time and resources in attempting to enable this select group of respondents to present themselves in ways that would be favourable to university admission tutors. The viewpoint expressed to me by this teacher, which was not expressed to the students themselves, was one that matched exactly Bourdieu's (1974) thesis about the primacy of middle-class 'values' and 'taste' within the education system. She was incredibly concerned that the lives that the girls led outside school would not fit well with middle-class expectations about what a 'good student' should be, and while investing time in helping some of the students produce well-written and interesting personal statements, she also entertained some doubts about the advantages that this would provide in a competition in which the requirements were often contingent upon particular class backgrounds.

Yet, the issue in this case was also one of ethnicity, for Mai's investments in her life outside school were valuable to her and had potential to create capital within those networks that shaped her everyday life. These investments did not fit with dominant Anglocentric, White 'values' about which hobbies create the 'right' kind of student and, in this case, she was penalised for her authenticity. The investments she was making, while providing her with cultural and social capital significant within her local social field were not capitals transferable to, or easily recognised, within the field of HE. This raises questions about the interactions between stereotyping of minority ethnic groups and the dis/advantageous investments that individuals from minority ethnic backgrounds make in different forms of capital. For instance, Modood and Shiner's (2002) research would suggest that Mai fits within those ethnic categories that are at an 'ethnic advantage' in gaining access to 'old' HE institutions, yet the experience outlined here suggests that the potential advantage attached to ethnic stereotyping was overridden by the disadvantage that accompanied her investments in the 'wrong' (feminine/working-class/shaped by ethnicity) hobbies.

Mai's experience with this university would support the view that particular cultural preferences impact upon the evaluation of students by admission tutors within particular institutions (Allen et al., 2010; Burke and McManus, 2010b). Indeed, it shows the extent to which the personal statement offers a 'self' to be read by an admission tutor. The authenticity and readability of the text is implicated, yet quite *how* extra-curricular activities come to indicate intelligence and aptitude is unclear. What *is* clear in this instance is that these activities can be used as proxies and symbolic markers that work against non-dominant class and ethnic positions. In addition, this raises questions about the control of 'rules of the game' that govern the admission process and how these rules are largely determined by members of a particular class and with a system of values that may not be transparent to those of different cultural backgrounds.

Beth's authenticity and reflexivity

'Authenticity' was an issue for many of the young women to whom I spoke who wanted to retain their class and ethnic identities alongside succeeding in HE. The dissonance between working-class *habitus* and the field of the elite university has been widely addressed by sociologists, not least, Reay et al. (2009), who have uncovered how this potential dissonance is negotiated by working-class students. Here I will turn to Beth, who sought to retain her working-class authenticity and, indeed, perhaps to exploit it as the very attribute that might be considered to be that 'something special' by admission tutors and university lecturers.

Beth wanted to become an actor and to undertake a degree in theatre studies at a prestigious central England university. Among the respondents in this study, it was Beth who most obviously demonstrated the 'awakening of consciousness' that Bourdieu has written about (Bourdieu, 1977, p. 83) as occurring when social actors react to the conflicts in terms of requirements of the different social fields they may be traversing. Indeed, she confessed at one point during the interviews that she had, in the past, considered pursuing elocution lessons as she had thought that neutralising her strong south-London accent would be advantageous in her pursuit of an acting career; particularly as it would serve to help mask her class origins. At the point of interviews, however, Beth expressed a strong desire to try to 'make it as a working-class person'. That she had been considering such measures in order to bring ambiguity to the embodied aspects of class is supportive of those aspects of Bourdieu's thesis that link critical reflexivity and social transformation with a thinking consciousness (ibid., p. 204): indeed, the problem of accent as a class 'giveaway' has been written about as a common cause of dilemma for working-class people entering a middle-class field (Hey, 1997; Hughes, 2004; Mahony and Zmroezek, 1997; Reynolds, 1997). Beth anticipated that moving away to study would allow separation from those aspects of the local field that she felt would impede her ability to study in a focused way:

> *Beth:* [...] I think, working-class people don't have that much ambition – there's only a certain few that do [...] they're so concerned with having money and material goods that I think comes from working-class mentality.

At the same time, she perceived that in fact this separation would enable a unique perspective, which would allow her to retain those aspects of her class identity that she valued, in ways that would be beneficial to her sense of self. In a discussion about role models, Beth pointed towards the actress Kathy Burke[8] as embodying the kind of class authenticity and success to which she aspired:

> *Beth:* [...] Kathy Burke I suppose [is a good role model]. Anyone who kind of rises from, erm, working-class to – not necessarily fame, because I'm not concerned with fame, but just someone who has a very good reputation in their field. Because that's basically just what I want.

The kind of success that Kathy Burke has achieved was a good example to Beth of a working-class woman 'making it' within a middle-class field;

Burke is seen as able to lay claim to success without compromising her authenticity, which endears her to her fans – from both minority and dominant groups. It was this form of recognition that Beth hoped to unpick and achieve in her own career, using her working-class authenticity as a form of capital that might have exchange value within the field of professional acting. However, as Valerie Hey (2008) has noted, being 'authentic' by 'being oneself' rarely works in working-class girls' favour. Indeed, there is a delicate balance between being valued for 'working-classness' by the middle-class groups, and being viewed with 'contempt', as was the case for Jade Goody and continues to be the case for Jordan (Katie Price).[9] The kind of recognition for her working-class authenticity that Beth hoped to achieve was one that would be difficult to convey during the application process itself, because the authenticity that she hoped to lay claim to depended heavily on an embodied performance and an interruption of the performative norms embedded within the application encounter. Not only did Beth want to be able to demonstrate her worth as an intellectual, as understood by the dominant class, but she wanted also to do so in such a way that would not supersede other, equally valuable, aspects of her identity.

The university interview

The university interview, however, might offer opportunities to present the kind embodied performance upon which Beth hoped to capitalise in her pursuit of authenticity and career success. The university interview for undergraduate applications remains highly differentiated and even within different HE institutions, a range of policies and procedures may apply, with interviews being compulsory for some subjects and not for others (UCAS, 2011).[10] Many universities now offer online guidance on their interview process to potential students – in part as a response to the policy drive to make university admissions more transparent (e.g. Schwartz, 2004). For example, both Oxford and Cambridge universities have published online handbooks, which outline the process, give advice about how to prepare for an interview and offer case studies from students who successfully achieved a place following their interview. Both explicitly mention the interviews as a means to assess 'potential'[11] and describe how the interview can be a means to do this beyond the written record of the UCAS application and other written work.

That cultural capital and having the right 'cultural heritage' can impact significantly on the university application interview process has been subject to scrutiny in a number of books, plays and films that have focused on working-class entry into HE. For example, Alan Bennett's 2004 play (made into a film in 2006), *The History Boys*, focuses on this recognition with respect to Oxbridge and on the impact of various approaches to pedagogy as a means of navigating this. The play is set in the 1980s (although the setting and language of the play often alludes to other time periods, particularly the 1950s) and follows a group of eight state comprehensive sixth-form boys in the north of England as they prepare to take the Oxbridge entrance exam and interviews for under-graduate entry. The boys are from working-class and lower middle-class backgrounds. Their school is led by a headmaster who places consider-able value upon Oxbridge entry for his students – not least because of the reputational enhancement he anticipates it will bring to the school. A young male teacher, Irwin, who identifies himself as an Oxbridge graduate, is employed to train the boys for their entrance exams and interviews. Here he describes that very 'something' that my respondent Jo recognised:

> Irwin: Has anybody been to Rome? No? Well, you will be competing against boys and girls who have. And they will have been to Rome and Venice Florence and Perugia, and they will doubtless have done courses on what they have seen there [...] their essays, unlike yours, will not be dull.
>
> (Bennett, 2004, p. 19)

Later in the play, there is considerable dispute between Irwin and an older teacher, Hector (who has quite a different pedagogical approach), around the issues of mis/recognition and authenticity – understood to be determining factors in both the Oxbridge entrance exam and the interview. Irwin favours an approach in which the students would abandon their authenticity as young working-class men to undertake a performance of middle-class 'potential', 'talent' and 'merit' in order to achieve entry. For him, success in the university interview is predicated on a successful performance of the 'right' kind of student. Hector advo-cates a more authentic (although perhaps more risky) representation and expression of self:

> Hector: May I make a suggestion? Why can they not all just tell the truth?
>
> Irwin: It's worth trying, provided, of course, you can make it seem like you're telling the truth.
>
> (Bennett, 2004, p. 83)

These issues are precisely those that Beth grappled with but, until recently, little academic work in the UK has explicitly investigated the way in which working-class and minority ethnic young people respond to the performative requirements of the university application process. Two important pieces of work, by Allen et al. (2010) and Burke and McManus (2010a, b) have, however, started to address this issue significantly. While Allen et al.'s work does not examine the university interview process per se, it does examine the practices of power that shape interviews for student work placements in the creative industries. As spheres of employment, the creative industries are spaces that historically privilege the White, middle-class, male subject (Skeggs, 2004) and thus can make the space between this 'ideal worker' and the reality of intersected identities of class, ethnicity, dis/ability and gender complex to navigate for those who do not fit the ideal type. Allen et al.'s work therefore provides a valuable point of reference for those interested in the university interview process. Burke and McManus' (2010a, b) recent work examines processes of misrecognition and exclusion in the university admissions practices for art and design subjects. They examined this within the context of the drive towards widening participation and the focus on transparency recommended by Schwartz's review (2004). Their work draws considerable and welcome attention to the way in which working-class and minority ethnic students are subject to misrecognition during the university admissions process, examining the institutional technologies of assessment and practices of power that classify individuals (Burke et al., 2010b).

Allen et al. (2010) found examples of students who found ways to exploit aspects of their identity in ways that connect to Beth's hope to perhaps capitalise on her own authenticity. Allen et al. provide the example of Ed, a young man who was from a Black and minority ethnic (BAME) background and also middle-class. During the interview process, Ed used his ethnicity successfully as his 'unique selling point' (ibid.), and thus recognised that certain kinds of 'difference' are deemed to 'have value' within middle-class spaces. Indeed, his insightful reading of how subjectivities are read, and identities made, within middle-class spaces matches exactly Bryne's (2006) analysis of how particular middle-class groups value ethnic difference as a means of affirming their own liberalism. Allen et al. (2010) suggest that during this kind of interview, middle-class advantage can supersede anxieties over gender (when female) and ethnicity (when non-White). But what then for working-class girls like Mai and Beth – from minority ethnic and White backgrounds, whose intersecting identities do not match those which are attributed value within the White, middle-class space? And, in cases where such young women recognise the extent of their subjectification, upon what resources and performances can they draw to interrupt the processes of power at play? Furthermore, how can the subtleties of this kind of exclusion be adequately understood and responded to during practices that are inherently class-ridden, and increasingly complex?

Conclusion

These snapshots of Mai and Beth's experience, alongside recent work that draws on Butler, Bourdieu and a feminist post-structural framework, open up a set of questions about the vested stakes in making class, background and merit intelligible. The examples given demonstrate difference about how and why 'background' – namely class and ethnicity – are taken into account during the university application process. The cases of Mai and Beth draw attention to the performative nature of applying to university and the subtle issues of misrecognition that may reproduce inequalities in access to HE. By way of an epilogue, it is worth turning briefly to *what happened next* for Mai and Beth. Both Mai and Beth did achieve university places studying the subjects of their first choice. Beth achieved an offer for her first choice of university (a member of the Russell Group) and moved out of London. Her website indicates that she has been active in performance, direction and visual arts and she appears to have found ways to negotiate her working-class identity within an essentially middle-class academic space. Mai stayed in London to study dentistry. Thus, Mai's experience of rejection to her first choice of university did not adversely affect her entry to HE long-term. Although, of course, this positive outcome for Mai only further serves to hide the misrecognition to which she was subject during the application process.

University admission tutors and academics are expected to 'take class into account' in the decisions they make about prospective students, and to be able to understand how background and context can impact on academic 'success' (Schwartz, 2004). However, 'class' within this discourse still only seems to be that which is marked on working-class bodies: the relational aspect of class remains difficult to recognise for many (although, of course, not all) of those middle-class bodies who preside over the HE system. Thus, while the notion of 'taking class into account' may be well-meaning, it works to reproduce class privilege rather than to disrupt it. It locates 'aptitude', 'potential' and 'intelligence' as characteristics that are best determined and identified in working-class and minority groups by those in dominant class positions.

In doing so, it reproduces a hierarchy in discourses of intelligence and knowledge that misrecognises alternate versions of intelligence and skill, often working to penalise authenticity among non-dominant groups. Therefore, we can see how, even when attempts are made to take class into account, this is done so in such a way as to reject the working-class subject as a reflexive subject in their own right. This discourse, therefore, denies the extent to which class difference is recognised by those who most greatly suffer from its effects. It raises a number of issues for institutions who must denaturalise their own specific class and ethnic capitals and privileges if they are to genuinely offer opportunities to those from minority groups. It also raises issues for schools and pupils from minority groups themselves: should schools prepare students for the possible effects (and affects) of class and ethnic privilege, and if so, how? This chapter identifies the work of Pelletier (2009) and Hey (2008, 2009) as particularly valuable in offering a space that works with and against Bourdieu to address these issues.

Finally, it is worth returning to the context of these acts of misrecognition within the increasing marketisation of the HE system. The university application process includes a range of forms of assessment: including predicted A-level results, the personal statement, essays and portfolios and the university interview. The introduction of tuition fees in 1998 put university applicants in the unusual position of being subject to these various forms of scrutiny in order to be granted entry to a service *for which they would be paying*. The threshold of tuition fees will be raised to £6,000 per annum (with a cap at £9,000) to be implemented from the academic year 2012–2013. At the time of writing, both the universities of Cambridge and Oxford have announced that they plan to charge the higher rate from 2012 in order to make up the deficit to the teaching budget, which has been a result of government cuts to HE funding (Shephard, 2011). If it is to be accepted that university students are now consumers of HE, then it must also be recognised that they are a group of potential consumers who are in the bizarre position of being assessed before consent is given for them to spend these considerable amounts. Within this context, it is likely that we will see the admissions process further lauded as one of the ways through which equity in access will be assured. The work of sociologists such as Burke, Allen, Hey, Reay, Pelletier and others offers significant evidence to contest this. Although the data provided here is limited, I hope that it at least points to the bigger question of how to support working-class and ethnic minority groups through new social fields and towards questions of how to ensure equality in access in an increasingly differentiated

HE system. In particular, I hope that the experiences of Mai and Beth will enable us to find ways to support young women like them without at the same time marking them with difference, or as not having that 'something special'.

Acknowledgements

I would like to thank Professor Valerie Hey for enabling me to reproduce parts of our 2009 Society for Research into Higher Education (SRHE) paper here, as well as for the considerable support, advice and important work of her and her colleagues at the Centre for Higher Education and Equity Research (CHEER), University of Sussex. Thank you too to Dr Kim Allen for alerting me to the brilliant seminars at the Institute for Policy Studies in Education (IPSE), London Metropolitan University, and for her feedback on a draft of this chapter.

Notes

1. A shorter version of some of the ideas in this chapter was presented in December 2009 at the Society for Research into Higher Education (SRHE) conference with Valerie Hey (Hey and Evans 2009), whose work has been considerably important for the interpretation used here. An extended paper was presented at the University of Neweastle in March 2010.
2. *Office of National Statistics*, available online: www.statistics.gov.uk/cci/nugget.asp?ID=9&Pos=1&ColRank=2&Rank=192.
3. For example, the *Aimhigher* national programme run by the Higher Education Funding Council for England (HEFCE) with support from the DfES was launched in 2001 largely in order to 'raise the aspirations' of 'young people from disadvantaged social and economic backgrounds' (according to the programme website: http://www.aimhigher.ac.uk/home/index.cfm, accessed 17 June 2007). Also refer to the DfES (2004) paper on *Widening Participation*. See also, Evans (2010).
4. Before the tuition fees act was passed, Professor Claire Callender, author of a study commissioned by education ministers, wrote: 'Variable fees increase both the costs of higher education for students and their debt. Both deter low-income groups' participation.' She said that the new reforms would 'reassert elitism in higher education. Privileged students who populate top universities will pay high fees, but get highly valued degrees. Low income and access students who populate universities at the bottom of the hierarchy will pay less and get less, but still end up with large debts' (Lawson, 2006).
5. http://www.ucas.com/students/applying/howtoapply/personalstatement/ [accessed February 2011].
6. In general, the respondents demonstrated very little sense of 'entitlement' in terms of access to higher education.

7. For example, one respondent Ellen said:

> '[…] the only way I know [how to write my personal statement] is because one of my mates have already done it, because she wants to do Dentistry and it had to be off early: she kind of sent me her one and I've looked at it and just kind of wrote my own.'

While Jane's experience was very different: 'With the personal statements Miss Elliott has helped me so much … it's unbelievable, because English isn't exactly my best subject, hence, I'm not doing it at A-level, but like […] I just done what I done and Miss Elliott just sort of helped me with the wording and then putting it all together.'

8. Kathy Burke is a popular and critically acclaimed British character actor and director. She is a Londoner who has retained her 'cockney' accent and can be considered to offer a rejection of feminine ideals, both in terms of the characters she has played and her presentation of self.

9. Jade Goody was a contestant in the UK version of the television programme 'Big Brother' in 2002. She became a national celebrity for what was regarded by the media as her 'working-class ignorance', supposed unabashed sexuality and authenticity (Hey, 2008). She subsequently became wealthy via business ventures and media appearances, for which she was admired and vilified in equal measure. She died of cervical cancer in 2009. Katie Price is a glamour model and business woman who is generally held in contempt by the middle-class media but delights the tabloid newspapers. Both of these women have been located in the middle-class imagination as sexually unruly, ignorant and excessive in a way that fixes them at a distance from middle-class morality and spaces (Gidley and Rooke 2010).

10. See: http://www.ucas.ac.uk/students/offers/interviews [accessed 29 December 2010].

11. See: http://www.cam.ac.uk/admissions/undergraduate/publications/inter views.pdf; http://www.ox.ac.uk/admissions/undergraduate_courses/how_to_ apply/interviews/index.html [accessed 29 December 2010].

References

Adkins, L. and Skeggs, B. (Eds) (2004) *Feminism After Bourdieu*. Oxford: Blackwell/The Sociological Review.

Allen, K., Quinn, J., Hollingworth, S. and Rose, A. (2010) *Work Placements in the Arts and Cultural Sector: Diversity, Equality and Access*. Report for the Equality Challenge Unit. Presented at London Metropolitan University, 10 December.

Bagwell, S., Hitchcock, M. and Nguyen, K. M. (2003) *Vietnamese Business in London*. BME Knowledge Centre, Business Link for London, May 2003.

Bennett, A. (2004) *The History Boys*. London: Faber and Faber.

Bourdieu, P. (1974) The school as a conservative force: Scholastic and cultural inequalities. In J. Eggleston (Ed.), *Contemporary Research in the Sociology of Education* (pp. 32–46). London: Methuen & Co.

Boudieu, P. (1977) *Outline of a Theory of Practice*. Cambridge: Cambridge University Press.

Browne, L. J. (2010) *Securing a Sustainable Future for Higher Educa-tion: An Independent Review of Higher Education Funding and Student Finance*, 12 October. http://hereview.independent.gov.uk/hereview/report/; http://www.bis.gov.uk/assets/biscore/corporate/docs/s/10-1208-securing-sustainable-higher-education-browne-report.pdf [accessed 1 January 2011].

Bryne, B. (2006) In search of a 'good mix'. Race, class gender and practices of mothering. *Sociology*, 40(6): 1001–1017.

Burke, P. J. and McManus, J. (2010a) *Art for a Few: Exclusion and Misrecognition in Art and Design Higher Education Admissions*. NALN Research Report.

Burke, P. J. and McManus, J. (2010b) Art for a few: Exclusion and misrecognition in art and design HE admissions. *Who Fits in the Creative World? How Higher Education Practices Mirror and Perpetuate Inequalities in the Arts and Cultural Sector* at IPSE, London Metropolitan University, 10 December.

Butler, J. (1994) Gender as performance: An interview with Judith Butler. Interview by Peter Osborne and Lynne Segal. *Radical Philosophy*, 67: 32–39.

Department for Education and Skills (DfES) with foreword by C. Clarke. (2003) *The Future of Higher Education*. http://www.dfes.gov.uk/hegateway/uploads/White%20Pape.pdf [accessed 14 April 2006].

Department for Education and Skills. (2004) *Widening Participation in Higher Education*. http://www.dfes.gov.uk/hegateway/uploads/EWParticipation.pdf [accessed 21 May 2007].

Evans, S. (2008) *Becoming Somebody: Higher Education and the Aspirations of Working-Class Girls*. Unpublished Thesis, University of Kent, Kent.

Evans, S. (2009) In a different place: Working-class girls and higher education. *Sociology*, 43(2), 340–355.

Evans, S. (2010) ' "Becoming somebody": Working-class girls and higher edu-cation'. In Y. Taylor (Ed.), *Classed Intersections: Spaces, Selves, Knowledges* (pp. 53–71). Surrey: Ashgate Publishing.

Fraser, N. (2007) 'Reframing justice in a globalizing world'. In T. Lovell (Ed.), *(Mis)recognition, Social Inequality and Social Justice* (pp. 17–35). Oxon and New York: Routledge.

Frean, A. (2009) Impressive personal statement – Pity that Cambridge doesn't believe you. *The Times*, 18 May, p. 4.

Galindo-Rueda, F., Vignoles, A. and Machin, S. (2004) *Sectoral Analysis of the Economic Effects of Qualifications and Basic Skills*. Nottingham: DfES.

Gidley, B. and Rooke, A. (2010) 'Asdatown: The intersections of classed places and identities'. In T. Yvette (Ed.), *Classed Intersections: Spaces, Selves, Knowledges* (pp. 95–115). Surrey: Ashgate Publishing.

Hey, V. (1997) 'Northern accent and southern comfort: Subjectivity and social class'. In P. Mahony and C. Zmroczek (Eds), *Class Matters: 'Working-Class' Women's Perspectives on Social Class* (pp. 140–151). London: Taylor & Francis.

Hey, V. (2008) 'Educating jade?' 'Class, ignorance, desire and knowledge' the social and educational significance of not/understanding in higher education. *SRHE Conference* Adelphi Hotel, 11–13 December.

Hey, V. (2009) 'Framing girls in girlhood studies: Gender/classifications in con-temporary feminist representations'. In C. Jackson, C. Paechter and E. Renold (Eds), *Girls and Education 3-16: Continuing Concerns, New Agendas* (pp. 210–222). Basingstoke: Open University Press.

Hey, V. and Evans, S. (2009) Destined for success?: Who is made intelligible in the discursive configuration of class and background. *CHEER Symposium (University of Sussex)* at the Society for Research into Higher Education Annual Conference, Newport, 8 December.

Hodgson, A. and Spours, K. (1999) *New Labour's Educational Agenda*. London: Kogan Page.

Hughes, C. (2004) Class and other identifications in managerial careers: The case of the lemon dress. *Gender, Work and Organizations*, 11(5): 526–543.

Lawler, S. (1999) 'Getting out and getting away': Women's narratives of class mobility. *Feminist Review*, 63: 3–24.

Lawson, N. (2006) Market logic turns a degree into a share certificate. *The Guardian*. 10 August.

Leach, J. (2006) Lessons one in student life – Money. *The Observer*, 20 August.

Lovell, T. (2000) Thinking feminism with and against Bourdieu. *Feminist Theory*, 1(1): 11–32.

Lovell, T. (2007) *(Mis)recognition, Social Inequality and Social Justice*. Oxon and New York: Routledge.

Mahony, P. and Zmroczek, C. (Eds) (1997) *Class Matters: 'Working-Class' Women's Perspectives on Social Class*. London: Taylor & Francis.

Modood, T. and Shiner, M. (2002) Help or hindrance? Higher education and the route to ethnic equality. *British Journal of Sociology of Education*, 23(2): 209–232.

Pelletier, C. (2009) Emancipation, equality and education: Rancière's critique of Bourdieu and the question of performativity. *Discourse: Studies in the Cultural Politics of Schooling*, 30(2): 137–150.

Reay, D. (2001) Finding or losing yourself?: Working-class relationships to education. *Journal of Education Policy*, 16(4): 333–346.

Reay, D., Crozier, G. and Clayton, J. (2009) Strangers in paradise: Working class students in élite universities. *Sociology*, 43(6): 1103–1121.

Reay, D., David, M. E. and Ball, S. J. (2005) *Degrees of Choice: Social Class, Race and Gender in Higher Education*. Stoke on Trent: Trentham Books.

Reynolds, T. (1997) 'Class matters, "race" matters, gender matters'. In P. Mahony and C. Zmroczek (Eds), *Class Matters: 'Working-Class' Women's Perspectives on Social Class* (pp. 8–17). London: Taylor & Francis.

Savage, M. (2000) *Class Analysis and Social Transformation*. Buckingham and Philadelphia, PA: Open University Press.

Schwartz, S. (2004) *Fair Admissions to Higher Education: Recommendations for Good Practice*. Higher Education Steering Group. http://www.admissions-review.org.uk/downloads/finalreport.pdf [accessed 12 December 2007].

Shephard, J. (2009) Personal statements 'not scored' by Cambridge tutors. *The Guardian*, Tuesday 19 May.

Shephard, J. (2011) Oxford and Cambridge to join £9,000 club on fees. *The Guardian*, Wednesday 9 February. http://www.guardian.co.uk/education/2011/feb/09/oxford-cambridge-9000-fees [accessed 9 February 2011].

Skeggs, B. (2004) *Class, Self, Culture*. London and New York: Routledge.

Tapper, T. and Palfreyman, D. (Eds) (2005) *Understanding Mass Higher Education, Comparative Perspectives on Access*. Oxford: Routledge-Falmer.

UCAS (2011). *UCAS website*. www.ucas.ac.uk [accessed February 2011].

7
Beyond 'Inclusion': Mainstreaming Equality Within the Curriculum

Kath Bridger and Jenny Shaw

Introduction

In this chapter we explore a number of different responses to issues of inequality within higher education (HE) and go on to argue, with reference to an extended case study, that a 'mainstreaming' approach provides an effective and progressive way of addressing these inequalities within the context of learning, teaching and assessment in HE, and moreover transcends some of the limitations of other approaches. Our geographic focus is mainly on the UK but we draw on a number of international studies and examples to develop our argument, with particular emphasis on attempts in the USA to embed 'multiculturalism' within the curriculum.

We have argued previously (Shaw et al., 2007) that a 'diversity' rather than 'equal opportunities' approach is required to deal with the complexities of identity among students, and to address the patterns of privilege and disadvantage that have been embedded in the HE system for centuries. Our argument, which built upon the model devised by Wilson and Iles (1996) contrasted the externally driven, peripheral, group-focused and operational 'equal opportunities' model with the internalised, central, individualised and strategic 'diversity' model. We have continued to explore the implications for this approach within the HE sector (May and Bridger, 2010; Shaw, 2008; Shaw, 2009; Shaw et al., 2008), drawing on a 'business case' approach that demonstrates the benefits to individual institutions and – crucially – to all students. Throughout our research we were consistently struck by the importance placed on social justice issues by HE institutions (HEIs), and the way in which staff, especially senior staff, were at pains to draw on the history and culture of the institution to present it in a favourable light in terms of its social justice credentials. This led us to an understanding of the importance of drawing on this drive for social justice in addressing inequality at the most fundamental level – the inequalities that are still, after many decades of equality legislation, embedded within the structures, strategies, policies and practices of HEIs.

The notion of social justice is a defining factor in an increasingly popular approach to equality and diversity, namely the 'mainstreaming' approach. 'Mainstreaming equality' in its current form has been linked in part to the Fourth United Nations World Conference on the Status of Women in 1995 (see Rees, 1997) though it undoubtedly has much deeper roots in feminist theory and for this reason is often still linked to gender equality alone. The approach explicitly seeks to build a more just society as well as to improve individual outcomes and is characterised by attempts to challenge current patterns of power and privileges within social and organisational structures, rather than simply helping specific groups to negotiate a path through these structures (see Goodman, 2001). The approach has received sustained attention within the European Union (Hinds, 2006; see also Equinet, 2007 and Shaw, 2004), although its adoption across the different member states has been uneven. It is also a strong feature of policy in the USA, though under different names such as 'multiculturalism', where it builds in particular on the civil rights movement and the resulting focus on race equality. As we will go on to discuss later, practice in US institutions drawing on a 'multiculturalism' approach has many parallels with the more European 'mainstreaming' approach and there is strong potential for mutual learning, particularly in relation to diversity practice in the HE sector, which is the main focus of this chapter.

Within the UK HE sector, which has been our primary area of focus, the dominant debate relating to equality and diversity has been around the ability of students to access the limited resource of a higher level education, in other words the 'widening participation' or 'widening access' debate. The emphasis has been for many years, and still is, on the point of access for students, and therefore on increasing the actual diversity of the student body without necessarily changing any of the policies, systems or structures within institutions or the national HE systems.[1] A challenge to this was posed by the Universities UK/Standing College of Principals publication *From the Margins to the Mainstream* (Thomas et al., 2005), which argued for the need to 'embed' an approach to widening participation in HE and this ran alongside an increasing programme of incentives to retain rather than simply recruit students from lower socio-economic groups and those with disabilities. However, there was little real consideration given to the need to address at the more fundamental level the inequalities enshrined within the HE system and individual institutions.

In 2006–2007, we led a team that undertook research for the UK's Higher Education Academy to establish whether a business case could be made for embedding widening participation and promoting student diversity in the UK HE sector. This study involved a comprehensive international literature review and in-depth case study research with eight institutions across the UK. An interesting and somewhat unexpected finding from this study was the relatively weak impact of equality legislation on the case study institutions' responses to widening participation and student diversity. Only senior managers mentioned legislation, particularly the Special Education Needs and Disability Act (SENDA) 2001, with one senior manager's entire discussion of the matter being limited to: 'well we don't want to get sued!'. There was a general disjunction between practitioners within an institution who set out to widen participation and those with an institutional role in equality and diversity, the latter role often being focused on staff rather than student issues.

A mainstreaming approach to equality explicitly incorporates considerations of social justice, and integrates equal opportunities principles, strategies and practices into all aspects of an institution's operation on a day-to-day basis (Mackay and Bilton, 2003). This requires that dominant ideologies be challenged and institutional policies and practices be changed accordingly (Goodman, 2001). In relation to the experiences of students in HE, a challenge to the status quo may be posed by questioning what kind of student the existing learning, teaching and assessment practices have been designed for – in other words, what does a 'normal student' learner look like? As Archer et al. (2003) have argued, the 'normal' student may be constructed as male, White and middle-class (to which we may also add heterosexual, able bodied and, arguably, either non-religious or Christian) thus placing those who do not fit this description at a disadvantage within existing institutional cultures. This kind of thinking is embedded in the frequently used terminology 'non-traditional students'. Such students, argues Liz Thomas (2002), are a poor fit with the traditional university 'habitus'. The term 'habitus' (Bourdieu and Passeron, 1977) is usually used in relation to individuals, describing how the culture of a social group or social class can become embodied in an individual, influencing (though not determining) their choices throughout life. Thomas explores the way in which the norms of a social group may be mediated through an organisation, in this case a HEI, in a way that favours the knowledge and experience of dominant social groups to the detriment of others. We would argue that understanding how this conception of a 'normal' student plays out within the strategies, policies and practices of an institution and, furthermore, in the behaviours of staff and other students, is a vital element of any attempt to mainstream equality within HE.

Student diversity: understanding difference

In line with a mainstreaming approach, we propose that individual initiatives alone are insufficient to create an environment in which all students are able to flourish and achieve to the best of their ability. As Clayton-Pederson and Musil have argued, in relation to student diversity, 'One frequently can identify educational innovations, but rarely can one detect structures that link them' (2005, p. vii). We would suggest that effective linking structures go beyond tools, techniques, initiatives and policies. Rather, there is evidence to suggest that an institution that is serious about diversity and inclusion needs to embrace this as part of its mainstream work (May and Bridger, 2010) and use it as a positive force to drive up standards and achieve excellence across all parts of the HE mission (Milem et al., 2005).

As has been previously mentioned, work in the USA under the 'multiculturalism' banner has many parallels with the more European project of mainstreaming, and lessons from US research, policy and practice may cautiously be examined for relevance to the UK and wider European context. Indeed, not to do so would be to miss out on potentially valuable comparators, particularly when it comes to understanding the impacts of diversity measures and, furthermore, what is possible in challenging the concept of what it is to be a 'normal' student. Researchers in the USA have demonstrated a range of benefits accruing to students as a result of their interaction with a diverse student body. The level of interaction with a diverse student peer group has variously been correlated with the development of critical thinking skills (Gurin, 1999; Hurtado, 2001; Pascarella et al., 2001), self-reported gains in intellectual skills, general education and personal/social development (Hu and Kuh, 2003), self-rated aspirations for postgraduate education (Gurin et al., 2002) and the development of academic self-concept (Chang, 2001). In all of these studies, the educational benefits are linked in one way or another to the notion of 'difference' as a resource for learning. The perception of difference as a resource to be valued is a key element of the Wilson and Iles (1996) diversity model, contrasted with the equal opportunities approach that can view difference as a problem to be managed. Within the UK HE system – and more widely – both approaches flourish, and sometimes side by side in the same institution. This may be for good reasons. The US literature makes it clear that these benefits do not arise as a result of the mere presence of a diverse peer group; rather, other factors come into play relating to the way in which the institution supports and works with student diversity. This encompasses psychological, behavioural, historical and structural aspects of the institution, referred to collectively in the USA as 'campus climate' (Hurtado et al., 1998, 1999; Milem 2001). In the UK, this is more likely to be referred to as the institution's 'culture' (May and Bridger, 2010) and although the context and research approaches differ considerably, there is remarkable congruence in findings across the two countries (Shaw, 2008).

This is, we believe, an important finding for the HE sector across a range of international contexts, especially given that access to a university education is a privilege limited to a few, and not seen as a basic entitlement in the same way that primary education is. HEIs have a choice in the approach they take to student diversity issues. One approach can lead to an enriched and improved educational experience for all students but may require substantial investment in organisational change; the other may result in a series of compensatory measures that have no (or negative) effects on the majority of the student body and in some cases may represent symbolic violence against students identified as 'different' (see Bowl, 2003; Quinn, 2004; Reay, 2001 for UK examples).

This is where the external environment can play a critical role. The US-based research on the benefits of student diversity owes a great deal to the ongoing political and legislative climate surrounding the controversial policy of affirmative action, which in turn has been devised in response to the historical legacy of race relations in that country. In the UK, pressures to increase the diversity of the student body have come to bear both financially and, more recently, legislatively. The huge expansion of student numbers in the UK over the last two decades inevitably meant a widening of participation to those who would not previously have accessed HE. Allied to this have been financial incentives for institutions both in terms of carrying out access activities, and as a 'reward' for recruiting and retaining students from under-represented groups, particularly lower socio-economic backgrounds. The introduction of tuition fees in the UK seems to have further complicated this issue. Tuition fees were introduced in 1998 to the expression of concerns about the impact they would have on participation in HE by students from lower socio-economic groups. At the same time, student grants were replaced by means-tested student loans. Since 1998, the level of tuition fees has risen sharply, from £1,125 in 1998 to a maximum of £9,000 in 2011. Initially, there did not appear to be an impact on the rates of participation (Higher Education Statistics Agency, 1999) and numbers accessing HE have continued to rise in the years to date. The Office of Fair Access was established to ensure that, at the same time as charging fees, institutions were carrying out widening participation activities that would militate against the potential financial deterrent for students from poorer backgrounds. However, with fees now reaching their current level, concerns are growing about their impact on participation. The UK government therefore now appears to be placing a greater emphasis on widening access as a prerequisite for charging the maximum level of tuition fees. On a legislative basis, the SENDA legislation in 2001 placed a 'duty to promote equality' on HEIs as public bodies, and most recently the 2010 Equality Act placed a general duty in all public institutions to consider the needs of all individuals in their day-to-day work, with 'specific duties' in relation to people with particular characteristics (age; disability; gender reassignment; marriage and civil partnership; pregnancy and maternity; race; religion or belief; sex; sexual orientation) likely to become law in 2011.

All this means that, for more and more HEIs in the UK, a 'tipping point' is being reached beyond which adopting a more mainstreamed approach is going to be in their direct financial interests. Furthermore, as we have argued above, the impact of the greater diversity of the student body resulting from over a decade of widening participation initiatives has the potential to be transformed from a problem to be managed to a positive resource for student learning under a mainstreaming approach.

Achieving a mainstreamed approach is never going to be easy in organisations as complex and diverse as HEIs. However, recent work undertaken by the Higher Education Academy across the UK HE sector (May and Bridger, 2010) and by the Equality Challenge Unit in Scotland (Bridger and Shaw, 2011) has begun to support institutions in mainstreaming a diversity approach in a more holistic manner, and offers insights into both the approaches necessary to bring about change, and the potential impacts of a fully mainstreamed approach to equality on the experience of students in HE.

Mainstreaming equality in student assessment: a case study

The Higher Education Academy's facilitated change programme *Developing and Embedding Inclusive Policy and Practice in Higher Education* was launched in April 2007 and was open to all HEIs in the UK. It provided a framework to facilitate and support HEIs in the development and embedding of inclusive policies and/or practices to improve the learning experience of students from under-represented groups. It was a longitudinal programme spanning a period of 14 months with 10 participating HEIs and resulted in a report based on research carried out on an ongoing basis throughout the programme. The action-based research set out to explore the participating institutional teams' experience of developing and implementing an initiative, designed by each team specific to their institution, in order to develop and embed an aspect of inclusive policy and practice. Each initiative was intended to bring about change, whether on an institutional (strategy and policy), departmental/faculty (policy and procedure) or individual (practice) level. The pieces of work carried out by each participating institution were referred to as 'change initiatives'. Kath Bridger provided an independent consultancy led for the research aspect of the programme. The report itself provides an analysis of the diverse ways in which 'inclusion' was conceptualised, managed, developed and embedded across the participating institutions and highlights the various strategies used by the teams to manage the mainstreaming of inclusive policy and practice (May and Bridger, 2010). The case studies contained in the report were designed to provide a resource for other institutions, contributing to a greater understanding of the processes involved in developing inclusive policy and practice in HE. Indeed, our most recent research with Scotland's HE sector suggests that such case studies are very important to other institutions in helping them to formulate their own vision for mainstreaming equality.

Drawing from this research and its case studies, an example of an effective mainstreamed approach to curriculum reform for student diversity is provided by the University of Bradford. This example demonstrates how the university has moved from dealing with a specific aspect of its policy and practice in isolation to addressing it as part of a whole-institution approach to mainstreaming equality.

It is important to note the contextual environment for the delivery of this initiative. Researchers in the USA have focused considerable attention on 'campus climate' (Hurtado et al., 1998, 1999) arguing that institutional history and context is a factor in the way the climate of the institution is perceived differently by different groups of students. This has parallels with the 'institutional habitus' proposed by Thomas (2002) as noted above, in that it encompasses a range of structural, behavioural and psychological factors that affect the student's relationship with the institution and their perceived place within it. These contextual, and perceptual, factors should not be ignored by institutions seeking to mainstream equality across the organisation as a whole, or within a specific area. We have previously suggested that the way in which staff perceive aspects of the organisational climate, including its history and tradition of inclusion, appear to be an important influence on their approach to diversity and inclusion in practice (Shaw et al., 2007). To this we would further add that engaging with the perceptions of *different* groups of students and staff are an important aspect of any mainstreaming initiative.

The particular significance of this example is seated in the position of the University of Bradford when it embarked on the development and delivery of the 'change initiative'. Its commitment to widening participation and ensuring the success of its students through the whole student life cycle is well documented in its mission and Corporate Strategy. Previously a well-established technical college, the University of Bradford was founded in 1966, and as such can be regarded as a 'plate glass' university with an innovative academic heritage. It is situated in the ethnically diverse environment of West Yorkshire and has a long history of widening participation. When joining the Higher Education Academy programme approximately 48 per cent of its students came from lower socio-economic groups, 54 per cent from minority ethnic groups and approximately 70 per cent of new students were in receipt of a 'fees grant', which reduces or waives tuition fees for students from families with low incomes. The University of Bradford characterises itself as an inclusive institution, stating on its website 'We have a firm commitment to confronting inequality and celebrating diversity' (University of Bradford, 2011). It regards itself and is regarded by others as a good example of an institution that has successfully incorporated equality and diversity. This is reflected in the fact that it has consistently met the performance indicators imposed by the Higher Education Funding Council on all English universities in respect of ethnicity and socio-economic background of its student body. This 'history of inclusion' (Hurtado et al., 1998) forms a positive building block in any attempt to ensure that all students have a positive perception of the institution and their relation to it, within which more inclusive learning, teaching and assessment practices can be developed.

However, despite the positive history of inclusion described above, there was a clear rationale for change within the University of Bradford. The proportion of disabled students at the university had fallen below the sector average over the previous two years. The university's Corporate Strategy identified widening participation and inclusive learning, teaching and assessment as key priorities. The aim of developing inclusive practice was highlighted within its Learning, Teaching & Assessment (LTA) Strategy. In addition, the university had worked in partnership with the Disability Rights Commission to enhance learning, teaching and assessment practice in order to ensure greater inclusivity for disabled students. Specialist consultants had been engaged to assist in this process, feeding into the development of inclusive policy and practice and particularly the university's Disability Equality Scheme.

The university had identified that, in order to ensure that the impact of this work did not become the responsibility of just one particular department or function, it needed to find a way in which to engage with the whole university in order to embed and secure change. Therefore, the vision that drove Bradford's 'change initiative' was an 'inclusive campus' in which equality, diversity and inclusion become mainstreamed into all aspects of the institution's operation and delivery and culture. The resulting initiative *'Changing Together'* was kick-started by the work that the university was already undertaking with the Disability Rights Commission to address the needs of disabled students. It took a holistic approach across the whole university with initial actions centred on enhancing a key strategy and policy area for all HEIs, namely the LTA Strategy with particular emphasis on disabled students.

The initiative set out to develop, implement and embed a whole university approach to deliver greater inclusivity for disabled students through the University's LTA Strategy and practice. It built on the university's commitment to the implementation of change management through the development and embedding of innovative practice into mainstream activities, supported by comprehensive staff development in order to facilitate a university-wide inclusive culture. In the context of the University of Bradford's initiative and the drive of the Academy's programme to embed equality and diversity, the institutional team convened to take forward Bradford's initiative identified in their key message as 'support to succeed', encompassing the need, as identified by the project team, to ensure that both students and staff are able to access appropriate support to succeed – students in their programme of study, whatever their background or circumstance, and staff in the delivery of excellence in an inclusive environment, whatever their job role within an institution. This message reflects the movement towards a cultural shift within the institution that recognises the need to take account of a student's journey as a whole on a very practical level, rather than deal with issues of equality and diversity through the implementation of isolated interventions that are not connected in any central strategic fashion. It is important to note the makeup of Bradford's implementation team as this gave the change initiative the status it needed to have an impact across the institution. The team was spearheaded by the Pro Vice Chancellor for Learning and Teaching, and managed by the Head of the university's Educational Development Unit. It also included senior academic staff at faculty level, a member of student support staff and students themselves. This pan-institutional mix, together with the seniority of the staff involved ensured that the significance of the changes required were understood and acted upon.

The University of Bradford's approach therefore addressed the whole of the student life cycle, from access, through participation, experience and success to employability. It identified at an early stage that the employment of a holistic approach to create an inclusive institution meant that it needed to build on work already ongoing across the institution, both with regard to its infrastructure and the support it offers to disabled students both centrally and at school level. In this way, relevance and impact could be strategically identified as bringing benefit to the institution as a whole. A key part of this work focused on enhancing the learning experience for students and a review of policies to identify how disability issues are being addressed. This was informed by qualitative and quantitative research into learning, teaching and assessment practice and which drew on the experiences and views of both staff and students through both structured and semi-structured focus groups and forums. This provided data on equality issues for disabled students, highlighting not only the areas of deficiency, for example, in respect of access to materials and the provision of reasonable adjustment for disabled students, but also where effective delivery and good practice were taking place. On the basis of this data, the university was able to develop a specific action plan to ensure greater inclusivity of practice for disabled students. It was also recognised that the initiative would make a significant contribution to the institution's commitment to widening participation, enhancing an inclusive learning, teaching and assessment experience for all students.

In terms of process, the development and delivery of the University of Bradford's change initiative was an iterative one. The Higher Education Academy programme enabled the team that was leading the University of Bradford's inclusion initiative, through honest and open debate, to undertake a process of understanding and analysing the concept of inclusion and practical elements of the changes to be made across the institution. This has some parallels with education tools developed in the USA, notably Privileged Identity Exploration (Watt, 2007), which suggests that 'difficult dialogues' create the conditions for individuals to raise their critical consciousness and confront social injustices. At the University of Bradford, this process resulted in the vision of 'an inclusive campus' in which all strategies, policies and practices across the whole of the university's operation took into account the needs and views of all students. In order to address what was clearly an ambitious aspiration for this initiative, those leading the change initiative recognised that they needed to break down and understand all aspects of the process of change they wanted to initiate. This was achieved through the visual articulation of 'an inclusive campus' in the form of a concept map. The concept map was drawn as a flow diagram, which gave the team a comprehensive pictorial overview of the process of change, enabled them to understand the impact of the changes to be made and to identify where barriers might occur and develop solutions to tackle them. The concept map became the team's project management tool, supported by an action plan, which included regular reporting on progress towards achieving milestones and measures of success. It was revisited and developed on an iterative basis and provided a means through which to articulate, demonstrate change and engage others in the process.

As a result of the work delivered over the 14 months of the Higher Education Academy's programme, the university has already seen significant change and, in line with a mainstreaming approach, this change has taken place within the core of the institution rather than at the periphery. For example, a university-wide policy on 'inclusive assessment' (2008) has been adopted as an integral part of the university's LTA Strategy. Inclusive assessment provides for a flexible range of assessment methods, capable of assessing the same learning outcomes in different ways and which are made available to all students. It is an approach that recognises that students have different learning styles and offers a range of assessment methods necessary to assess the different ways in which students can demonstrate the achievement of the learning outcomes required by their programme of study. This approach to assessment has required a change in mindset and a development of understanding about the principles of assessment and a demonstration of how it can benefit both the student experience and academic outcomes. In addition, revisions were made to various university policies, programme specification templates and guidance to support staff in developing inclusive methods of assessment. The disability disclosure procedure was reviewed and further developed, supporting students in the disclosure of their disability in order to ensure that disabled students are able to access the reasonable adjustments they need in order to succeed. Providing an environment whereby students do not feel threatened or stigmatised as a result of disclosing their disability is again changing the university's attitude towards the inclusion of disabled students as part of its 'mainstream' student body. In other words, students with disabilities are considered as 'normal' students of the institution and are not seen as out of place or 'special'.

All these developments are indicative of the movement across the University of Bradford's core culture towards a 'campus climate' that recognises a wider range of actual and potential students as part of its mainstream, and embeds good equality, diversity and inclusion practice in pursuit of social justice aims. Such a move represented a significant challenge to dominant ideologies, such as notions of meritocracy, but has succeeded in bringing about change to policy and procedure at the centre of the institution rather than on the periphery.

Conclusion

It was recognised by the University of Bradford at the outset that it would take longer than the 14-month programme to bring about the required change and, in fact, the work is still ongoing at the time of writing. At present, the longer-term impact of what the changes will be on students with disabilities or the wider student body is not yet known. More generally, it may be valuable, for example, to understand the impact of the new approaches to assessment on students whose first language is not English, or who are from lower socio-economic groups. Warren (2002) has provided evidence to support the idea that mainstreamed approaches to academic support could prove of value to all students, not just those for whose needs it was specifically designed. The study offered evidence in support of an embedded or a semi-embedded model of academic support, supporting the conclusion that 'embedding "academic development" in mainstream teaching and learning, is more likely to enhance student retention, progress and achievement' (Warren, 2002, p. 94). Furthermore, some commentators have sought to present a mainstreamed equality approach as common-sense good practice in curriculum design, where:

> Identifying the characteristics of prospective learners is one of the first steps in course design. It is vital to understand the motivation and the existing skills and knowledge that students bring. This is a principle for all teaching but becomes foremost when working with a non-traditional group.
>
> (Powney, 2002, p. 22)

Parker et al. (2005), moreover, effectively distinguished between academics who embraced a mainstreaming equality perspective (though without using this term) and those who worked with a compensatory mindset. Their study determined that some practitioners routinely made adaptations and extended the curriculum to make it more accessible to a wider group of students. However, a problem with this approach is that it relies on the goodwill of individuals and departmental funding, as such approaches are not usually mainstreamed throughout the institution. They contend that practitioners committed to widening participation hold a particular view of the curriculum and how it should be taught, and that this view is likely to differ from accepted practice within their institution. They go on to conclude that extra effort is required to work with a broader diversity of student, but that this is because institutional norms have not kept pace with changes in the student body, rather than because of any deficiencies on behalf of the students themselves.

The University of Bradford's mainstreaming approach to curriculum reform was founded on social justice principles and challenged the basis on which the institution's existing approach to its core delivery – learning, teaching and assessment, the student experience and student success – as founded. We may hypothesise that the changes put into place would provide a context in which a broader diversity of students is able to succeed academically, and that these effects may not simply be confined to students with a disability. However, the data is not yet available to test this hypothesis.

The mainstreamed approach to equality within teaching, learning and assessment contrasts with an approach that seeks to help certain students to 'compensate' for their perceived deficiencies. This compensatory approach is based on conceptions of what a 'normal' student should be, as discussed previously. Influential policy literature of the early 2000s demonstrates a resistance to a more broadly mainstreamed, inclusive curriculum on the grounds that it was resource intensive (JM Consulting, 2004; Layer et al., 2002) and may compete with other, higher status, institutional priorities such as research (Powney, 2002). For example, as identified in Shaw et al. (2007), responsibility for equality and diversity issues was often placed within a specific unit and seen as separate and not relevant to what we might regard as core delivery across an institution. This past reluctance to embrace a mainstreaming approach may be attributed to a number of factors including the steer and direction being provided by the Funding Councils in the UK informed by the funding structure across the sector itself , which, in respect of widening participation and equality and diversity, provided for specific time-bound project activities, which remained at the margins of an institution's mainstream operation.

Examples such as the University of Bradford case study presented above, and other case studies arising from the same programme (May and Bridger, 2010), challenge this previous stance by demonstrating a viable mainstreamed approach to dealing with diversity and 'difference' among students in the UK's HEIs. A particular feature of the Bradford example as it was put into practice was their willingness to move on from basic compliance with legal requirements towards a vision-led embedding of an inclusive culture across all aspects of the organisation in pursuit of an enhanced experience for all students. In particular, the drive for greater inclusiveness in assessment not only affected the learning, teaching and assessment strategy, but also became embedded within the staff development programme, the Quality Enhancement Strategy and, perhaps most significantly, resulted in academic scholarship and research. A pilot was carried out to review learning outcomes in the context of inclusion using Bloom's taxonomy (Bloom, 1956), in order to support the development of inclusive curriculum. Moreover, the change initiative itself was grounded in empirical research in order that it could become an academic initiative in recognition of the fact that academic staff are key stakeholders in ensuring that change is achieved, for example, the collection of evidence in respect of the experience of disabled students alongside research into the experience of all diversity groups. This continues to be supported by the publication of journal articles and conference papers and the dissemination of the initiative, thus challenging the notion that a mainstreamed equality approach necessarily diverts resources away from research.

This and the other case studies from the Higher Education Academy programme provide a strong contrast to the findings of our 2007 study, in which issues of curriculum inclusivity, and the needs of 'non-traditional' or 'widening participation' students were largely seen as an entirely different issue from the requirements of equality legislation and, with one exception, not a central concern. Attitudes towards curriculum inclusivity tended to focus on an understanding of the changing needs of the student body and the pursuit of social good. On the other hand, attitudes to legislative equality requirements were focused on demonstrating compliance with the law and therefore the avoidance of litigation, rather than based on any business case or social justice motivation. Moreover, the two were not explicitly linked in any of the case study organisations we interviewed, despite the fact that a mainstreamed approach to curriculum inclusivity would satisfy legislative requirements. In essence, legislation was not acting as a springboard for potentially beneficial change as we had anticipated, but rather appeared to be regarded as a hoop to jump through. This was a particularly interesting finding given that a purposive sample had been selected of institutions with a good track record of widening participation in HE. It suggests that understandings of issues of equality within the curriculum have continued to develop in the UK and, perhaps, that given the changed legislative framework and the ongoing diversification of the student body, a mainstreamed approach is now a more attractive proposition than one that seeks to compensate for the deficiencies of specific groups, whereas previously the converse was true. Moreover, mainstreaming is an approach that effectively resolves tensions between selecting approaches for the general social good or for the success of the individual institution, because it may be seen as contributing to both. There is, therefore, a real opportunity emerging for HEIs that are prepared, at every level, to undertake the difficult work of identifying the inequalities that remain within their very fabric, and to take action to address them.

Note

1. It should be noted that the UK has devolved administrations in Scotland, Wales and Northern Ireland and that the HE systems within the four nations of the UK show some structural differences. However, unless otherwise stated, our analysis applies to the whole of the UK.

References

Archer, L., Hutchings, M. and Ross, A. (2003) *Higher Education and Social Class: Issues of Exclusion and Inclusion*. London: Routledge/Falmer.

Bloom, B. S. (1956) *Taxonomy of Educational Objectives: The Classification of Educational Goals* (pp. 201–207). Chicago: Susan Fauer Company.

Bourdieu, P. and Passeron, J.-C. (1977) *Reproduction in Education, Society and Culture* London: Sage.

Bowl, M. (2003) *Non-Traditional Entrants to Higher Education: 'They Talk About People Like Me'*. Stoke-on-Trent: Trentham Books.

Bridger, K. and Shaw, J. (2011) *Mainstreaming: Equality at the Heart of Higher Education*. London: Equality Challenge Unit.

Chang, M. L. (2001) 'The positive educational effects of racial diversity on campus'. In G. Orfield (Ed.), *Diversity Challenged: Evidence on the Impact of Affirmative Action* (pp. 175–186). Cambridge, MA: Harvard Educational Publishing Group.

Clayton-Pederson, A. and Musil, C. M. (2005) 'Introduction'. In J. Milem, M. Changand A. Antonio (Eds), *Making Diversity Work on Campus: A Research-Based Perspective* (pp. iii–ix). Washington, DC: Association of American Colleges and Universities.

Equinet. (2007) *Equality Mainstreaming, A Perspective from the Equality Bodies*. Brussels: Equinet Secretariat.

Goodman, D. J. (2001) *Promoting Diversity and Social Justice: Educating People from Privileged Groups*. Thousand Oaks, CA: Sage.

Gurin, P. (1999) The compelling need for diversity in education. *The University of Massachusetts Schools of Education Journal*, 32(2): 36–62

Gurin, P., Dey, E. L., Hurtado, S. and Gurin, G. (2002) Diversity and higher education: Theory and impact on educational outcomes. *Harvard Educational Review*, 72(3): 330–366.

Higher Education Statistics Agency. (2000) *Higher Education Management Statistics – Sector Level 1999/2000*. Cheltenham: HESA.

Hinds, B. (2006) Mainstreaming sex equality. *Keynote Presentation Given at ECNI Annual Conference*, Belfast, 22 November.

Hu, S. and Kuh, G. (2003) Maximizing what students get out of college: Testing a learning productivity model. *Journal of College Student Development*, 44: 185–203.

Hurtado, S. (2001) 'Linking diversity and educational purpose: How diversity affects the classroom environment and student development'. In G. Orfield (Ed.), *Diversity Challenged: Evidence on the Impact of Affirmative Action* (pp. 187–204). Cambridge, MA: Harvard Education Publishing Group.

Hurtado, S., Milem, J., Clayton-Pedersen, A. and Allen, W. (1999) *Enacting Diverse Learning Environments: Improving the Climate for Racial/Ethnic Diversity in Higher Education*. ASHE-ERIC Higher Education Report, Volume 26, No. 8. Washington, DC: The George Washington University.

Hurtado, S., Milem, J. F., Clayton-Pedersen, A. R. and Allen, W. R. (1998) Enhancing campus climates for racial/ethnic diversity: Educational policy and practice. *Review of Higher Education*, 21(3): 279–302.

JM Consulting. (2004) *The Costs of Widening Participation (A Report to HEFCE)*. www.hefce.ac.uk/pubs/rdreports/2004/rd03_04/ [accessed 7 July 2011].

Layer, G., Srivastava, A., Thomas, L. and Yorke, M. (2002) 'Student success: building for change'. In Action on Access (Ed.) (2003), *Student Success in Higher Education* (pp. 73–136). Bradford: Action on Access.

Mackay, F. and Bilton, K. (2003) *Learning from Experience: Lessons in Mainstreaming Equal Opportunities*. Governance of Scotland Forum, University of Edinburgh, Scottish Executive Social Research.

May, H. and Bridger, K. (2010) *Developing and Embedding Inclusive Policy and Practice in Higher Education*. York: Higher Education Academy.

Milem, J., Chang, M. and Antonio, A. (2005) *Making Diversity Work on Campus: A Research-Based Perspective*. Washington, DC: Association of American Colleges and Universities.

Milem, J. F. (2001) 'Increasing diversity benefits: How campus climate and teaching methods affect student outcomes'. In G. Orfield (Ed.), *Diversity Challenged: Evidence on the Impact of Affirmative Action* (pp. 233–249). Cambridge, MA: Harvard Education Publishing Group.

Parker, S., Naylor, P. and Warmington, P. (2005) Widening participation in higher education: What can we learn from the ideologies and practices of committed practitioners? *Journal of Access Policy and Practice*, 2(2): 140–160.

Pascarella, E., Palmer, B., Moye, M., and Pierson, C. (2001). Do diversity experiences influence the development of critical thinking? *Journal of College Student Development*, 42(3): 257–271.

Powney J. (Ed.) (2002) *Successful Student Diversity Case Studies of Practice in Learning and Teaching and Widening Participation*. Bristol: HEFCE: 2002/48.

Quinn, J. (2004) Understanding working-class 'drop-out' from higher education through a sociocultural lens: Cultural narratives and local contexts. *International Studies in Sociology of Education*, 14(1): 57–74.

Reay, D. (2001) Finding or losing yourself? Working-class relationships to education. *Journal of Education Policy*, 16(4): 333–346.

Rees, T. (1997) *Mainstreaming Equality in the European Union*. London: Routledge.

Shaw, J. (2004) *Mainstreaming Equality in European Union Law and Policy Making*. Brussels: European Network Against Racism.

Shaw, J. (2008) 'Towards an inclusive higher education: Crossing the boundaries of research traditions in widening participation and student diversity'. In J. Storan et al. (Eds), *Challenging Isolation: The Role of Lifelong Learning*. London: Forum for Access and Continuing Education.

Shaw, J. (2009) The diversity paradox. *Journal of Further and Higher Education*, 33(4): 321–332.

Shaw, J., Brain, K., Bridger, K., Foreman, J. and Reid, I. (2007) *Embedding Widening Participation and Promoting Student Diversity: What Can Be Learned from a Business Case Approach?* York: Higher Education Academy.

Shaw, J., Brain, K., Bridger, K., Foreman, J. and Reid, I. (2008) 'Student diversity = student success'. In F. Ferrier and M. Heagney (Eds), *Higher Education in Diverse Communities: Global Perspectives, Local Initiatives* (pp. 30–37). London: European Access Network.

Thomas, E. (2002) Student retention in higher education: The role of institutional habitus. *Journal of Education Policy*, 17(4): 423–442.

Thomas L., May H., Harrop H., Houston M., Knox H., Lee M. F., Osborne M., Pudner H. and Trotman, C. (2005) *From the Margins to the Mainstream: Embedding Widening Participation in Higher Education*. London: UUK/SCOP.

University of Bradford. (2011) The University of Bradford. www.bradford.ac.uk/about/ [accessed 17 May 2011].

Warren, D. (2002) Curriculum design in a context of widening participation in higher education. *Arts and Humanities in Higher Education*, 1(1): 85–99.

Watt, S. K. (2007) Difficult dialogues, privilege and social justice: Uses of the privileged identity exploration (PIE) model in student affairs practice. *College Student Affairs Journal*, 25: 114–125.

Wilson, E. and Iles, P. (1996) *Managing Diversity: Evaluation of an Emerging Paradigm.* Proceedings of the British Academy of Management Annual Conference Aston.

8
Mapping Exclusion in Undergraduate Psychology: Towards a Common Architecture of the Minority Student Experience

Ian Hodges and Sanjay Jobanputra

Introduction

This chapter addresses the issue of diversity in higher education (HE) within the context of the experiences of psychology students with ethnic and sexual minority identifications. Although recent years have seen an increased focus in the UK on equality of access and the promotion of a policy of widening participation in HE, especially with regard to Black and minority ethnic (BME) students and those from residential areas which have a higher representation of people with lower incomes (Higher Education Funding Council for England, 2000; Zinkiewicz and Trapp, 2004), we still have only a limited understanding of the learning and teaching experiences of minority students in UK universities. Here we explore the experiences of minority students with a particular focus on UK university psychology departments and make reference to two recent studies carried out by the Westminster Diversity in Education Research[1] group, which explored the experiences of BME and sexual minority (male Gay and Bisexual (GB)) psychology students.[2] Primarily, we seek to identify commonalities in the ways that students from these groups are positioned and framed through their teaching and learning experiences of psychology. We also aim to address the questions: Does psychology, through its teaching and learning practices, at both the individual and institutional levels, properly and meaningfully encompass the diversity of its student population? How can psychology (and other disciplines/institutions) facilitate an inclusive and rewarding learning experience for minority students? Although our research specifically focuses upon the discipline of psychology and its related (evidence-based) practices (e.g. educational, clinical and counselling psychology), our research has implications for HE more generally, which we discuss later.

While widening participation is a laudable initiative, there are growing concerns that minority students, once they enter HE, experience a range of challenges and problems. Existing literature, primarily from the USA, has repeatedly shown that these problems are many and varied, and include general discrimination, for example, on the basis of ethnicity or sexual orientation; difficulties of expression in classroom interaction with majority students; feelings of fear, isolation and alienation; and discomfort and detachment involving the curriculum (e.g. Feagin and Sikes, 1995; Rhoads, 1995). Research suggests that minority students continue to face challenges that are additional to the regular problems and stresses that all students experience as part of their learning, and shows that the overall impact on the student may range from struggling within a sometimes unfriendly, unsupportive and alienating university environment, to dropping out of their degree altogether, (Ortiz and Santoz, 2006; Reid and Radhakrishnan, 2003). We begin with a brief survey of relevant literature in relation to the two groups we discuss in this chapter, BME and male GB students.

BME students

In the USA, a study by Kraft (1991) found that the interaction between mainly White faculty and minority students was problematic for Black students. Similarly, Love (1993) showed that 'The experience of Black students in White institutions is substantially and qualitatively different than the experience of White students in White institutions.' Furthermore, Feagin and Sikes (1995, p. 93) argued that 'a university setting... [would appear] to be a cosmopolitan place generally free of overt racial discrimination... yet the reality in all parts of the country seems to be that some White and other non-Black professors can create major hurdles'.

A focus on the experiences of BME students studying psychology is particularly interesting given that psychology has made strenuous attempts to study racial prejudice as evidenced by the wide range of theoretical explanations of racial prejudice disseminated over the past 60 years or so. At the same time, however, it has been argued that psychology has continuously been affected by, and in turn reflected and reinforced, the very prejudices and discrimination that it purports to understand and challenge (Garvey, 2001; Howitt, 1990).

Owusu-Bempah and Howitt (1999, p. 26) have commented that: 'psychology continues to play its part in supporting racism rather than seeking to undermine it.' Although the precise forms of racism have changed over time, its manifestation has continued in a variety of settings, including teaching, research and practice (Cook, 2010; Richards, 1997).

In light of this situation, it is crucial to systematically explore the ways in which BME students experience psychology in HE, given their unique position as minority members studying the very discipline that appears to hold a conflicting and potentially problematic (including, at times, racist) stance towards these groups. Those BME students that do decide to study psychology are likely to find themselves not only in a numerical minority, but exposed also to psychological material that may be potentially difficult or even offensive or degrading (Howitt and Owusu-Bempah, 1994; Phoenix, 1994). An exploration of minority experiences in the UK is a useful exercise not only in assessing the impact of psychology on BME students, but also in actively engaging their often silenced voices.

Lesbian, gay and bisexual students

Lesbian, gay and bisexual (LGB) experiences and issues remain a neglected area in HE. It can be argued that this is partly due to the effects of Conservative government policy during the 1980s and 1990s, in particular the now repealed Section 28 of the Local Government Act[3] and partly because those who work as teachers and lecturers still routinely avoid the issue – education, it is often suggested, belongs to the public domain whereas sexuality belongs in the private domain – and such beliefs make it difficult to address the needs and concerns of LGB people in an educational setting (Epstein, 1994; Hodges and Pearson, 2008). Moreover, the effects of such a public/private dualism are manifested not only in individual behaviour, for example, some teachers and lecturers still take an explicit position against LBG persons and lifestyles, though this appears to be somewhat less common now (Equality Challenge Unit, 2009), but they exert also an influence upon the operation of institutions, including the relations between institutional policies and practices and those individuals who are subject to them.

Survey research continues to show that the majority of lesbians, gay men and bisexuals in the UK have experienced some form of homophobia[4] and in many cases even violence and physical assault (Jarman and Tenant, 2003; Moran et al., 2004). In a national LGB survey conducted by Stonewall[5] (Mason and Palmer, 1996) it was found that one third of all men and one quarter of all women had experienced violent attacks, while 32 per cent of all respondents had been harassed, 73 per cent had been verbally abused, 31 per cent had visited the police, and 40 per cent of violent attacks on participants aged 18 and under had taken place in school (in 50 per cent of these attacks, the perpetrators were fellow students).

In an online survey of lesbian, gay, bisexual and transgender (LGBT) staff and students in HE, based upon 4,205 responses, it was shown that LGB students reported 'significant levels of negative treatment on the grounds of their sexual orientation' (ECU, 2009, p. 4), 49.5 per cent reported such treatment from other students and 10.4 per cent from tutors and lecturers. Transexual students reported the highest levels of negative treatment (for a single group) with 22.6 per cent reporting having been bullied or discriminated against since starting university.[6]

Other research from the UK has examined LGB students' experiences of living in halls of residence (Rivers and Taulke-Johnson, 2002), heterosexism in teaching materials such as textbooks (Barker, 2007; Peel, 2001) and the construction of sexualities in schools and universities (Epstein et al., 2003). Current UK research provides a picture of life for LGB students in HE where the university environments are, for some, a safe place in which to come out and express themselves, while others still experience exclusion, discrimination or even bullying and abuse. The majority of students in HE still fear the consequences of and avoid coming out to staff (and less commonly to other students).

Westminster diversity in education research projects

Our research in the Westminster diversity in education research WiDER group is based upon the premise that the current policy emphasis on increased access to HE, while valuable in many ways, fails to address the specific experiences of minority groups, and has produced a conceptual and policy framework in which the needs of many minority students have been almost completely erased. Our research programme aims to contribute to an evidence-based discussion of these issues, through detailed documentation of the experiences of minority psychology students. The programme has so far included three separate studies (with a total of 59 participants) looking at lesbian and bisexual women (Pearson and Smith, 2006), gay and bisexual men (Hodges and Pearson, 2005; Pearson and Hodges, 2006) and ethnic minority students (Jobanputra, 2005, 2006). We have also explored all three data sets aiming to map the experiences of the three groups together (Smith et al., 2006). In what follows, we further explore the data looking at BME and male GB students.

Methodology

Design

Our studies utilise a qualitative design within a social constructionist framework. We are primarily interested in the subjective meanings that participants ascribe to the experiences and events under examination, where language is conceptualised as in part constructing the subjects and objects referred to in participants' accounts. We take a somewhat relativist stance to our data and do not assume these accounts represent a more or less accurate version of events but rather conceptualise them as versions relative (and bound) to their social, cultural and temporal location. Given that these were exploratory studies, we sampled for diversity to secure as many viewpoints and experiences as possible. Thus, we were aiming to include as varied a range of participants as possible within a sampling frame conditioned by the requirement to represent a range of institutions (within the restricted remit of the study) and limited by participants' self-selection.

We sought to analyse our data using a form of thematic analysis (cf. Boyatzis, 1998) influenced by grounded theory coding procedures, (cf. Bryant and Charmaz, 2007). Thus we aimed to uncover the recurring patterns in the data through an iterative process of 'open' and 'focused' coding derived from a process of constant comparison to provide maximum flexibility in generating themes and categories from participants' accounts. We also sought, however, in line with our constructionist position, to interpret those accounts in relation to the wider institutional and social context. In this way, a more detailed, in-depth understanding of the learning and teaching experiences of students may be assembled in a form suitable to contribute to resources for interventions that are relevant to the lived-experience of ethnic and sexual minority psychology (and other) students. Interviews were conducted during the period 2002–2007. Overall, 11 different universities were represented in the sample and these included 'old', 'new' and 'red brick' universities.[7]

Participants

GB students

In total, 18 participants were recruited through informal contacts – for example, poster campaigns and via student publications – with ages ranging from 19 to 45 years (mean age of 27.7) Of those, 14 self-identified as gay and four as bisexual. Their ethnicities/nationalities were as follows: White UK (10), Black UK (1), White Irish (1),

Argentinean (1), Danish (1), German (1), Greek (1), Iraqi (1) and White American (1). All participants had completed at least two years of their degree course or had graduated less than five years prior to inclusion in the study.

Black and minority ethnic students

There were 14 African Caribbean and South Asian students who participated (12 were female and 2 male), recruited through poster campaigns and informal contacts. The age range was 20–50 years (mean age of 28). Six of the participants were of African Caribbean origin, and the remaining eight were from the Indian subcontinent. Most of the participants were born in England; three were born outside of England, but had been living there for a considerable period of time.

Procedure

Data were collected using semi-structured one-to-one informal and confidential face-to-face and telephone interviews, which took place at the University of Westminster. The interview protocol consisted primarily of open-ended questions, such as: (1) Have your expectations changed over the period of your degree? (2) Do you relate to more than one identity category, for example, gay/bisexual, and Black? (3) Did you experience any prejudice either overt or covert from staff (students)? (4) Did you find any of the teaching material to be problematic? (5) Did you come out to or talk to other students (staff) about being gay/bisexual? The interviews were transcribed verbatim without editing, according to accepted conventions (O'Connell and Kowal, 1995). The transcripts were then scrutinised by our research assistant[8] using a thematic analytic approach drawing upon grounded theory coding techniques to identify themes and categories with the greatest explanatory power. Two other members of the research team (involved in other WiDER projects) and the authors also provided input to the coding process. This consisted of an initial phase of line-by-line (open) coding where detailed and primarily descriptive codes were produced for each entire transcript. This was followed by focused (axial) coding where the codes from the first phase were re-analysed for common themes and higher-order meanings.

Results

The results of our studies indicated that individual and institutionalised homophobia, heterosexism and racism have a detrimental impact on students' experience through exclusionary practices that are evident in areas such as curriculum content and departmental and broader university environments. However, most students reported a positive overall experience of their degree course, although there were some exceptions to this including several cases where LGB students had experienced very severe problems relating to homophobia, primarily from other students.

Participants also appeared loyal to psychology both as discipline and practice and as an eventual career path. However, there was broad disaffection and frustration regarding the exclusion of ethnicity and minority sexualities course content and the experience of estrangement while studying as an ethnic or sexual minority student in the university setting. Put another way, psychology as a discipline – through its institutional and learning and teaching practices – appears to produce a complex (and potentially contradictory) set of subject positions for minority students. In what follows we further explore the data from our studies looking at BME and male GB students, explicating the commonalities of experience between these groups using two main categories, which we term: (1) the dynamics of marginalisation and (2) valuing and problematising psychology.

The dynamics of marginalisation

Participants reported many instances of exclusion and feelings of marginalisation, which occurred in a variety of forms and settings. These experiences were reported with respect to the overall subject and curriculum, as well as the learning/teaching and social environments – where students, especially GB students often engaged in a variety of forms of self-exclusion in order to protect themselves from homophobia and other forms of prejudice and discrimination. Participants also referred to the ethnocentric and heteronormative nature of what they were taught. Often, material conveyed in the classroom tended to focus on research based on White participants, and from a White perspective:

> It's this white supremacy kind of mentality; everything is seen from a white perspective. And the reinforcement all the time of whiteness, anything else doesn't exist or is abnormal.
>
> (Valerie, 48)[9]

A key experience of difference related to a lack of understanding from the other (here, White), students:

I find it really frustrating when white people say 'you're too paranoid' or 'you're too this', or 'you're thinking about it too much'. But they don't really know what it's like to grow up and to have that responsibility and to have that shade of skin and know that some people treat you differently, completely differently. You've got that added thought at the back of your head.

(Chris, 42)

Numerous references were made to stereotyping tendencies among White psychologists (this included lecturers and authors), both in college interactions, as well as in the context of teaching. For example:

My tutor was asking if my parents will force me to get an arranged marriage, and I thought: what a thing to ask.

(Nuria, 20)

While the statement that Nuria cited was most likely to have been uttered in a seemingly benign manner by the White member of staff, its impact was felt in a very potent way. Overall, the data showed that stereotypes tended to reflect oppressive discourses and indicated an element of the dynamics of marginalisation insofar as the emphasis within psychology as a discipline was perceived as highlighting the negative assumptions of minority cultures. This tendency has also been identified by Foster (2005), who reported experiences of alienation of Black students that result from a racist campus climate (see also Feagin and Sikes, 1995).

There were criticisms of psychology course material perceived as overtly racist. The powerful impact on BME students of this type of course content is illustrated in the selection of quotes below:

And when he [author of journal article] was talking about genetic differences around intelligence and brain sizes and things, I didn't think that these kinds of things were actually happening. It opened up my mind, that there was a lot of prejudice going on... [I was] really shocked. Because I had never experienced any direct racism like that.

(Roohi, 20)

For instance some of the magazines like *The Psychologist*, like that Rushton chap put an article in there, which to me, I couldn't really understand why that was really in there. Even though it was research, but I didn't really feel it was, I thought it was quite primitive in other words. We shouldn't really be dealing with that sort of thing in this day and age.

(Michele, 27)

Not only was this material felt to be problematic in its own right, but it had also a profound impact on these students. The revelation of racism in what is researched and taught came as a shock, because it was not expected to occur within an academic setting. Academia was perceived to be an enlightened institution above and beyond ideological afflictions such as racism. Instead, the stark reality was that it was reflecting and reproducing this injustice. Furthermore, there was a sense that this racism was felt directly by the students and penetrated them in a painful way.

There was strong support for greater inclusion of material relating to minority experience in the syllabus to more accurately reflect students' lived experience though this was modulated by an ambivalence among male GB (gay and bisexual) students that appeared to normalise the lack of representation of sexual minority concerns. The following excerpts are typical reports of exclusion from the curriculum for GB men in the study:

If the course had been more open about kind of sexuality or addressed more issues to do with sexuality then I might have felt more comfortable talking about *my* sexuality.

(Ben, 35)

...as I've said and there was not much lesbian or gay kind of issues that came up within psychology. I had to search elsewhere to identify as a gay 18-year-old at University...There was nothing on my course to kind of...build it up or reiterate who I was as a gay student....

(Paul, 19)

There was also a sense that LGB issues were generally excluded from the learning/teaching environment, that is, they was simply not talked about in the university environment and that there were implicit and explicit messages signalling that they should not be talked about (we explore this in more detail in the next category). What might be termed 'obligatory invisibility' led to feelings of fear within and estrangement from the learning/teaching and social environments. However, when minority sexuality was spoken about, this was often difficult and left participants not knowing how to deal with (manage) the interaction, for example:

> There were quite a big group of kind of youngish Indian guys who were really, really homophobic and the guy in my group that I worked with, just an ordinary kind of London guy who was really homophobic, but it did feel like, it felt like the group was more menacing and more vocal about the homophobia and they'd say things like, they'd say really homophobic things and they'd say, 'Oh you're not like that are you?' to different people and it was a bit...a bit weird. So at that age I didn't really know what to say.
>
> (John, 32)

In this excerpt we also see a positioning of race/ethnicity and (possibly) class 'ordinary kind of London guy' with homophobia. While the participant did not develop this account further, there is a potential but not explicit link here and we can ask why these identity categories form a key element of this account. It appears that for this participant these labels may help the listener to make sense of the incidents described.

Participants did not routinely volunteer extended discussion about their multiple identifications, even though we asked about this explicitly during the interviews. A common response, however, to the question of intersection, was for participants to position themselves as resistant to any labelling and categorisation, the following excerpt is a useful example:

> ...I don't like to be categorised generally, and I say when I'm (.) thinking whatever, you know, why do you have to give it a name and define it and you know whatever it is, it's like it is. So I wouldn't combine, I wouldn't say gay, Arabic, I wouldn't give it a name, I am who I am....
>
> (Farhan, 26)

There was a sense from some participants that talking about identifications other than that currently being discussed (sexual identity) was a label too far. The notion of an intersecting identity or identities did not seem to provide a desirable representation of these participants' lived experience. Here, and in other interviews, the complexity of and inherent tensions within the lived experience of minority identity (and intersectionality) is illustrated, where identity categories themselves are constructed as constraining (labelling) but necessary, valued but problematised.

All GB male participants described an awareness of the heteronormative nature of the university environment – though in different ways and to differing extents. Experiences ranged from overt homophobia from both staff and students to a general feeling that the environment was not conducive to being open about one's sexuality. Direct experiences of homophobia usually took the form of prejudiced comments ('Are you fucking gay?', Kevin, 21); for example, it was very common for participants to report anti-gay or anti-lesbian comments from fellow students:

> ...but I just remember I was always working in the same group of people. One of them was okay, one was really, really homophobic and kind of expected me to join in with his homophobic comments, and the other person, in the small group was someone I was having this sort of relationship with and he was having a lot of problems with himself, and I just feel generally it was a very, very unsafe environment.
>
> (John, 32)

One student spoke of death threats (investigated by the police), which he received because of his involvement in a student union LGB organisation, while another had dropped out of HE altogether because of the level of homophobia (primarily from other students) that he experienced at university. It was more typical, however, for students to describe a more subtle and complex experience of heteronormativity where staff and students made routine assumptions that all people are heterosexual, that this is the only normal type of sexual relation and that any other form of sexuality required some kind of explanation (personally and/or theoretically).

The sense of exclusion from the curriculum, the feeling of estrangement from the university environment and the lack of acknowledgement of minority identities reported here may be conceptualised as a means through which psychology, as a discipline, marginalises those who fall outside the White, male, heterosexual norm. Where minority issues were included, for example, in the curriculum, they were almost always mentioned in the context of the unquestioned requirement to provide an explanation for 'different' identities and lifestyles. Here, students are reporting a process of what might be termed normalised absence and pathologised presence, and this we argue indicates a deep-rooted ethnocentricity and heterocentricity within psychology both as discipline and with respect to educational practices at universities more generally. Foucault (1989, pp. 65–66) famously argued that universities provide an 'artificial' environment for all students through which they are rendered 'safe and ineffective, socially and politically castrated'. The 'rituals of exclusion' to which Foucault refers are operating here in a much more selective way. Here, it is minority identities that are marginalised or erased from the university environment. Put another way, they are powerfully and routinely regulated through a process of 'Othering', that is a process whereby minority identities are, at best, marked as problematic in some sense and, at worst, repressed, stigmatised or pathologised.

Valuing and problematising psychology

While all students described some negative experiences as explicated in category one, when asked to sum up their experience almost all said that overall they had a positive experience of studying psychology at university. In general, students described a strong investment in the value and significance of psychological research and practice and remained loyal to the discipline despite their reservations concerning its treatment of minority identities and their experiences of marginalisation and exclusion. Thus, the difficulties and frustrations of studying in HE as a member of an ethnic and/or sexual minority did not appear to have a detrimental impact on participants' loyalty and commitment to psychology as discipline and practice.

In this vein, the accounts from BME students tell a vivid story about the complex and often problematic nature of studying psychology (Jobanputra, 2003). BME students, on the one hand, genuinely enjoyed studying psychology and could see its transformative benefits; at the same time, aspects of psychology were felt to be problematic; BME students often experienced difficulties and a sense of marginalisation by White staff and White students in the context of their everyday academic experience. Furthermore, BME students tended to seek each other out for emotional and academic support; they expressed a need for more BME staff and students and a more inclusive teaching program. While sexual minority students expressed similar concerns, they also tended to self-censor and self-exclude from the university and learning and teaching environments. This simultaneous valuing and problematising of psychology can be seen in the two comments below from the same participant:

> I do feel that I've learnt a lot from it. If I didn't learn anything from it, then I think I would be wasting my time. It's made me more

aware and conscious of a lot of things, and I think that's really good. It shows that I'm learning.

(Nuria, 20)

Yeah, it would be nice if every so often, [if] psychology adopted a different perspective, it would be nice to see what black psychologists have to say. However, the way things are taught, you would think that all psychologists in the whole world are white. I think you need awareness of black psychologists, because everybody uses a role model.

(Nuria, 20)

In addition to the overall positive reports of 'disciplinary loyalty' (Hodges and Pearson, 2008, p. 43), participants' accounts of how psychology should deal with issues of diversity were complex and sometimes ambivalent. While the vast majority of students in our studies expressed a desire for more minority research, issues and experiences to be included in the curriculum, some GB male students also suggested that given GB men are a small minority, it may not necessarily make sense to do so:

...I'm in a minority and psychology is a discipline and most of the research and stuff is done on the generalized populous....

(Joseph, 37)

But I think it's one of those things when you are the minority that obviously some of the curriculum is you know, sort of have to cover everything and probably take more consideration to the majority and that's just how it is... if you really want to deal with those issues there are opportunities for it, but it's not in any of the core modules. It's not sort of any mainstream thing that's taught... I feel. I don't know if it should be, you know I think it's good that the opportunities are there and you can take them if you want to, but again it might not be as relevant for other people.

(James, 30)

The excerpt above also provides a typical example of the ways in which some participants constructed a notion of the 'mainstream' as excluding minority concerns. In this sense, we can ask, 'Who is psychology for? Who are psychology's audience?'

In contrast to clear calls for greater inclusion of LGB material in the curriculum were arguments from some GB participants that it was not appropriate to reveal or discuss sexuality and sexual identity ('your gay life', Harry, 45) in a university environment 'because in the end you are giving an answer as a professional, not as a gay man...' (Brad, 32):

> In the same way that I would feel that a lecturer who was focused on their political beliefs or their race or their gender, if a lecturer was, unless it was a specific course was sort of sexuality sort of oriented, a lecturer who focused solely on that when they could have been providing a much broader base of knowledge I would feel would be a flaw to teaching....
>
> (Robert, 24)

What is interesting here is the presentation of 'race' and 'gender' as some kind of bias or flaw. Implicit here, we suggest, is the distinction between political (value laden, biased) and disinterested (value free, neutral) subject positions in which only the latter produces a (scientific) basis for disciplinary authority. This finding contrasts with the much more politicised position of participants in the WiDER study of lesbian and bisexual female psychology students, who described the dominance of majority concerns in psychology as one of the key shortfalls within the discipline and a powerful barrier to equality (Pearson and Smith, 2006, 2011).

Our findings in this study point to the ways in which the construction of the 'individual' (as subject and consumer) embedded in psychological theory and practice (including educational practices) does not properly reflect the cultural complexity of the communities and societies to which research conclusions and practical interventions are often applied. Thus, we argue that to make broader sense of the findings here we need to reflect on the 'psychological' subject and its exclusions. We argue that the assumed 'subject' of psychology rather than belonging to a general 'non-social' category, is in fact highly specific. Thus people identifying as other than White, male, heterosexual, and are somehow made 'Other', that is, they become subject to a variety of forms of regulation, whether, for example, through the notion that occupying 'Other' identities necessarily leads to bias in the researcher's own position, through the processes of normalised absence and pathologised presence identified above or through the discipline's discursive construction of a 'mainstream' audience (or consumers) who are White, and heterosexual. This is more complex than an issue of competing models of the person (cf., Chapman and Jones, 1980). Rather it points to the unspoken, taken-for-granted characteristics of those models (and subject positions) that reflect the unmarked nature of certain (central, dominant) identity categories within western culture and the ways that these are bound up with notions of disinterest and neutrality within psychological scientific theory and practice.

Given the importance of the psychological subject and its exclusions, we interpret this second category (valuing and problematising psychology) in relation to a process of alignment with the core ('mainstream') values of psychology. This process appears to be bound up with students' personal investments in the accounts that psychology routinely offers about itself as scientific, disinterested and thus apolitical and which are articulated with culturally embedded understandings of scientific (and academic) authority. In particular, if minority issues (and subjectivities) are conceptualised as fundamentally political, they cannot then count as an element of an apolitical discipline. Hence, while there were clear calls for greater recognition and inclusion of minority issues and experiences within course content (and a more open atmosphere with respect to gay and bisexual identity), there was also – for some male GB students – a desire to limit these changes to ensure that the key values of psychology were upheld and protected, such that the discipline's claims to authority were not undermined.

This process of what has been termed 'disciplinary value alignment' (Hodges and Pearson, 2008) raises difficult questions about the ways in which (any) students may 'buy into' the potentially oppressive aspects of psychological research and practice. We argue that this provides an example of the powerful means through which psychology (and possibly other disciplines) can partially incorporate issues of difference and diversity without having to properly challenge its foundation in ethnocentric and heteronormative values. Moreover, this is particularly powerful because students themselves – in some sense – come to identify with the values of scientific neutrality that psychology promotes and not least because any evidence that psychology has not (historically) been disinterested is rarely found in the content of psychology degree courses.

Discussion and implications

Our research provides evidence of experiences of stereotyping, marginalisation and pathologisation among minority students while studying psychology, where students voiced a lack of an authentic sense of inclusion as part of their learning experience. Such an experience was far from conducive to full and proper self-expression. Hence, it is important that attempts are made to address such issues in teaching and learning practices in psychology (and possibly across the sector). One example may be critical self-reflections, on what it means to be White and/or heterosexual, what it means to be prejudiced, and how the power and privileges that are ascribed to such dominant subject positions could be recognised, discussed and possibly abused, wittingly or otherwise. For White students, this opportunity may arise through appropriate modules, such as psychology of prejudice and racism. Indeed, a study by Aveling (2002) found that those White students who had received exposure to an examination of 'race' issues felt a greater sense of empowerment in being able to recognise, address and confront racist incidents around them and within themselves. Such exposure for White staff could similarly lead to transformed approaches to teaching, research and practice.

Another consideration is the recruitment of more BME students in order to achieve a critical mass. A critical mass occurs when students feel comfortable, at ease, and connected with other BME students on college campus. In the absence of such critical mass, as Fries-Britt and Turner (2001) argue, students are less likely to engage in social and academic activities on campus. For some students, this may result in dropping out of college altogether. In relation to academic staff, it would appear that currently very few BME psychologists are employed in psychology departments and yet our studies suggest that BME psychologists could play an important role in opening up academia to BME students. However, as we mentioned earlier, improving the minority student experience takes us beyond the current narrow policy focus on recruitment and, as our research has shown, we need a range of policies both nationally and locally that add up to a cultural shift in the both discipline and the sector itself.

For sexual minority students, our analysis indicates that individual and institutionalised homophobia and heterosexism can have a detrimental impact on students' experience through exclusionary practices evident in areas such as curriculum content and the departmental and social/personal environments. A key issue here relates to students (and staff) feeling welcome and able, within the university environment, to be open and authentic in relation to their sexuality. Such a move towards a more accepting, more welcoming environment would require a significantly greater degree of (pro)action with regard to institutional and departmental policies and practices than is currently the case.

Above all, the experiences of BME and sexual minority students that emerged in this exploration have one key element in common; they reflect what we might term 'silencing practices'. Such practices close down opportunities for openness and recognition not only of the ways in which the learning and teaching practices of university psychology fail to reflect the experiences, needs and concerns of minority students but also the very recognition of their presence within university departments and psychological research itself. Moreover, we have argued that the 'disciplinary loyalty' described by most of the students in our sample may also, in part, reinforce these silencing practices through limiting or censoring those aspects of identity that are perceived as incompatible with neutrality and should, therefore, remain in the private domain. Such an institutional and disciplinary context can only serve to reinforce the oppression of minority students even when universities claim to implement equal opportunities policies and other strategies of inclusion.

Although our research has been discipline specific, it is likely that our findings offer useful hypotheses for further work within other disciplines or for looking at HE more broadly. Over two decades ago, Apple (1982) argued that education, in general, and the curriculum, in particular, are essential components of those apparatuses that sustain existing patterns of structural inequality and social privilege, thus preserving a social order stratified by class, gender and ethnicity. One of the key barriers to change, he suggested, related to the ways in which those apparatuses are not recognised as such. This lack of recognition has been and remains a powerful barrier to the development of learning and teaching practices that properly cater for the needs of minority students. We must identify and recognise the effects of our practices – both within psychology and across the HE sector – not only with respect to our departmental/institutional learning and teaching practices but also through the messages and models that we, as academics, (intentionally and unintentionally) provide concerning the worth and value of ethnic and sexual minority people and their lifestyles.

Conclusions

The research reported here suggests a number of key goals for psychology as a discipline and for university departments in particular, especially with respect to learning and teaching practices. For example: psychology must operate in ways which affirm minority experience and identities rather than problematising or pathologising them. Psychology departments need to create a climate of genuine inclusion for all ethnic groups. Minority research, concerns and issues should be meaningfully incorporated into university curricula without ghettoising or pathologising minority identification and expression. Psychology departments must foster safer and more open environments for LGB students. From the accounts of students given here, we suggest that, in order to achieve these goals, the following needs to happen. First, psychology, and, we would argue, the UK HE sector, needs to fully recognise ethnic and sexual minority people and their lifestyles as an entirely normal reflection of the diversity in our societies and cultures. Second, both universities and the institutions that govern psychology (in the UK, the British Psychological Society and the Health Professions Council) must implement procedures and policies that will enable more inclusive teaching and learning practices. Third, there is an urgent need to implement staff training programmes in this regard. Moreover, as we have said, the experiences documented here offer a range of questions and hypotheses that may be useful for other disciplines and more generally with respect to learning, teaching and research in UK universities. We hope that, if the above recommendations are effectively implemented across the sector, in time minority affirmative learning and teaching practices will become taken-for-granted aspects of best practice in the provision of all forms of psychology and HE.

Notes

1. The *Westminster Diversity in Education Research* group includes Ian Hodges, Sanjay Jobanputra, Carol Pearson, Corriene Reed and Sue Smith. Website at: http://www.westminster.ac.uk/schools/humanities/research/psychology/ psychology-in-higher-education/westminster-diversity-in-education-research-group. This research was originally funded by the Higher Education Academy.
2. A paper reporting a further WiDER project exploring the experiences of Lesbian and female Bisexual psychology students is forthcoming (Pearson and Smith 2011).
3. 'Section' or 'Clause' 28 refers to an amendment to the UK Local Government Act 1986 which took place in May 1988 initiated by the then Tory government under Margaret Thatcher; it was eventually repealed in November 2003.
4. Homophobia is normally defined as some form of irrational and persistent fear or dread of 'homosexuals' (there are debates as to who from the LGBT community this term includes) or their lifestyle/culture.
5. Stonewall is a UK-based LGB campaigning organisation founded in 1989, see their website at: http://www.stonewall.org.uk.
6. Although we invited transsexual students to take part in this research none came forward.
7. So called 'redbrick' universities were established during and after the 1960s, 'new' universities were established post-1992 and tend to be ex-polytechnics (HE institutions that specialised in technical and vocational education) and less commonly ex-colleges of further education.

8. We would like to thank Anna Jessen for her dedicated work for these projects.
9. The names of all participants have been changed and any potentially identifying features within excerpts have also been removed or altered.

References

Apple, M. W. (1982) *Education and Power*. London: Routledge and Kegan Paul.

Aveling, N. (2002) Student teachers' resistance to exploring racism: Reflections on 'doing' border pedagogy. *Asia-Pacific Journal of Teacher Education*, 30(2): 119–130.

Barker, M. (2007) 'Heteronormativity and the exclusion of bisexuality in psychology'. In V. Clarke and E. Peel (Eds), *Out in Psychology: Lesbian, Gay, Bisexual, Trans and Queer Perspectives* (pp. 86–118). Chichester: Wiley.

Boyatzis, R. E. (1998) *Transforming Qualitative Information: Thematic Analysis and Code Development*. London: Sage.

Bryant, A. and Charmaz, C. (Eds) (2007) *The Sage Handbook of Grounded Theory*. London: Sage.

Chapman, A. and Jones, D. (1980) *Models of Man*. Leicester: British Psychological Society.

Cook, C. (2010) *Experiences and Perceptions of Racism among Minority Students in Doctoral Psychology Training Programs*. Unpublished PsyD, University of La Verne, La Verne, CA.

Epstein, D. (1994) *Challenging Lesbian and Gay Inequality in Education*. Buckingham: Open University Press.

Epstein, D., O'Flynn, S. and Telford, D. (2003) *Silenced Sexualities in Schools and Universities*. Stoke-on-Trent: Trentham Books.

Equality Challenge Unit (ECU). (2009) *The Experience of Lesbian, Gay, Bisexual and Trans Staff and Students in Higher Education*. Research Report Downloaded from: http://www.ecu.ac.uk/publications/files/Experiences-of-lgbt-staff-and-students-in-he.doc [accessed 21 February 2011].

Feagin, J. and Sikes, P. (1995) How black students cope with racism on white campuses. *Journal of Blacks in Higher Education*, 8: 91–97.

Foster, K. (2005) Diet of disparagement: The racial experiences of black students in a predominantly white university. *International Journal of Qualitative Studies in Education*, 18(4): 489–505.

Foucault, M. (1989) *Foucault Live*. New York: Semiotext(e).

Fries-Britt, S. L. and Turner, B. (2001) Facing stereotypes: A case study of black students on a white campus. *The Journal of College Student Development*, 42(5): 420–429.

Garvey, D. (2001) 'Boongs, bigots, and bystanders: Indigenous and non-indigenous experiences of racism and prejudice and their implications for psychology in Australia'. In M. Augoustinos and K. Reynolds (Eds), *Understanding Prejudice, Racism and Social Conflict* (pp. 43–56). London: Sage.

Higher Education Funding Council for England (HEFCE). (2000) *Funding for Widening Participation in Higher Education: New Proposals 2000–01 to 2003–04*. Bristol: HEFCE. http://www.hefce.ac.uk/Pubs/hefce/2000/00_50.htm [accessed 21 June 2011].

Hodges, I. and Pearson, C. (2005) *Out from the Margins: Exploring Gay Men's Accounts of Learning and Teaching in U.K. Psychology Departments*. Paper

Presented at the BPS Quinquennial Conference, Manchester, UK, 30 March–1 April.

Hodges, I. and Pearson, C. (2008) Silent minority: Exploring gay and bisexual men's accounts of learning and teaching in British university psychology departments. *Hellenic Journal of Psychology*, 5: 33–57.

Howitt, D. (1990) *Concerning Psychology*. Milton Keynes: OUP.

Howitt, D. and Owusu-Bempah, J. (1994) *The Racism of Psychology: Time for Change*. London: Harvester Wheatsheaf.

Jarman, N. and Tenant, A. (2003) *An Acceptable Prejudice? Homophobic Violence and Harassment in Northern Ireland*. Belfast: Institute of Conflict Research.

Jobanputra, S. (2003) *Psychology and Racism: A Study of Black Students' Experiences*. Unpublished PhD Thesis, Fairfax University, Fairfax, VA.

Jobanputra, S. (2005) *Giving Voice to Black Students in Psychology*. Widening Participation Symposium. Paper Presented at the BPS Quinquennial Conference, Manchester, UK, 30 March–1 April.

Jobanputra, S. (2006) *How Do Ethnic Minority Students Experience Psychology in Higher Education?* Poster Presented at the 4th Annual Conference on Teaching and Learning, Galway, Ireland, 8–9 June.

Kraft, C. (1991) What makes a successful black student on a predominantly white campus? *American Educational Research Journal*, 28(2): 423–443.

Love, B. (1993) Issues and problems in the retention of black students in predominantly white institutions of higher education. *Equity and Excellence in Education*, 26(1): 27–36.

Mason, A. and Palmer, A. (1996) *Queer Bashing: A National Survey of Hate Crimes Against Lesbians and Gay Men*. London: Stonewall.

Moran, L., Paterson, S. and Docherty, T. (2004) *'Count Me In!' A Report on the Bexley and Greenwich Homophobic Crime Survey*. London: GALOP.

O'Connell, D. and Kowal, S. (1995) 'Basic principles of transcription'. In J. Smith, R. Harré and L. Van Langenhove (Eds), *Rethinking Methods in Psychology* (pp. 93–105). London: Sage.

Ortiz, A. M. and Santoz, S. J. (2006) *The Ethnic Experience of College: Learning from Students to Create Successful Diverse Communities*. Stirling, VA: Stylus Press.

Owusu-Bempah, K. and Howitt, D. (1999) Even their soul is defective. *The Psychologist*, 12(3): 126–130.

Pearson, C. and Hodges, I. (2006) *Psychology at the Crossroads: Gay and Bi Men's Accounts of Learning and Teaching in UK Psychology Departments*. Poster Presented at the 4th Annual Conference on Teaching and Learning, Galway, Ireland, 8–9 June.

Pearson, C. and Smith, S. (2006) *Lesbian and Bisexual Psychology Undergraduates' Experiences of Studying Psychology*. Poster Presented at the 4th Annual Conference on Teaching and Learning, Galway, Ireland, 8–9 June.

Pearson, C. and Smith, S. (2011) *Is There a Lesbian Spectrum in Psychology? Lesbian and Bisexual Women Voice Their Experiences of Undergraduate Study*. Unpublished Manuscript, Department of Psychology, University of Westminster, London.

Peel, E. (2001) Neglect and tokenism: Representations of violence against lesbians in textbooks. *Psychology of Women Section Review*, 3(1): 14–19.

Phoenix, A. (1994) Positioned differently: Issues of 'race', difference and commonality. *Changes*, 12(4): 299–305.

Reid, L. D. and Radhakrishnan, P. (2003) Race matters: The relation between race and general campus climate. *Cultural Diversity and Ethnic Minority Psychology*, 9(3): 263–275.

Rhoads, R. (1995) Learning from the coming-out experiences of college males. *Journal of College Student Development*, 36(1): 67–74.

Richards, G. (1997) *'Race', Racism and Psychology: Towards a Reflexive History.* London: Routledge.

Rivers, I. and Taulke-Johnson, R. (2002) Listening to lesbian, gay and bisexual students on-campus: Experiences of living in university accommodation. *Journal of Institutional Research*, 11(2): 14–23.

Smith, S., Jessen, A., Hodges, I., Jobanputra, S., Pearson, C. and Reed, C. (2006) *Mapping Exclusion in Undergraduate Psychology: Towards a Common Architecture of the Minority Student Experience.* Paper Presented at the 4th Annual Conference on Teaching and Learning: Challenge of Diversity Conference, Galway, Ireland, 8–9 June.

Zinkiewicz, L. and Trapp, A. (2004) *Widening and Increasing Participation: Challenges and Opportunities for Psychology Departments* (Report and Evaluation Series No. 5). York: Learning and Teaching Support Network in Psychology, The University of York.

9
Embodying Diversity: Pedagogies of Transformation

Kay Inckle

Introduction

I work (without tenure) in a traditional, conservative, high-status, third-level institution, where the vast majority of students hail from upper middle-class families, private schools and privileged backgrounds. That is not to presume, however, that these students have not faced challenges and difficulties in their lives. In recent years there have been efforts to promote diversity within my college and to recruit 'non-traditional' students: those from working-class backgrounds, mature students and people with disabilities through a range of access programmes and by monitoring the percentage of minorities within the overall student population. (Non-European Union (EU) students have always been actively recruited on account of the inflated fees they pay.) I have often remarked that I quite literally embody diversity (female, queer, disabled, not of the majority nationality, visibly non-normative (i.e. tattooed and pierced) – to name but a few of the identity markers that could be applied to me). In my work I attempt to operationalise these locations not as rigid oppositional identity positions from which to argue against the normative/privileged Other but, rather, as portals through which to interrogate epistemological, empirical and pedagogical ethics and practices. For me, this is also a movement into embodiment; a holistic and transformative ethos that offers a radical alternative to dualistic notions of diversity in teaching, learning and research.

In this chapter I explore this holistic alternative to positivistic approaches to diversity that are based on identity politics and quantitative models of measuring and counting 'difference'. Quantitative approaches generally operate via target quotas, so that, for example, in my institution there is an aspirational policy to have 3 per cent of the staff population made up of people with a disability.[1] Here, 'people with a disability' includes physical, sensory and intellectual disability as well as people with diagnosis of mental illness. However, both the definition and target actually endorse discrimination since 10 per cent of the population have a physical disability alone (Morris, 1991).

An alternative, holistic approach to diversity that emerges through non-normative embodiment fosters a radically transformative pedagogy. This alternative position reflects a move from dualism to holism; from identity politics to a spiritually based equity; from democracy to co-operacy. The move away from democracy is essential, as quantitative approaches to diversity, democratic ideology and practice perpetuate oppression and inequality. Democracy is founded on 'the belief that the majority is right' and that 'the minority can be overruled and marginalised' (Hunter, 2007, p. 22).

For me, the move from dualism to holism is enacted via the position of embodiment that informs my research and theoretical practice (see Inckle, 2007) and which also operates as a model for radical pedagogy. Thus, in the same way in which embodied methodologies are based on an ethos of radical engagement that integrates body, heart, mind, soul and lived experience and creates the possibilities for personal and social transformation, so too is an embodied pedagogy. Indeed, a holistic and embodied approach to teaching and learning is inseparable from research in that both are processes of inquiry, discovery and transformation. They are 'an alternative means for creating inquiries compatible with a critical pedagogy project that nurtures rather than alienates the individual internally and his or her connections with larger society ... [and] connects human kind through its social and spiritual relevance' (Finley, 2002, p. 175; see also Leavy, 2009). In this pedagogical encounter, diversity and transformation are experienced and enjoyed rather than conceptualised and counted. For bell hooks this is 'liberatory education' that 'connects the will to know with the will to become' (1994, p. 19), while Tobin Hart defines it as an approach in which 'we gain the capacity not only to gather the facts of our life but also to transcend and transform them; this is where the deepest moments in education lead' (2001, p. 12). Working through my own embodiment, I conceptualise (or incorporate) this as an ethos of 'lying with' that subverts the position of normative objectivity of 'standing against'.

In framing an embodied pedagogy of diversity, I draw heavily on the work of two very different writers who both advocate for education that promotes a transformation in consciousness. bell hooks' (1994) pedagogical ethos, 'teaching to transgress: education as the practice of freedom', arises from the combination of critical race theory and politics, Buddhism, feminism and the critical pedagogy of Paulo Friere. Tobin Hart advocates for education that is 'a movement towards increasing wholeness that simultaneously pushes towards diversity and uniqueness' (2001, p. 150). For Hart this 'replaces radical disconnection with radical amazement' and 'is an education of the mind and heart, that balances intuition with intellect, mastery with mystery, and cultivates wisdom over the accumulation of facts' (2001, p. 2). For Hart the move from information to transformation is primarily a spiritual practice, and indeed many radical pedagogies are shaped in conjunction with radical spirituality (Hart, 2001; hooks, 1994; Snowber, 2002). This is not a dualistic, transcendent spirituality (as promoted by hierarchical and patriarchal religions), but one that, like the ethos of the radical pedagogies themselves is present-time, embodied and communitarian, it is: 'an inquiry of body and soul, a place where a space is opened up for the possibilities of inquiry to be transformative' (Snowber, 2002, p. 21).

In the final section of this chapter, I explore how I have used the ethos of co-operacy to embody a holistic approach to diversity and create a learning community. I draw on my students' experiences of my pedagogical practices through data from course feedback forms, which I specifically designed with this chapter in mind. However, the results of the survey did not highlight the identity-based aspects of the course material as I had presupposed, but rather, focused on my pedagogical ethos and practice and challenged me to think more deeply about the issues I explore here. The responses also draw attention to the tensions that underlie my ongoing ambivalence in regard to identity-based politics, the practice of education and a more holistic or spiritual ethos of diversity. Identity politics are powerfully seductive as a means to name and oppose the oppression and inequality I experience. Yet by embracing identity categories, I also shore up systems of dualism and division. A holistic approach, however, recognises that all human beings, by virtue of our sentient embodiment, are equally vulnerable. And while this vulnerability is structured into particular inequalities (such as sexuality, disability) it also provides an opportunity for generosity, to use that experience to touch and transform the raw and wounded places of all our experiences and to create a transformative learning community based on an ethos that recognises and nurtures uniqueness and diversity. What follows is then quite literally a new chapter in my movement towards an embodied pedagogy of diversity.

Standing against or lying with? Dualistic knowledge and pedagogies of transformation

> To feel is to be inferior, for in the dualism of Western metaphysical thought, ideas are always more important.
>
> bell hooks (1994, p. 80)

> Without the appropriate emotions underpinning and supporting reason, reason turns into its opposite.
>
> Jack Barbalet (Inckle, 2007, p. 86)

Dualism divides the world into categories of opposing binary opposites, for example: mind/body; reason/emotion; culture/nature; science/art; fact/fiction; male/female. Dualism (like democracy) is integral to the ways in which we conceive and organise our inner and outer worlds and is foundational to positivism and objectivity/objectification. Yet as a system of binary opposites, dualism is inevitably a system of dominance because it operates via a norm (the ideal) against which the Other is positioned as opposite and thereby unequal to. Dualism dictates which knowledge and which persons have status and impacts notions of diversity through reifying positivistic identity-based approaches. It is also central to the structure, function and ethos of contemporary education. Dualism privileges separation and rationality over connectedness and feeling, and eschews lived realities, embodied subjectivity, desire and affect in favour of abstract, cognitive discourses (Kazan, 2005; Zembylas, 2007). The dualism of valid knowledge (truth) and invalid knowledge (fiction) plays out across conceptual and corporeal binaries in which certain characteristics embody the 'correct' position. 'The production of "truth" – and the disqualification of "non-truth" – is thus critical to the exercise of power' (Seymour, 2006, p. 462).

In education settings, dualism permeates intricate systems of power and value that predetermine what constitutes, and who produces, valid knowledge. These structures locate not only the reified side of the dualism within a particular form of normative embodiment (male, able-bodied and so on), but insist also on the primacy of abstract disembodied knowledge. Enshrined within dualism is a positivistic ethos that reifies a mind-based, single 'truth', usually referred to as objectivism. Objectivism literally means 'standing against' (Hart, 2001, p. 91) and promotes distance, separation and opposition. This distance creates dysfunction and destruction because it means to be constantly in opposition to the devalued side of the dualism (body, emotion, connectedness) and therefore the self: 'The most insidious source of violence are the ideologies of objectivism and materialism which treat the Other (person, object, the natural world or ever some disowned part of the self) as an object to possess, measure and control' (Hart, 2001, p. 115). This 'non-relational' knowing is always separated, disembodied – standing against – and inevitably destructive to the self and others. This destructiveness is evident in the systems of knowledge production, the type of knowledge produced and the personal limitations that are imposed on those teaching and learning in this way.

The destructiveness of dualistic systems are epitomised by the current 'banking system' or 'assembly-line' approach to education where 'facts' are deposited in students to be regurgitated in examination and awarded with a dividend (a degree) (Hart, 2001; hooks, 1994). Here, teaching and learning are purely cognitive practices (i.e. disembodied and impersonal) that reify rigidity over fluidity and openness, and fixity over applied wisdom (Hart, 2001; Zembylas, 2007). Positivism and objectivity require control and prediction and Hart argues that this creates 'intolerance and fear of ambiguity and the unknown [which] contributes to the sterilization and commodification of knowledge' (Hart, 2001, p. 120). This leads to a 'distortion and fixing of view' (2001, p. 121) and creates passive and ethically bankrupt students who surrender their power of discernment to authority (a person, text or discipline). This ethical bankruptcy (as well as the failure of the banking model – and not just in education!) is endemic in contemporary society where, notwithstanding the explosion in the availability of information, individuals are bereft of the critical and creative capacities necessary for ethical and independent discernment.

Congruent with the ethos of the banking system of education, valued knowledge is positivistic, hierarchical and quantitative: 'the world is something to be controlled (objectivism) and possessed (materialism)' (Hart, 2001, p. 94). Separation from the self, the world and the Other are essential in this system where detachment is synonymous with credibility, and abstract knowing of a non-experiential nature (the mind) is validated over 'doing' and experiential knowledge (embodiment) (Seymour, 2006). Doing is construed as corporeal, bodily, feminised, while knowing is a product of the rational, transcendent, masculine mind. Thus, 'gendered notions of rationality' and the 'feminization of doing' mitigate against explicitly working from and through embodiment and lived experience (Seymour, 2006, p. 458). A female or an embodied pedagogical subject violates dualistic value structures where a body of knowledge is both literally and figuratively male (hooks, 1994;

Kazan, 2005; Seymour, 2006). This shores up the dichotomy between theory and practice (hooks, 1994) and also demands a negation or loss of self (Seymour, 2006).

This system of knowledge, which values the accumulation of abstract 'facts' over personal learning and transformation, reproduces domination and dysfunction and mitigates against holistic learning experiences with negative consequences for the wellbeing of teachers and learners (Hart, 2001; hooks, 1994; Seymour, 2006). This can be seen in the lack of 'well-being' or 'self-actualisation' (hooks, 1994, p. 15) of teachers and learners in the university system where the focus is on learning the 'one right answer' that will guarantee exam performance, or meeting positivistic performance measures. This fosters passivity, compliance and conformity rather than critical, creative and reflective teaching and learning and stifles ethical development (Hart, 2001; hooks, 1994). Hart describes the result as a 'constriction in human consciousness' (2001, p. 5) characterised by feelings of alienation, resentment, disappointment and resignation as well as the fundamental loss of self that Seymour described earlier. Thus, universities become 'a haven for those who are smart in book knowledge but who might otherwise be unfit for social interaction' (hooks, 1994, p. 16). The toxicity of this environment is evident in the psychological and emotional disease that is experienced with increasing frequency among staff and students in educational settings (see Sparkes, 2007).

The dualistic way of being in the university system is so life-negating that both hooks (1994) and Seymour (2006) experienced a deep ambivalence at the prospect of gaining tenure (despite the material and social rewards of this) and a subsequent profound sense of loss on entering the academy. This ambivalence is something I share. I have been in academia in various capacities for a decade now and, while the benefits of security that tenure would offer are undeniably attractive (assuming, of course, I would be offered a position), I also experience a deep anxiety regarding constriction that permanent, full-time status may impose on my wellbeing and my creativity, and its potentially negative impacts on my work both within and outside the classroom – particularly if this involved relocating to a culture where universities are even more absorbed in the banking system of education than my present location. At the same time, I love teaching and feel privileged, inspired and uplifted by the opportunity to work with students and support their learning. I also have a deep commitment to education as a fundamental right and also as radical potential for the transformation of lives.

My own approach to teaching and learning is one that promotes a holistic and embodied ethos and that incorporates reflection, subjectivity and spirituality. Here, spirituality is an inner experience rather than an external identity or practice and engages energy, wellbeing, creativity and life-meaning and purpose. Spirituality can be accessed via a whole range of practices, from devotion to a deity to playing music or sport, and incorporates experiences of intuition, wonder, inspiration, faith and hope linked to a holistic sense of wellbeing and purpose regardless of external structures and circumstance (Myss, 1997). In this way, it becomes a means to foster non-identity-based diversity where experiences of constriction can be portals to learning and growth rather than opposition or dualism (below). Embodiment is equally crucial to my teaching and learning ethos. Embodiment exceeds dualism; it incorporates the material (body), intangible (soul/psyche/intuition) and non-rational (emotional) and enables diversity beyond oppositional, identity-based dualisms. Embodiment integrates experiences from both sides of the normative binary and accommodates paradox, fluidity and ambiguity as precisely the tensions from which insight, learning and transformation occur (Hart, 2001; Inckle, 2007; Snowber, 2002). However, embodiment is an anathema to the mind/body dichotomy that permeates academic culture. Indeed, part of the mechanism through which privilege functions is to render the normative disembodied and the non-normative Other as innately corporeal and hyper-visible. In this way, educators are expected to conform to a normative, middle-class presentation of self, one that absents the body, the self, the private and the subjective (hooks, 1994; Zembylas, 2007). For example, in 2009 the British Broadcasting Corporation (BBC) reported how some UK universities now impose strict appearance codes on academic staff that prohibit tattoos, multiple and facial piercings, bright or 'scruffy' clothes and 'messy' hair, insisting that lectures wear business suits in sombre colours (http://news.bbc.co.uk/ 2/hi/uk_news/education/8292429.stm). Such codes co-exist with policies that claim to honour diversity, while simultaneously prohibiting religious and traditional dress from many cultures. Furthermore, what happens where teachers embody characteristics that cannot be absented through appearance codes, such as gender, 'race' and physical disability? hooks (1994) describes how she is, for many of her students, their first experience of being taught by a Black, working-class woman. Likewise, I imagine that I am probably the first experience that my students have of being taught by a visibly disabled, queer, tattooed and pierced woman and these are certainly not characteristics that I can hide in a performance of a normative academic with neat hair and a grey suit.

There are inevitable constrictions that result from my embodied identity in terms of the reception of my work, where I could apply for a job, my career prospects and so on that certainly would be very different if I was an able-bodied, straight, suit-wearing middle-class man. But because this chapter (and my practice) is an effort towards an embodiment of a 'politics of hope' (Halpin, 2003) rather than an oppositional identity-based argument, I want to focus on the ways in which teaching, learning (and researching) through non-normative embodiment has radical and transformative potential. When one does not occupy and thereby simultaneously transcend a spectral, normative body, it can become the means via which radical and transgressive teaching and learning takes place. For example, as a young pupil in a segregated school system, hooks experienced 'learning as revolution' where, inseparable from racial politics, 'teaching – educating – was fundamentally political' (1994, p. 2). hooks' teachers embodied a radical pedagogy, infusing their students with transformative potential: 'my teachers were enacting a revolutionary pedagogy of resistance that was profoundly anti-colonial' (1994, p. 2). But conceiving a pedagogical politics and practice that is based on minority identity/marginalised experience raises questions regarding the productivity of identity-based approaches to radical teaching and learning and the embodiment of diversity within the classroom. Here I tease out some of the issues integral to this dilemma and that have been formative for me in attempting to move beyond an identity-based approach to a more holistic ethos of diversity.

Postmodernism and identity-based politics are commonly positioned as binary opposites, yet both are criticised for inhibiting diversity and liberatory practice: postmodernism via its hyper-individualism, and identity-politics through replicating dualism in a quasi-essentialism. I will explore these positions and also suggest a move beyond them into what might be framed as a spiritually based equity where identity is neither fixed nor denied but becomes a portal for a community-based ethos of transformation. I integrate these approaches in a position of disabled embodiment, 'lying with', as an ethos of teaching and learning that enacts (rather than espouses) diversity.

In university settings, and certainly in my institution, diversity (which is usually coupled with 'equality') is construed around fixed identity categories and the monitoring of staff and student populations to ensure that minority or marginalised/disadvantaged groups mirror their per capita representation in the wider population. In Ireland, there are nine categories through which diversity is measured and discrimination is recognised. These are: gender, age, family status, marital status, disability, sexual orientation, religion, race and ethnicity, membership of the Traveller Community.[2] All of these identity categories, as with identity markers more generally, integrate what are in many instances (such as gender) defined as innate corporeal features with social structures and cultural determinants (of value, for example) and produce what are enshrined in policy as clearly demarcated fixed identities. At the same time, these policies also recognise that all of these categories, except (by their definition) 'race and ethnicity' and 'membership of the Traveller Community', are fluid and a person may move in and out of any number of them over the life course – marital status and age being the most obviously transient of these categories, but this is also true for gender, age, sexual orientation, religion and disability.

Identity categories and identity politics have been central to rights movements and academic disciplines (in Ireland and internationally), notably in terms of gender, sexual orientation, disability, 'race' and social class. However, within these identity-based movements, there has also been recognition of the limitations of single-issue identity politics, which create a homogenous identity and result in exclusion, discrimination and hierarchy both within and outside the movement. Debates around these issues have been particularly intense within feminism (which is often construed as a movement of middle-class, White, heterosexuals) (hooks, 1994) and in disability studies, where issues of gender and sexuality have been hotly contested (Morris, 1991). Furthermore, where inequality is seen to result from hierarchical social structures that oppress and inhibit the freedom of essentially defined groups, the question of agency becomes problematic. If an identity category is based on innate or essential features (which are already contested in feminism, critical race theory and so on) and which are then structured within a rigid hierarchical system of dominance, how has critique and change emerged? How can we understand agency?

Postmodernist approaches potentially offer a radical alternative to the limitations of identity-based approaches, their lack of agentic possibility, and the dualism they reproduce. By their 'breaking down of disciplinary boundaries and the use of reflexive and situated accounts' (Leavy, 2009, p. 123), postmodernists have formed the catalyst for contemporary embodied, reflexive, interdisciplinary and deconstructive approaches that challenge universalist approaches and create diversity.

Yet, at the same time, postmodernism, and in particular queer theory, has been seen as the antithesis of social action and merely propagating reactionary, hyper-individualist ideals that reinforce hierarchy and oppression.

Queer theorists adopt a highly critical relationship to identity politics. Judith Butler problematises identity politics on the grounds that they reproduce the dualistic and exclusionary structures that limit rather than promote diversity. In identity politics, the

> power to establish what qualifies as 'being' – works not only through reiteration, but through exclusion as well. [So that while] terms of identity have in recent years appeared to promise . . . a full recognition [the] impossibility of an identity category to fulfil that promise is a consequence of a set of exclusions which found the very subjects whose identities such categories are supposed to phenomenalize and represent.
>
> (1993, p. 188)

Identity politics reproduce dualism and hierarchy because they necessitate a self/Other binary. For this reason, Lee Edelman describes queer as 'the appropriately perverse refusal . . . of every substantialization of identity' (2004, p. 4). 'Queerness undoes identities. . . . Queerness could never constitute an authentic or substantive identity' (2004, p. 24). It is 'a constant *no* in response to the law of the symbolic . . . whose value resides in its challenge to value as defined by the social, and thus [a] radical challenge to the very value of the social itself' (2004, pp. 5–6). Queer is more accurately understood as a verb, as a doing rather than an identity – or, perhaps more appropriately as an '*un*doing'.[3] Thus, rather than being (a) queer, we *do* queer; a deconstructive political strategy of postmodernism: 'betraying what ought to remain concealed, "queering" works as the exposure within language – an exposure that disrupts the repressive surface of language' (Butler, 1993, p. 178). But here, the imperative to queer begins to become somewhat diluted within the academic imperative to detachment and abstraction: 'it implies that language is more important than agency and thought more important than action' (Kirsch, 2000, p. 58). Queer theorists have been criticised for focusing on abstract, disembodied and elitist subversions of cultural productions that are not productive of change and that reinforce reactionary politics, slipping into dangerous conceptual territory where 'the *mind* can reframe the significance of harm' (Kirsch, 2000, p. 114 [original emphasis]).

Max Kirsch is highly critical of the queer anti-identity project. For him, queer is not a liberatory practice but a re-dressing of conservative, hyper-individualist politics that suggest society is a meritocracy where everyone is equally free to be and do as they chose. This individualism is not radical or new, but merely a reflection of the contemporary spin of capitalist ideology. Theory that 'reifies the self, serves the *goals* of the capitalist enterprise by promoting the isolation of the individual and the fragmentation of resistance. Fragmentation and isolation are strategies of capitalist management' (2000, p. 114 [original emphasis]). Furthermore, the queer tactics of deconstruction and performance – the doing – are pretentious and self-defeating; an academic version of self-help culture, which insists that you can become whatever you desire regardless of external structures or circumstances. 'The idea that performance and parody are radical activities encapsulates a grandiose ambition: if we can convince ourselves that we are making a difference, perhaps we are. After all, the power of positive thinking has been emphasised in US culture' (2000, p. 90). This belief in the power of the individual, and in particular the individual mind to create reality is dualistic and dangerous as Kirsch soberly reminds us: 'soldiers do not exist for abstract reasons' (2000, p. 90).

Kirsch argues that social change is fundamentally rooted in communities that identify with an issue or struggle and form social movements around them. These communities are not tied to rigid identity politics but rather to a recognition of the impact of structures of inequality and a collective will to enact change in people's lives. These communities foster an 'energetic level of alliances' between them (2000, p. 115) rather than an identity-based one through mutual recognition. From this perspective, queer theory has become part of the destruction and fragmentation of communities and the promotion of individualism: 'with the language of past radical movements queer theory works against the struggle it claims to engage, and as reified self-involvement it militates against the construction and building of communities' (2000, p. 115).

Likewise, Halpin (2003) sees the postmodern project of deconstructionism as the enemy of hope – hope being the essential energy of social change and transformation (particularly within education). 'Discourses about hope that stress social aims and progress are generally frowned upon by postmodernists because they imply that universal or foundational truths are both discoverable and applicable as guidelines for political action, something which they deny is either possible or necessary' (2003, p. 3). However, Halpin's anti-postmodernist critique is based upon a remarkably similar premise to the postmodernist anti-identity rhetoric, in that both positions define the other as self-fulfilling inhibitors of change. So that while identity politics are seen to shore up the very structures that create unequal identity categories, in Halpin's terms postmodernist approaches pose a very real danger of producing the valueless, hyper-individualist, meaninglessness that they claim do not include values or ideological positions – much like the stuff of Margaret Atwood's dystopic futures (2003, 2009). In this vein, Halpin cautions that 'postmodernism's mockery at the possibility of social progress along such lines [i.e. value-based politics] and its scornful dismissal of the idea that specific standards of validity are worth searching for is likely to be self-fulfilling if we are not careful' (2003, p. 5).

Ultimately, however, the identity-politics/postmodernism debate has become exactly one of the dualisms that promote the anti-progressiveness that they both oppose. However, both positions also share a focus on *doing* and the 'vital energy' (Halpin, 2003, p. 26) for transformation that is materialised both in radical communities and individual queer/postmodern practices. This energy, like desire or affect, is embodied and experienced and is resistant to dualistic splitting. It can be harnessed as a holistic/spiritually based approach to diversity where structures and identities are not fixed and inevitable but form portals through which recognition and the energy for transformation occur. This energy can form a bridge from rigid identity politics or abstract postmodern conceptualisations into a model of spiritually based equity grounded in lived embodiment and community. Here, I frame this through my own non-normative and disabled embodiment in a pedagogical ethos of 'lying with'.

To 'call attention to the body' is already a political and transgressive act, it is to 'betray the legacy of repression and denial that has been handed down to us' (hooks, 1994, p. 191). To make the non-normative body visible and central to pedagogic, empirical and epistemological processes, and to embody within that the desire for an intimate, engaged and transformative teaching and learning experience is a radical act that opens up new possibilities for knowing and being. In this way, for bell hooks, her raced, gendered and classed embodiment offers a 'privileged standpoint' from which to engage with and productively critique and transform the world she inhabits (1994, p. 90). Likewise, my own non-normative, disabled embodiment illustrates the way in which 'radical freedom emerges in the midst of complete external restriction' (Hart, 2001, p. 162). The physical and social barriers that I encounter on a daily basis are not only sources of opposition, hurt, anger, frustration and restriction but require also strength and creativity in order to continue my life in a way that is positive and hopeful. Similarly, for Celeste Snowber, radical freedom emerged within constriction during her own experience of temporary physical limitation and her exclusion from the privileges that her dancer's body usually affords her. The experience of physical restriction became 'a point of reference for the place where my research questions were most challenged, explored and opened up' (in Cancienne and Snowber, 2009, p. 209). This experience was the catalyst for her to *un-learn* her own most profoundly held and unquestioned preconceptions about 'limitations'. Snowber had 'always thought of limits as places not of possibilities but places of obstacle, something to be jumped danced or skipped over. I certainly could not have seen how a place of extension and openness could be sustained and fostered by a limit' (2009, p. 209). To me, these experiences highlight how the most marginalised often have strengths and resources that far exceed normative conception, and these are resources that we can offer to those who remain limited by privilege/dualism or who are compelled to hide and transcend their vulnerabilities, embodiment and sentience.

The lived embodiment of disability and its potential to expose and exceed the limitations of dualistic culture is integral to radical crip projects in which disabled embodiment becomes a force through which normativity is interrogated, challenged and transgressed in much the same way as queerness engages heteronormativity. For Robert McRuer, bringing 'severely disabled/critically queer bodies' (2006, p. 31) to the fore is the means to produce and transmit alternative ways of knowing and being.

> A severe critique is a fierce critique, a defiant critique, one that thoroughly and carefully.... [and] loudly call[s] out the inadequacies of a given situation, person, text, or ideology. 'Severely disabled,' according to such a queer conception, would reverse able-bodied understanding of severely disabled bodies as the most marginalised, the most excluded from a privileged and always elusive normalcy, and would instead suggest that it is precisely those bodies that are best positioned to refuse 'mere toleration' and to call out the inadequacies of compulsory able-bodiedness.
>
> (2006, p. 31)

I would like to extend McRuer's crip gesture in two ways. Firstly, to suggest that the conceptualisation 'severely disabled' could be expanded into the term 'profoundly disabled', for the knowledge and practice to which disabled embodiment forms a portal. Here, my use of 'profound' highlights the way in which the adjective is reified when applied to a normative, dualistic context, such as a profound theory (the mind), and degraded when applied to disability (an abject body). Moreover, in diagnostic terms, 'profoundly disabled' indicates a more chronic state of disability than 'severely disabled'. In this way I both rework/crip its meaning and simultaneously expand severely disabled practices. This move is also intended to render it unintelligible/incomprehensible in the normative dualistic categories of either a purely discursive (postmodernist) act or an identity category (dualism).

Secondly, and following on from this, I would like to use the position of disabled embodiment, of being profoundly disabled, as a pedagogic ethos to counter the positivism and objectivity that are reified in normative teaching, learning and research. Objectivity, literally 'standing against' (Hart, 2001), embodies both an ableist (standing) and oppositional (against) position of hierarchy and defensive combat – neither of which are conducive to diversity, learning and growth. In its place, I would suggest the ethos of 'lying with' to capture the essence of progressive pedagogies and diversity. The two possible meanings of 'lying', as either a universally possible, and vulnerable, physical posture, or as an 'un-truth', suggest an intimate and subversive relation to the rigid and upstanding one-truth of dualistic and positivist discourses. Furthermore, being 'with' rather than against offers a sense of community and equality that challenges hyper-individualist and competitive approaches to identity, identity politics and pedagogical success. Indeed 'being-with' is integral to an embodied ethos in which normative structures of power and relations 'become complicated, responsive, undone' (La Jevic and Springgay, 2008, p. 67) and which opens possibilities for radical and transformative knowledge and practice.

You teach what you are: embodying diversity

We do not have the power to control how bodies are made intelligible in our culture. But we do have the power to control how bodies are read and responded to in our classrooms and whether students are as active, vocal and mobile as the teacher.

Tina S. Kazan (2005, p. 394)

Creating spaces for embracing affective connections in educational settings is an act of ethical and political practice.

Michalinos Zembylas (2007, p. 30)

For me, learning communities that honour and promote diversity and transformation are embodied within Dale Hunter's (2007) ethos and practice of co-operacy. Co-operacy is a principle of community government or decision making that moves beyond the traditional binary system of autocracy and democracy. Traditional teaching practices tend to be autocratic, with the teacher in control of the content, process and environment of the learning and many radical pedagogical theories – including Hart (2001) and hooks (1994) – aspire to democratic education systems. However, democracy like identity politics reiterates dualism, objectification and hierarchy through a self/Other; majority/minority dualism. The principle of co-operacy, a model used by 'indigenous cultures', therapy groups, peace and environmental movements (Hunter, 2007), is transferable to the classroom. It creates a facilitative approach to teaching and learning based on the premise that 'every person has the right to speak and participate' and creates learning communities that refuse any practice 'that includes having power over others' (Hunter, 2007, p. 21). Full embodied presence is essential for working in a model of co-operacy, which accesses all levels of experience, learning and wisdom. 'It involves the head, heart, belly, (brain, emotions, intuition) and powers of listening, being-with and mindfulness' (Hunter, 2007, p. 38). As such, it counters the dualistic approach to teaching and learning that reifies the disconnected ingestion and regurgitation of abstract 'facts' at the expense of whole-person/holistic development.

Co-operacy is based on accessing the positive energy within each individual, the 'power within' (rather than power over) and learning that enables all individuals within the group 'to value, express and develop a full sense of self and being in authentic relationship with others individually and as part of a group' (Hunter, 2007, p. 21). This creates diversity where the uniqueness of every individual and their equal value and contribution is appreciated: 'all persons are of equal worth, difference is valued, honoured and celebrated' (Hunter, 2007, p. 23). Hunter also highlights the importance of 'group synergy' in fulfilling the ethos of co-operacy, this group synergy is akin to the 'vital force' or 'doing' energy that informs radical alternatives to inequality and dualism, and in Hunter's work is deeply rooted in ecological spirituality. In all of these approaches, it is essential that politics and practices are enacted/embodied now, in the present, rather than conceptualised for a future-oriented agenda. The future, as both radical queer theorists (Edelman, 2004) and radical spiritual teachers (Tolle, 2001) remind us will never materialise – tomorrow never comes. Futurism, like dualism, condemns us to project the exact oppressions that we struggle against into our present moment and thereby reiterate them within the only temporal context – now – in which we have agency at personal, social and global levels (much like the Buddhist concept of Samsara). As such, contemporary classrooms within systems of constriction are locations of possibility for openness and transformation and 'the most radical space of possibility in the academy' (hooks, 1994, p. 12).

But how does this ethos translate into student experience? When I knew I would be writing a chapter for this collection, I decided to include the experiences of students I was teaching qualitative methods and ethics on a one-year full-time MSc in Applied Social Research. I chose this course because I was only teaching for one year and was therefore constrained to a greater extent than in my other work by a course and structure that was not my own. Nonetheless, as much as possible on a one-year contract, I attempted to practice an embodied pedagogy of diversity. That said, I should also confess that the focus of the students' responses surprised me. When I converted my course feedback forms to research instruments to elicit students' experiences, I had already presupposed that responses would be focused on the identity-based aspects of their classroom experience rather than the deeper pedagogical ethos I have been exploring in this chapter and was attempting to practice with them.

When I framed the question 'How much do you feel that my values, interests and experiences influenced the teaching and learning experience and how do you feel about that?' I expected answers oriented towards the politics and content of the research theory and practice I used during the course. This included the politics and practices of disability, feminist research, and embodied research with lots of content around sexuality and sexual politics, self-injury and social marginalisation. However, only one student made direct reference to any of these areas, positively citing the feminist input: 'I was also happy to see a feminist perspective represented in the teaching and learning experience'. All of the other responses to this question, while recognising that my personal values, interests and experiences were central to the content, reflected on this more broadly with responses falling into two major themes. The first theme focused on the 'real-life learning' of how to be a researcher, where my values and experiences offered a window into researcher life and how (in my work at least) the messiness of the process and the unforeseen pitfalls and possibilities of research often contrast with the 'polished' text book accounts or initial research proposal.

There was a lot of influence...I thought this added greatly to the class, as I think your values are similar to mine and your interests and experiences are fascinating! Also a good insight into 'real-researcher-life'.

I think they influence the teaching and learning, I thought you made your own views and position obvious. I thought this was beneficial to see how a researcher can use their position/views to inform their research, follow their interests and locate themselves in theoretical debate.

The second theme that emerged from these responses focused on the learning environment that resulted from explicitly drawing on my values, interests and experiences in the classroom, which three students described as follows:

I believe they were extremely influential in the teaching and learning experience to the absolute benefit of the class.

I do think it makes a positive difference when a person is passionate about what they are teaching and that did come across in class with you.

You always brought humour to the class which was great...You seem very encouraging and open to other people's interpretation of things, I know this made people feel they could contribute to classes.

The other main themes that are relevant to this chapter (as opposed to the structure and content of the specific course) emerged from answers to the questions 'what did you like best about the qual classes', 'overall experience' and 'any other comments'. These produced a remarkable similarity of response, which focused on the interactive nature of the classes, the ways in which everyone was engaged and involved in the learning process, the participatory ethos and my own attitude and orientation towards students.

Students highlighted the importance of the interactive nature of the classes where 'student input [was] not treated as a nuisance but valued', and which also had impacts for the group as a learning community: 'your classes were a really good way of getting to know the other people in the class'. My efforts towards inclusivity seemed to pay off as students particularly noted how in each class I 'engaged and involved everyone' and, furthermore, that involvement and engagement are mutually productive: it 'made classes engaging as you weren't just talking at us, you got us all involved'. Participation was also a key theme in terms of the 'creative' and 'fun' ways to learn that my efforts towards a participatory classroom incorporated, alongside the impact of participatory learning on the breadth and depth of learning experience: 'it challenged me to participate fully in the class, to learn more, to expand my views and challenge my own norms and think about things differently'. Students appreciated that I was enthusiastic and motivated about the topic and felt that it made a difference when a teacher 'enjoys it and is passionate about it'. Interaction, participation, involvement and engagement were the key themes of the students' responses to the learning process. Students noted personal qualities of openness and warmth in my approach, which they also felt were very important to the learning experience. They described me as 'honest, open and accepting', 'friendly and open' and providing a 'very friendly, positive and open atmosphere' and a 'friendly and welcoming experience'.

My aim in reporting this is not purely self-serving, but rather that it came as an unanticipated affirmation that my deepest values and beliefs are more formative of my classroom practice than I had anticipated. It indicates (to me at least) that, even in circumstances of external constriction, it is possible to move beyond the surface identity politics – which I had expected to be more dominant – and open up another layer of connection and response. The students named the very qualities that are integral to an embodied pedagogy of diversity and a co-operatic community. The contrast between their responses and my initial expectations also functions to remind me of how easy it is for me to place identity politics before our shared humanity and the constrictions I re-impose on myself and others when I do so. To this day, I am often seduced by the (oppositional) energy of identity politics, particularly when I am quite literally obstructed by the disabling environment and culture of the university, even though I also experience the ways in which identity politicking is a destructive and self-defeating cycle. I know it is very easy to passionately champion a cause or an approach, to highlight an injustice, and to simultaneously silence others and recreate an autocracy that is simply based on a reversal of values and majority/minority status. In this way, at the deepest level, it is our classroom culture and practice that students learn, rather than the content of our words and texts (Hart, 2001). Or, in Seymour's (2006) terms, students learn from what we do rather than what we know. Ultimately, then, 'we teach what we are' (Hart, 2001, p. 115), and I am heartened to know that, at least in this instance, I am embodying my deeper holistic values rather than being seduced by the mind-based, dualistic identity politics and hierarchy, which remain the currency of much educational policy and practice.

Conclusion: education as the embodiment of freedom

Processes of change are not binary.

Max Kirsch (2000, p. 115)

When our lived experience of theorising is fundamentally linked to processes of self-recovery, of collective liberation, no gap exists between theory and practice.... [They are] reciprocal processes where one enables the other.

bell hooks (1994, p. 61)

This chapter has travelled through my often ambivalent relationship with the issues, beliefs and experiences that shape me and my approach to teaching and learning. Here, an embodied pedagogy of diversity emerges from lived experience of the constrictions and limitations of dualism, identity politics and democracy; while from vulnerability and marginalisation emerge radical learning communities that are holistic, fluid and dynamic. Here, embodied experiences, my own disability for example, are not instances of oppositional identity politics but, rather, portals into lived experience that form the basis of holistic and trans-formative teaching and learning. It provides an opportunity to engage the vulnerabilities, desires and capacities that enable each individual's unique contribution. It is here that education becomes 'the practice of freedom' (hooks, 1994) and transformation at the individual and social level simultaneously occurs (Hart, 2001; hooks, 1994). bell hooks (1994) experienced this as a young student despite the constrictions of exter-nal circumstances, and access to education has certainly had a profound impact on my own life and indeed, that of many of the people who participated in my research on self-injury (Inckle, 2010). One research participant described education as 'even more important than therapy' in enabling her to ask deep questions and to create a life-enhancing reality for herself.

That is not to deny, however, the personal and professional vulnera-bility that an embodied approach to diversity creates. As hooks points out, 'it is not easy to name our pain, to perceive from that location' (1994, p. 74). Equally, nor is it easy to do so within a system that is hostile to the vulnerable, embodied subject who relinquishes autocratic or democratic power for a holistic pedagogical approach. Furthermore, it requires being 'genuinely free of a desire to impose ready-made truths' (Hunter, 2007, p. 27), including identity politics, and being open to facilitating rather than lecturing the learning community. Surrendering control and certainty are the antithesis of dualistic culture, but are central to the ethos of many contemporary holistic spiritual, epistemological, empirical and pedagogical practices. Dualism requires certainty and fixity while teaching from 'an embodied and affective pedagogy is both a *process* and a *product* of particular teaching practices' (Zembylas, 2007, p. 30). These processes and products cannot be controlled or predicted in the same way as autocratic systems and require deep engagement and trust in the learning community and the process of learning. Nonetheless, uncertainty, vulnerability and trust are the perquisites of transformation, and it is precisely this openness and fluidity that allows transgression and change to occur (hooks, 1994; Zembylas, 2007). Thus, when classrooms become communities where everyone is equally embodied, vulnerable and valued, diversity is realised. Here, the deepest forms of learning take place and education becomes, to rework hooks' (1994) phrase, the *embodiment* of freedom, which enables the experience (rather than the theory) of diversity and personal and social transformation.

Notes

1. Nonetheless, the majority of the campus and facilities remain inaccessible to staff and students with mobility difficulties.
2. The categories are particular to Irish history and culture: the focus on family status reflects that it was only in the 1970s that the category of 'illegitimacy' was removed from those born to unmarried mothers, while even today Travellers are not classed as an ethnic minority. Social class and rural/geographical background are not included in the criteria.
3. I owe this insight to Michael O'Rourke who made this suggestion during a discussion at Dublin Queer Studies Group, University College Dublin, 2 June 2006.

References

Atwood, M. (2003) *Oryx and Crake*. New York and London: Bloomsbury.
Atwood, M. (2009) *The Year of the Flood*. New York and London: Doubleday.
Butler, J. (1993) *Bodies That Matter*. New York and London: Routledge.
Cancienne, M. B. and Snowber, C. N. (2009) 'Writing rhythm: Movement as method'. In P. Leavy (Ed.), *Method Meets Art: Arts-Based Research Practice* (pp. 198–214). London and New York: The Guilford Press.
Edelman, L. (2004) *No Future: Queer Theory and the Death Drive*. Durham, NC: Duke University Press.

Finley, S. (2002) 'Women myths: Teacher self-images and socialisation into feminine stereotypes'. In C. Bagley and M. B. Cancienne (Eds), *Dancing the Data* (pp. 162–176). New York and Oxford: Peter Lang.

Halpin, D. (2003) *Hope and Education: The Role of Utopian Imagination.* London and New York: Routledge Falmer.

Hart, T. (2001) *From Information to Transformation: Education for the Evolution of Consciousness.* New York: Peter Lang.

hooks, b. (1994) *Teaching to Transgress: Education as the Practice of Freedom.* London and New York: Routledge.

Hunter, D. (2007) *The Art of Facilitation: The Essentials for Leading Great Meetings and Creating Group Synergy.* Auckland and London: Random House.

Inckle, K. (2007) *Writing on the Body? Thinking Through Gendered Embodiment and Marked Flesh.* Newcastle-upon-Tyne: Cambridge Scholars Publishing.

Inckle, K. (2010) At the cutting edge: Creative and holistic responses to self-injury. *Creative Nursing*, 16(4): 60–65.

Kazan, T. S. (2005) Dancing bodies in the classroom: Moving towards an embodied pedagogy. *Pedagogy: Critical Approaches to Teaching Literature, Language, Composition and Culture*, 5(3): 379–408.

Kirsch, M. (2000) *Queer Theory and Social Change.* London and New York: Routledge.

La Jevic, L. and Springgay, S. (2008) A/r/tography as an ethics of embodiment. *Qualitative Inquiry*, 14(1): 67–89.

Leavy, P. (2009) *Method Meets Art: Arts-Based Research Practice.* London and New York: The Guilford Press.

McRuer, R. (2006) *Crip Theory: Cultural Signs of Queerness and Disability.* New York: New York University Press.

Morris, J. (1991) *Pride Against Prejudice.* London: Women's Press.

Myss, C. (1997) *Anatomy of the Spirit: The Seven Stages of Power and Healing.* London and New York: Bantam Books.

Seymour, K. (2006) From 'doing' to 'knowing': Becoming academic. *Qualitative Social Work*, 5(4): 459–469.

Snowber, C. (2002) 'Bodydance: Enfleshing soulful inquiry through improvisation'. In C. Bagley and M. B. Cancienne (Eds), *Dancing the Data* (pp. 20–33). New York and Oxford: Peter Lang.

Sparkes, A. C. (2007) Embodiment, academics and the audit culture: A story seeking consideration. *Qualitative Research*, 7(4): 521–550.

Tolle, E. (2001) *The Power of Now.* London: Hodder and Stoughton.

Zembylas, M. (2007) The *specters* of bodies and affects in the classroom: A rhizo-ethological approach. *Pedagogy, Culture and Society*, 15(1): 19–35.

10
Doing Diversity and Evading Equality: The Case of Student Work Placements in the Creative Sector

Kimberly Allen, Jocey Quinn, Sumi Hollingworth and Anthea Rose

Introduction

'Diversity' has become an all-pervasive concept within Higher Education (HE). This chapter explores how the generic concept of diversity gets 'done' (Ahmed, 2006) within the particular context of HE work placements in the creative industries. It draws upon a recent qualitative study (Allen et al., 2010a) commissioned by the Equality Challenge Unit (ECU), the HE equality body in the UK. The study was designed to examine how Higher Education Institutions (HEIs) support students from 'equality groups' (defined by the ECU as disabled students, Black and minority ethnic (BME) students and students seeking to enter a labour market sector where there are significant gender imbalances) into positive and inclusive work placement experiences that will enhance their future employment prospects.

Neither HE work placements nor the creative industries (sectors including film, television, arts and music)[1] are in themselves the focus of this chapter, but rather provide interesting sites for critically examining how diversity and equality issues are understood within HE and how these conceptualisations position students within education and the labour market. Work experience is understood to be important to the employment prospects of graduates in all occupational areas but this is especially true for those seeking to enter the creative industries (La Valle et al., 2000). The highly competitive nature of the sector means that students must undertake (often unpaid) work experience as a way of 'getting a foot in the door' (Ball et al., 2010). Thus, work placements are a normalised part of the HE learning experience and preparation for the creative sector. Yet, opportunities to undertake work placements are unequally distributed, resulting in profound inequalities in students' experience and access to the sector.

In this chapter we consider how equality and diversity issues within HE work placements were understood and experienced by students, HEI staff and employers. Drawing on a poststructuralist framework, we identify and unpick the different discursive practices through which participants in the study positioned themselves in relation to equality issues in accessing and surviving work placements (and 'making it' in the sector itself). We discuss how these various conceptualisations constitute students as 'subjects of difference' (Mirza, 2006). Attending to the intersections of class, gender and ethnicity as well as disability, we argue that, despite calls for greater diversity within the sector, only some differences can be absorbed. While some differences can operate as an asset (or 'Unique Selling Point'), for other students being different only produces feelings of being 'out of place'.

'Variety anxiety': the turn to diversity in HE and the creative sector

Critical work on the 'turn to diversity' in HE (see Ahmed, 2006; Ahmed and Swann, 2006; Blackmore, 2006; Deem and Ozga, 1997; Mirza, 2006) has identified a shift away from discourses of equality towards an all-pervasive discourse of diversity. In the UK and internationally, 'diversity' is a term that increasingly features within university mission statements and policies, positioned as a desirable feature of HE. In current policy discourse in the UK, 'diversity' is understood as a recognition and respect for differences. In contrast, 'equality of opportunity' refers to attempts to ensure equality of treatment by eliminating barriers of discrimination, and promoting equal outcomes for different groups (ECU et al., 2009). Various legislation has been introduced in the UK with implications for HEIs, more recently the Equality Act 2010, which sought to consolidate and harmonise anti-discrimination legislation (such as the Race Relations Act 1976, Race Relations Amendment Act 2000; Disability Discrimination Act 1995; Equality Act 2006) through a single framework relating to a range of 'protected characteristics'.[2]

The term 'diversity' has been increasingly mobilised to refer to attempts to foster greater participation in HE among under-represented groups. The increasing significance of a language of diversity within HE has been attributed to the neoliberal marketisation of HE and rising audit culture, where 'diversity' becomes yet another performance indicator to be monitored, managed and showcased as a measure of good performance (Blackmore, 2006; Deem and Morley, 2006). Furthermore, under neoliberalism, inequalities in HE are rendered invisible: success and failure is understood at the individual level, often in terms of deficit and lack (Burke, 2007). While emerging from the demands of feminist and anti-racist social movements of the 1970s and 1980s, current articulations of diversity are understood to obscure such collective histories of struggle (Blackmore, 2006) and disavow the acknowledgement of structural disadvantage (Ahmed and Swann, 2006). Claiming diversity, in effect, becomes another way of 'doing advantage' as systematic inequalities can be concealed under the 'banner of difference' (Ahmed, 2006, p. 746). As Rosemary Deem and Jenny Ozga (1997, p. 33) argue, diversity discourses invoke and even celebrate difference but do not necessarily lead to redistributive justice.

While much critical work has traced the 'diversity work' being conducted within HE policy and practice, in this chapter we consider how discourses of diversity are mobilised by agents *across* both HE and sectors of the labour market associated with particular HE disciplines, as students contemplate and prepare for employment after graduation. Looking at what actors in different spaces (HE and the industry) do with diversity, we trace how discourses of diversity are reproduced across these two spaces to give them normative status. Our analysis is set within the context of HE students studying within arts and cultural disciplines and their experiences of and preparation for working in the creative industries, where a similar 'fetish for difference' (Mirza, 2006, p. 151) can also be identified.

The creative industries have in the UK, as in many Western countries, been highlighted as a key source of employment growth and central to the nation's competitive advantage (Confederation of British Industry, 2010). Work within this sector is highly individualised and precarious, characterised by informal and closed recruitment methods, portfolio careers, and a prevalence of unpaid work. These practices make it difficult for some groups to access and stay in the sector. Not surprisingly, BME groups, women, disabled people and those from lower socio-economic groups are under-represented in the UK creative sector (Creative and Cultural Skills, 2008). Over the past decade, there has been a growing 'variety anxiety'[3] within the creative sector, which has played out in the British media.[4] Across the industry and the UK government's economic and cultural policy, there have been calls to dismantle the barriers that may prevent particular groups from accessing and remaining in the sector (Panel on Fair Access to the Professions, 2009). HE and work placements are recognised as significant within this. The role of social networks in influencing entry and advancement in the sector and a lack of clear pathways into the industry have been identified as restricting access for people from under-represented groups (Department for Culture Media and Sport, 2008). The Widening Participation (WP) agenda in HE arts disciplines has responded to calls to enhance the diversity of arts students and the creative industries workforce by increasing the number and range of formal progression routes into the sector (Dann et al., 2009).

Yet despite so much talk of diversity within both HE and the creative sector, why do chronic divisions and exclusions remain along lines of class, gender, ethnicity and disability? In this chapter we examine how discourses of equality and diversity, mobilised across both HE and the creative sector, can operate to challenge or maintain disadvantage within HE work placements and the sector itself. First, we introduce the study and the conceptual framework that informs our analysis.

The study

This research primarily involved interviews with staff and students in five case study HEIs across England and Wales. Composed of both specialist and non-specialist institutions of varying size, including 'elite' and post-1992 institution, the sample was selected through an extensive call distributed to Equality and Diversity (E&D) and WP practitioners.[5] These practitioners acted as gatekeepers in many of the selected case study institutions. In this way, the case study institutions' decisions to participate may itself be understood as part of their 'diversity work' (Ahmed, 2006), an internal showcasing of their commitment to diversity, as well as more well-intended desires to understand and improve their practice.

Twenty-six students from 'equality groups' were interviewed,[6] including several working-class students as the research team recognised the significance of social class as a factor in equality.[7] Most students occupied multiple 'equality groups', for example, being a disabled BME student, and here we attend to the intersection of these multiple identities. Ranging from longer 'sandwich' placements to summer internships and shorter placements of several days,[8] students had undertaken placements across the sector, including design studios, architecture firms and television broadcasters.

Students were asked their views and experiences of placement/s; their views of the sector and future intentions for employment. Equality issues were approached carefully using a range of different techniques, including probing of students on specific experiences of the work placements and explicit questions about potential equality issues identified through the literature. Press cuttings about issues of equality and diversity across the UK sector were used as prompts that helped generate discussion as students used these examples to reflect on their own experiences. Some students more readily discussed and identified equality issues than others. However, students' accounts often appeared to reveal inequalities even when they might not be named as such by participants. Here and elsewhere (Allen et al., 2010b), we suggest that the hesitancy among some students to identify equality issues is bound up with both constructions of creative disciplines and organisations as liberal and inclusive, and the centrality of neoliberal processes of subjectification, where to position oneself through discourses of inequality or disadvantage invites the danger of being seen as weak and inadequate.

Interviews were also conducted with nine relevant members of staff. Interviews focused on the management of work placements; perceptions and experience of equality issues; and procedures for addressing these. Institutional material related to work placements (such as placement guidance, equal opportunities policies and monitoring data) was gathered and reviewed. Eleven employers were also interviewed, ranging from large employers to sole traders, spanning the sector. Employers were asked about their motivations for offering work placements, recruitment practices, perceptions and experience of equality issues, and procedures and policies for addressing these. Copies of diversity and equality policies and relevant material related to work placements were requested and analysed.

Interviews were audio-recorded, transcribed and made anonymous. Data were coded and analysed thematically to identify key issues and student data were contextualised using biographical data. The analysis was informed by poststructuralist theory, which allowed us to examine how student subjectivities were constituted through the discursive practices of HE creative work placements. Discourses are 'about what can be said and thought, about who can speak, when and with what authority' (Ball, 2006, p. 48). They are themselves constitutive of the social relations and subject positions they seek to describe (Foucault, 1972). While various discourses co-exist, some are more powerful than others, operating to reproduce 'particular social relationships that reaffirm the power and privilege of particular groups' (Robinson and Jones Diaz, 2006, p. 35). In this chapter we see various equality and diversity discourses as making available particular 'truths' or ways of understanding the nature and effects of inequalities in HE work placements in the creative sector (for example, that inequalities are inevitable or that diversity matters as an commercial asset). They inform to what extent inequalities can be seen and addressed and what 'differences' can be recognised. We consider which discourses of diversity and equality circulate in HE and the creative sector and examine how these may operate to maintain social inequalities and disadvantage, paying particular attention to how the constitutive effects of these discourses are classed, gendered and raced.

The positioning of students through such discourses is informed by their location within a complex web of identity positions, oppressions and relations of power. Drawing on the concept of intersectionality (Brah and Phoenix, 2004), we explore how 'social divisions combine to produce qualitatively different experiences, identities and positions' (Archer et al., 2001, p. 45). Gender, ethnicity, social class, disability and sexuality come together in different permutations that enable or deny recognition and advantage. This perspective facilitates a more nuanced analysis of how diversity and equality discourses operate to make it possible for particular classed, gendered and raced 'differences' to become valuable, while constituting others as undesirable.

Equality and diversity discourses in HE work placements

As we discuss in greater detail elsewhere (Allen et al., 2010a, b), this research found that students' success in finding and undertaking a 'good' placement depends on their access to a range of social, cultural and economic resources that are unequally distributed. Students without access to industry networks or the financial resources to undertake lengthy (and often unpaid) placements were disadvantaged in this process. Furthermore, the discursive construction of the ideal work placement student and potential creative worker – with a currency on flexibility, enterprise and self-sufficiency – privileges whiteness, middle-class-ness, masculinity and able-bodiedness. The lack of diversity in some parts of the sector also led to some students reporting that they felt a lack of 'belonging' on their placement. Consequently, the research pointed to how students from under-represented groups are excluded from the sector before they even graduate and thus how HE work placements contribute to the sector's 'diversity problem'.

Despite finding these equality issues, however, there was significant variation in how staff, students and employers identified and perceived these. In the rest of this chapter we unpick the different sets of discursive practices within which participants positioned themselves in relation to equality and diversity issues in HE work placements. We identify four discursive positions but recognise that discursive practices are complex. Thus, the way in which participants in the study discursively situated themselves was not fixed and many participants moved between different discursive positions. However, these four positions provide a heuristic device to examine the different ways that diversity and equality are mobilised and understood, and to critically illuminate their effects.

'It's a level playing field': the invisibility of inequality

One of the most common discursive positions taken up by interviewees in the research produced a denial of the existence of inequality. This was enabled through a celebration of diversity (within the student or staff body of the institution or organisation), which in turn negated questions of inequality, and through the mobilisation of discourses of individualisation and meritocracy.

Many participants struggled to identify barriers and inequalities in the work placement process. Most HEI staff and employers spoke positively about their arrangements and claimed that they were unaware of any equality issues:

> *Placement Officer:* We've had no issues at all in terms of equality in the workplace, and I think the fact that it's not something you think about it kind of highlights the fact that it's not an issue. It's not considered. You know everybody feels that they're being treated fairly and equally.

The inability of staff and employers to recognise equality issues because they have had no direct experience of students reporting these is deeply problematic because it fails to address the cultural practices and power relations that may prevent students from reporting experiences of inequality – such as not feeling entitled or not knowing how to express feelings of injustice.

One HEI staff member suggested that all students are equally 'eligible' to take up placements as part of their course. As such, he argued, equality issues were not at play:

> *Head of Department:* I struggle with this. If you've got students on a programme and you are offering placements or encouraging students to do them, I'm not sure there should be any values to equal opportunities.... When we enrol students we do so irrespective of their appearance or any other aspect of their personality

or orientation. If they're on the programme equally, they are all equally eligible for what the programme offers.

Such a statement mistakenly assumes that equality in the recruitment of students onto a course translates into equitable student experiences in finding and undertaking placements. As Louise Archer states, 'the achievement of a more diverse population of students entering HE does not straightforwardly equate with the achievement of equitable forms of participation' (2007, p. 646). Yet in this case and others, staff mobilised a 'diverse student body' as an indicator of equality of opportunity in the work placement process: 'I don't think there are [equality issues]. We have a wide variety of ethnicity and I have never come across a problem' (Placement Officer). Focusing only on equal *access* to HE courses negates the existence of inequalities within the HE experience once students arrive at an institution as well as how these experiences relate to inequalities in outcome, for example, in relation to employability. The presence of underlying bias and attitudinal barriers that may exist within the institution about what makes an 'ideal' student, and which inform recruitment and admission processes are thus concealed (see Burke and McManus, 2009).

Another interviewee stated that because of the area in which the university was located – and in which many of the students undertake their placement – was 'so diverse and multicultural', inequalities in work placements were 'very difficult to see' and thus do not exist. Again, diversity in a wider context – in this case in the locality of the HEI – is called upon as evidence of equality within work placement practices. However, the refusal to 'see' inequalities is underlined by a sense of ambivalence about how inequalities can be addressed: this interviewee went on to say, 'but sometimes those things are so subtle it's very difficult to show and prove'.

Claiming diversity is a way of producing a good image for the university, yet this 'politics of feeling good' (Ahmed, 2006) powerfully blocks action. To admit to the existence of identifiable inequalities in work placements would mean evoking 'bad feelings' and disrupting the ideal image of the university. Thus, claiming diversity allows HEI staff to avoid feelings of unease about a university's success (or lack of) at tackling inequality.

The refusal to recognise inequalities in students' work placement experiences across gender, ethnicity, social class or disability was also enabled through discourses of individualisation. Often discourses of merit, individual responsibility and personal choice were mobilised by interviewees when responding to questions about equality issues:

> *Employer:* I'm not really aware of those issues. Basically...in the creative industries [it's] down to the quality of the work and it's very easy to spot whether somebody's good enough to do it or not. If the portfolio's not good enough they don't get the job, simple as that.

Advantage is thus interpreted as a personal value, where success is 'all about attitude, attitude, attitude' (Employer). In constituting equality as something relating to individual personality or appearance, attention is not paid to how students have different choices and opportunities because of their different location in structural relations.

It has been suggested elsewhere that the creative sector, defined by micro-businesses, small and medium enterprises (SMEs) and informal working practices, has situated itself as immune from equal opportunity legislation: equality issues are thus 'unmanageable' (Jones and Proctor-Thomson, 2010). In her work on media workers, Rosalind Gill has also argued that an 'attachment to the notion of the sector as "diverse" and "egalitarian" with success based on merit [has] led to a reluctance, even a refusal, to see or speak of inequalities' (2010, p. 16). In this study we found evidence to support this: the discursive construction of working practices and cultures as creative, egalitarian and relaxed operated to negate the need for equality and diversity policies and practices or reflective engagement with equal opportunity legislation:

> *Employer:* No we don't really [have equality policies]...we are quite a relaxed company. If we take somebody on we interview them beforehand and if we feel they sort of fit in with the company then that's not a problem. We've got full range of [people] here, age, sex, so there's no sort of problem there at all...It's sort of quite tight knit. If anybody has got any issues then they air the views and it's brought to light, but yeah there's no well, there doesn't seem to be any issues.

The notion that equal opportunities do not require attention was also mobilised by HEI staff who explained an 'ad hoc' ('We're just "ad hoc" that's [our institution's] motto' (Head of Department)) approach to their work placement policies and practices. The attachment to the notion of creative organisations and disciplinary cultures as 'diverse', 'open' and 'inclusive' appears as a substitute for equality practices ('The arts community has always accepted gender and sexuality quite freely it's got a long tradition' (Head of Department)). Such statements obscure how judgements about which students and employees 'fit in' the company or institution can operate to exclude. Furthermore, the assumption that inequalities can be freely 'aired' and 'brought to light' negates and contributes to the very practices that make inequalities 'unspeakable' (Gill, 2010).

'Managing' difference and accepting inequality as inevitable

The 'unspeakability' of inequalities means that they have to be managed and accepted by individual students if they want to succeed. In interviews with employers and HEI staff, there was an emphasis on the students adapting to the needs of the workplace (especially the fast-paced, unpredictable and intensive nature of work in the creative sector), rather than the workplace adapting to meet the needs of students:

> *Placement Officer:* [In] post-production particularly, a lot of the companies are around the Soho area [of London] and in old houses, listed buildings and they simply don't have access for a wheelchair.... With this particular student, he is very realistic about what he can do and about the access and it's not a problem for him personally. He is quite happy to get experience wherever he can.

Another member of staff discussed the issues experienced by a student with a mental health condition, who couldn't cope with '...a very fast pace environment...'. Students must adapt to these 'barriers' or accept that the sector is not the right place for them. One employer described how dyslexic students can be incorporated into the workplace if they are able to 'manage' and in fact hide their disability:

> *Employer:* My current placement student has dyslexia. He is very good at checking his work and he's very articulate.... I had somebody else who desperately wanted to be a designer and he had dyslexia and it was hopeless. It just isn't going to happen. In this work, you're dealing with images and words and it was hopeless because he couldn't spell... so you basically had to do all the work for him and it didn't work, and I couldn't explain this to him. He got upset and said 'that's discrimination' and I said 'it isn't, it's practicality'. But with my current placement student, he's just so attentive to that sort of thing, it's not an issue. You wouldn't know he has dyslexia.

The practices that exclude some people are impenetrable to demands for change and claims that these may be unfair or discriminatory cannot be heard: 'it's not discrimination its practicality'. Inequalities in students' choice of and access to placement opportunities are not seen as such because they are naturalised and normalised: 'this is just the way the creative sector is'.

This non-recognition of inequalities fed into the ways in which students themselves talked about particular challenges they encountered in their work placement. Discourses of individualisation and self-determination were mobilised as students talked about 'just dealing' with unpaid work and other exploitative conditions such as long hours, 'being more driven' when encountering gender stereotypes, or disabled students creating their own solutions to challenges rather than asking for help. For example, Mary, a White middle-class student who was partially deaf explained: 'My general attitude is, being slightly hard of hearing, I just sort of ignore it or pretend like I'm fine.'

As Penny Jane Burke states, under neoliberalism, 'successful' individuals are 'those who are determined to rise above their problems through their own motivation, hard work and discipline' (2007, p. 418). Technologies of self-governance operate to individualise and obscure inequalities. Yet the self-governing subject is modelled on the image of a middle-class and masculine subject (Walkerdine, 2003) and some students could not 'rise above' or manage these inequalities so confidently. These experiences had profound emotional and psychological consequences as a 'bad' work placement becomes reinterpreted and experienced as an individual failing.

Mel, a White working-class student who was the first in her family to go to university, undertook a work placement at a design agency in central London. Mel described how she felt 'out of place' among the middle-class workers in the agency:

> *Mel:* I didn't really enjoy it to be honest. It was like...the feelings I got from people didn't settle me....You feel that you're lower than them...Oh God, it's funny, the [company director's] mum used to phone every lunchtime, 'is Rupert there?' or whatever his name was. It was those kinds of names...it was even the way they talked. You know, really 'proper'...it just throws you off a little bit when you arrive. [It's like] you've not got enough money and the [people you work with] have a totally different lifestyle...you know like the vibes you get off people.

Here, Mel's working-class self presents an unacceptable difference that must be given up in order to fit in. Feminist working-class scholars have written about their feelings of exclusion and difference in the elite spaces of academia, where to survive means having to 'adapt to an ethos and culture premised on middle-class values and attitudes' (Reay, 1998, p. 11; see also Skeggs, 1995). Mel was similarly aware that she lacked the lifestyle, culture and 'legitimate language' (Bourdieu, 1992) of her middle-class colleagues: that she was not 'proper' enough. In her compelling work on difference and space, Nirmal Puwar (2004) examines how women and ethnic minorities enter spaces of White male power, including academia, politics and the art world. She states:

> social spaces are not blank and open for anybody to occupy.... while all can, in theory, enter, it is certain types of bodies that are tacitly designated as being the 'natural' occupants.... Some bodies have the right to belong in certain locations while others are marked out as trespassers who are, in accordance with how both spaces and bodies are imagined, circumscribed as being 'out of place'.
>
> (2004, p. 8)

While focused on race and gender, Puwar's analysis is also relevant to understanding the positioning of working-class bodies as 'out of place'. Puwar argues that when 'alien' bodies enter spaces in which they have previously been absent, they evoke fear, anxiety and disorientation within the 'natural inhabitants' of these spaces. They are met with a gaze that 'abnormalises their presence and locates them as belonging elsewhere' (2004, p. 42). The 'vibes' that unsettled Mel are products of a gaze that, if it could speak, asks 'what are *you* doing here?'

We return to these experiences of 'out of placeness' at the end of this chapter. What is also significant here is how Mel interpreted these feelings. Mel compared herself to other students who had a more 'successful' experience:

> *Mel:* I found it really hard. I spoke to someone else who had done a placement at the same place and she had a much better time and experience of it. Maybe she had tougher skin. I don't know, it says something about me.

Not fitting in was relocated to the level of the individual, experienced as a deficiency of the self ('it says something about me') rather than the outcome of structural inequalities that contribute to parts of the sector remaining homogenously middle-class.

A 'commitment' to increasing diversity

Despite a denial of inequalities among some participants, the study revealed a strong commitment to increasing diversity in the sector among some HEI staff and employers who prided themselves on being part of an organisation with diversity and equality at its heart. One placement officer said, 'I think diversity and equality policy is important. . . . It shows everybody that equality and diversity is not something just we band about. It's essential.'

However, as Sara Ahmed (2006) warns, HEIs can claim diversity without actually changing institutional cultures and practices, when '. . . To be seen as "being diverse" leads to the failure to commit to "doing diversity", as the organisation says it "is it" or even that it already "does it" which means that it sees there is nothing left to do' (p. 753). In this study, commitments to diversity were variously translated and enacted in ways that did not address structural inequalities but actually reinforced them. There was a lack of reflective and critical thinking among HEI staff and employers in relation to equality. For example, while HEI staff spoke of having institutional equality and diversity policy, it was unclear how these policies extended to cover work placement procedures. Policies were, on the whole, institution-wide, covering student and staff diversity and equal opportunities. In some cases, policies were more specific to work placements but focused on delivering accessible *services* and *spaces* rather than *practices* that affect students' access to and experience of work placements (for example, providing wheelchair access and larger font materials for dyslexic students). Similarly, employers discussed organisational equality and diversity frameworks and policies concerning employees that were not specific to work placements. Some (mainly sole) employers did not have such policies.

In some interviews, we found evidence of the way in which diversity can be claimed while reproducing privilege. For example, one employer, who stated that equal opportunities is 'part of our ethos', spoke about a new placement scheme that was specifically designed to increase diversity in the organisation. The employer described how they had publicised the scheme to HEIs, colleges and community organisations in order to 'open up' their scheme to students from a range of backgrounds rather than 'going through the same group of people'. When asked further about what 'diverse backgrounds' meant, they explained:

> *Employer:* We're interested in people that are not just from a film and television background, [but] people with a history degree, a science degree…people who maybe just didn't think television was for them.
>
> *Interviewer:* So in terms of their ethnicity or social class background, how would you describe them?
>
> *Employer:* Well two of them are White, middle-class girls and the other one, he's of Russian descent.

Ahmed states that 'the openness of the term [diversity] also means that the work it does depends on who defines the term and for whom' (2006, p. 749). In this example, diversity thus becomes defined and translated by the company to denote diverse disciplinary backgrounds rather than diversity in relation to identity. The recruitment of students for this work placement scheme thus remains closed, and the exclusionary practices that restrict access for particular students are neglected.

There were also concerns that unequal practices were too embedded for HEI staff to challenge and that their institution's commitments to equality and diversity were limited in their capacity to affect real change. For example, staff described the dilemmas they faced in regulating employers to abide by fair practice in relation to pay. This included concerns that the culture of unpaid placements was an 'industry norm' and thus too difficult to counter, and that challenging employers who don't pay students fairly may negatively impact on the opportunities available to their graduates by discouraging employers to advertise opportunities with their institution.

HEI staff were uncertain around how HE diversity and equality duties extended to cover student work placements, where students are operating outside of the university. A careers service manager discussed making reasonable adjustments to ensure *their* services are accessible to disabled students, but stated that ensuring that these adjustments are made by employers was 'outside of their remit'. One placement officer argued that 'while we can ensure that the employer has diversity policies…we can't control who they do and don't take on, because…its sometimes very difficult to identify that they may not have taken on students because they're disadvantaged'. In an audit culture, diversity work becomes a box-ticking exercise, leaving inequitable practices unattended. Commitments to doing diversity are also inhibited by organisational boundaries between HEIs and employers and a lack of clarity about who has responsibility for ensuring equality in students' work placement experiences. These statements point to how HEI staff may be able to recognise the existence of structures of inequalities but may equally feel powerless within these very structures.

Diversity as valuable: capitalising on 'difference'

Framed within market agendas, the economics of diversity (widening the talent pool to increase local and national productivity) have become the driving force for diversity work in HE policy (Mirza, 2006; Archer, 2007). Economic drivers for a more diverse workforce are also highlighted alongside social justice or legal imperatives in diversity debates within the creative sector. Diversity has been increasingly framed as a 'driver' for economic growth (The Work Foundation, 2007; Department for Culture Media and Sport, 2008), where it matters not just as a moral or legal obligation but because it makes good 'business sense': a more diverse workforce provides a larger talent-pool and 'talent is money' (MediaGuardian, 2009, p. 1).

Several participants mobilised this discourse. For example, one broadcasting company spoke about the commercial benefits of a diverse workforce and cohort of work placement students:

> *Employer:* Our audience is actually really, really diverse and our staff [aren't] really as diverse and we're wanting to try and marry that up.... We want to produce good programming that wins commissions and is going to be successful.... If you have people from a similar background with all the similar values sitting within your development team they're going to come up with similar ideas. If you have other people thrown into the mix they're all going to come up with different ideas and that's when you get the brilliant ideas for brilliant programmes.

For this employer, a more diverse intake of placement students is good because it helps their organisation to capitalise on new markets. Yet when diversity matters most for commercial ends, social justice gets sidelined. As Stuart Hall (1991) states, there is a danger that the exotica of difference negates a language of disadvantage and discrimination. Furthermore, we must ask *which* differences are recognised as having value when diversity is constituted as a form of human capital to enhance the profitability of an organisation. And what if some groups are 'perceived to offer greater business advantages than others' (Squires, 2008, p. 59)? We argue that intersections of class, gender and ethnicity inform which differences can be recognised as economically valuable.

We can see this more clearly when we look at the different experiences of two BME students: Ed and Faheem.

Ed was a 20-year middle-class student of mixed ethnic heritage: his mother was Chinese and his father was native-American. Both were employed in professional occupations. Ed described himself as an 'entrepreneur' and had undertaken multiple work placements as well as set up his own music video production company with financial support from his father. Ed saw his ethnic 'difference' as an asset or 'unique selling point' (USP) that could work in his favour to make him stand out from the crowd from other potential employees:

> *Ed:* Sometimes you have to be realistic that it [race or gender] can stand against you but it can also work in your favour if you are sensible. I use my diversity in my favour, it makes me unique, different...and so I just see that as a positive rather than a negative thing...I think everybody has an equal opportunity and you just have to...not hold it against yourself because you will end up crippling yourself if you do. It doesn't make sense to behave like that.

For Ed, as with some other middle-class BME students, being a minority was perceived as an asset that gave them advantage over others. We suggest that this approach to exploiting one's ethnic difference as an asset is enabled by Ed's class advantage. Being middle-class protected Ed in some ways from feelings of racialised Otherness, helping to produce an 'exotic' difference that could be exploited.

Ed was laying claim to a very different ethnic identity to that available to working-class BME students in the study, for whom *not* being White merely produced feelings of alienation. Faheem was a 24-year-old working-class British Asian student from Birmingham. Faheem's mother was a full-time carer for his disabled sister and had 'been on benefits most of her life'. His father was a taxi driver. Faheem described the feelings of exclusion he experienced on both his placements:

> *Faheem:* There was a very middle-class guy who owned [the gallery] and...the majority of the time I'd be thinking 'I don't know what he's talking about'...there was a lot of elaborate words. I always kind of felt a little out placed (sic)...I was the only Asian person there....With the web design placement I didn't see or feel any discrimination, I just noticed that it was this big white building and this big white box and these big white tables and big

white computer... and they [the employees] were White. Well, the designer was Chinese but from South London so he was just 'from London'... and [the director was White] and from Crouch End [in North London] and he spoke so well and it was like 'OK, I need to be more like this.'

Difference is lived and experienced complexly across class, gender, ethnicity and locality. Faheem's feeling that he 'did not fit' in the sector was informed by the specific permutations of his identity. Like Mel, discussed earlier in this chapter, Faheem felt the need to change parts of his self in order to 'pass' (Lawler, 1999) within middle-class space of the creative sector. But his working-class Otherness was compounded by his Asian identity in a predominantly White sector, as well as his regional cultural background. While he was not the only non-White worker in the design agency, he did not feel that he could embody the metropolitan ethnic identity of this other BME worker. Faheem described the Chinese designer as being 'just from London', implying that some ethnic differences can accrue positive value because of their association with particular classed locales, which overrides their ethnic Otherness. Given the high concentration of the creative sector in London and the embeddedness of its cultural networks (with a third of the creative workforce working in the capital (Creative and Cultural Skills, 2008)), as well as the more general prestige of London itself as 'fashionable' and central to the knowledge economy, symbolic capital is transferred onto the body of the Chinese designer. For Faheem, who was from Birmingham, a city associated with Britain's industrial heritage and often ridiculed in public discourse, such symbolic capital was not available to him. As Bourdieu states '... the fashionable neighbourhood symbolically consecrates its inhabitants by allowing each one to partake of the capital accumulated by the inhabitants as a whole. Likewise, the stigmatized area symbolically degrades its inhabitants...' (1999, p. 129). Thus Faheem, like other White and BME working-class students, could not capitalise on his difference as a commodity to be exploited within the sector's fetish for diversity. Instead he felt marked as an outsider, a 'space invader' (Puwar, 2004) who simply did not belong.

Conclusion

While this chapter has focused on issues of diversity within the context of one area of HE practice (work placements) and one industry sector (the creative sector), we hope that our analysis provides useful insights into how discourses of diversity are encountered by and position students as 'subjects of difference' within education and the labour market, both in the UK and abroad.

We have identified and unpicked four different discourses of diversity and equality that participants mobilised. While some participants drew upon neoliberal discourses of meritocracy to deny the existence of inequality, there were signs of a commitment to diversity and equality among HEI staff and employers. Yet we have shown how these commitments get 'stuck' and do not always bring about the effects to which they purport (Ahmed, 2006). Rather, commitments to diversity and equality were differently translated in ways that served to reproduce inequalities. We have also shown how only some differences can be recognised while others get marginalised and have argued that this is informed by the intersectionality of class, ethnicity, gender and disability, which produces different experiences of exclusion or belonging.

The failure of diversity agendas within HE and the creative sector affects students profoundly. Feelings of being 'out of place' do much greater damage than simply influencing students' future intentions and opportunities for employment. There are also immense psychological and emotional costs to being 'different', when for some, 'out of place-ness' is experienced as individual failure rather than the outcome of inequitable practices.

This chapter has pointed to the ways in which discourses of diversity and inequality are reproduced by practices across both HE arts institutions and the creative sector. For example, the discursive constructions of the arts and of creative organisational practices and cultures as liberal, *laissez-faire* and 'inclusive' operates to disguise the existence of inequalities. The 'unspeakability' of inequalities produced interesting encounters with students, staff and employers within the interviews and recruitment process for this study. Some participants could not understand the point of the research and were perplexed as to why they were asked about 'equality issues'. But others welcomed the opportunity to give words to their feelings of exclusion. Faheem told us that when he saw the advert for this research he was excited about being able to talk to someone about issues of ethnicity, equality and discrimination. He claimed:

> It's a topic that people *don't* talk about. Discrimination . . . it's like: 'ah, I can't believe you used that word!'

Despite so much diversity talk, racial, gendered and classed inequalities remain unspeakable. Without such a language, issues of social injustice in both the student experience and the creative sector more generally cannot be addressed. We hope that this chapter can contribute to the development of a language that can more effectively address, rather than evade, inequalities.

Acknowledgements

The authors would like to thank the ECU, who funded this research, as well as the participants who shared their experiences. We are grateful to Professor Carole Leathwood and Ayo Mansaray for informative discussions that helped us to refine our arguments.

Notes

1. The sector includes advertising, architecture, the art and antiques market, crafts, design, designer fashion, film and video, interactive leisure software, music, the performing arts, publishing, software and computer services, television and radio (Department for Culture Media and Sport, 2008).
2. These include age, disability, gender reassignment, marriage and civil partnership, pregnancy and maternity, race, religion, sex and sexual orientation. Socio-economic status was removed as it passed through the UK parliament.
3. This phrase came from a *Media Guardian* publication on diversity in the Media (2009).
4. In 2001, Greg Dyke, the then Director General of the BBC famously called the organisation 'hideously white' (Hill, 2001).
5. HEIs were asked to complete a short questionnaire providing information on: the size of institution and student cohort; disciplines taught; work placements organisation and management; names of key staff responsible for work placements; and links to diversity and equality policies and other relevant documentation.
6. The sample included 11 BME; 20 female (11 of which undertook placements in sectors of female under-representation); and 13 disabled students. 'Disabled' students were defined using the definition of disability provided in UK disability equality legislation (Equality Act 2010) however a social model of disability (Oliver, 1990) underpinned the research. See Allen et al. (2010a) for further details on the sample.
7. Social class was assigned using biographical data gathered from the students in the form of a questionnaire (i.e. parental occupation, familial experience of HE) and additional information gathered within interviews.
8. 'Work placements' refer to formal, planned placements in the industry linked to a programme of study, and placements 'extrinsic' to formal programme of study but encouraged or expected by HEIs.

References

Ahmed, S. (2006) Doing diversity work in higher education in Australia. *Educational Philosophy and Theory*, 38(6): 745–768.
Ahmed, S. and Swann, E. (2006) Doing diversity: Introduction. *Policy Futures in Education*, 4(2): 96–100.

Allen, K., Quinn, J., Hollingworth, S. and Rose, A. (2010a) *Work Placements in the Arts and Cultural Sector: Diversity, Equality and Access. A Report for the Equality Challenge Unit.* London: ECU.

Allen, K., Quinn, J., Hollingworth, S., and Rose, A. (2010b) *Becoming the 'Ideal' Heroic Creative Worker? Subjectification, Higher Education Student Work Placements and Processes of Exclusion in the Creative Industries.* Presented at London Metropolitan University, 10 December 2010.

Archer, L. (2007) Diversity, equality and higher education: A critical reflection on the ab/uses of equity discourse within widening participation. *Teaching in Higher Education*, 12(5): 635–653.

Archer, L., Hutchings, M. and Leathwood, C. (2001) Engaging with commonality and difference: Theoretical tensions in the analysis of working-class women's educational discourses. *International Studies in Sociology of Education*, 11(1): 41–62.

Ball, S. (2006) *Education Policy and Social Class. The Selected Works of Stephen J. Ball.* London: Routledge.

Ball, L., Pollard, E. and Stanley, N. (2010) *Creative Graduates Creative Futures.* London: The Creative Graduates Creative Futures Higher Education Partnership and the Institute for Employment Studies.

Blackmore, J. (2006) Deconstructing diversity discourses in the field of educational management and leadership. *Educational Management Administration & Leadership*, 34(2): 181–199.

Bourdieu, P. (1992) *Language and Symbolic Power: The Economy of Linguistic Exchanges.* Cambridge: Cambridge University Press.

Bourdieu, P. et al. (1999) *The Weight of the World: Social Suffering in Contemporary Society.* Oxford: Polity Press.

Brah, A. and Phoenix, A. (2004) Ain't I a woman? Revisiting intersectionality. *Journal of International Women's Studies*, 5(3): 75–86.

Burke, P. J. (2007) Men accessing education: Masculinities, identifications and widening participation. *British Journal of Sociology of Education*, 28(4): 411–424.

Burke, P. J. and McManus, J. (2009) *'Art for a Few': Exclusion and Misrecognition in Art and Design Higher Education Admissions. A Report for the National Arts Learning Network.* London: NALN.

Confederation of British Industry (CBI). (2010) *Creating Growth: A Blueprint for the Creative Industries.* London: CBI.

Creative and Cultural Skills. (2008) *Creative and Cultural Industry: Impact and Footprints 08–09.* London: Creative & Cultural Skills.

Dann, L., Ware, N. and Cass, K. (2009) *Tackling Exclusion in the Creative Industries: An Enterprise Led Approach.* London: NALN.

Deem, R. and Morley, L. (2006) Diversity in the academy? Staff and senior manager perceptions of equality policies in six contemporary UK higher education institutions. *Policy Futures*, 4(2): 185–202.

Deem, R. and Ozga, J. (1997) 'Women managing diversity in a postmodern world'. In C. Marshall (Ed.), *Feminist Critical Policy Analysis* (pp. 25–40). London: Falmer.

Department for Culture Media and Sport. (2008) *Creative Britain: New talents for a New Economy.* London: Department for Culture, Media and Sport.

Equality Act. (2010) *Equality Act 2010.* London: HM Stationery Office.

Equality Challenge Unit, the Association of University Administrators and the Higher Education Equal Opportunities Network. (2009) *A-Z of Equality & Diversity*. http://www.aua.ac.uk/networks/sigs/current/e_and_d/docs/azguide2009.pdf [accessed 13 November 2010].

Foucault, M. (1972) *The Archaeology of Knowledge and the Discourse on Language*. A. M. S. Smith, transl. New York: Pantheon Books.

Gill, R. (2010) ' "Life is a pitch": Managing the self in new media work'. In M. Deuze (Ed.), *Managing Media Work* (pp. 249–262). London: Sage.

Hall, S. (1991) 'Old and new identities, old and new ethnicities'. In A. D. King (Ed.), *Culture, Globalization and the World-System* (pp. 41–68). London: Macmillan.

Hill, A. (2001). Dyke: BBC is hideously white. *The Observer*, 7 January 2001. http://www.guardian.co.uk/media/2001/jan/07/uknews.theobserver1 [accessed 28 November 2010].

Jones, P. and Proctor-Thomson, S. (2010) Unmanageable inequalities: Gender and power in the 'creative industries'. *Gender, Work and Organisation*. 6th Biennial International Interdisciplinary Conference 21–23 June 2010, Keele University, Staffordshire.

La Valle, I., O'Regan, S. and Jackson, C. (2000) *The Art of Getting Started: Graduate Skills in a Fragmented Labour Market*. Report 364, Institute for Employment Studies. Grantham: Grantham Book Services.

Lawler, S. (1999) 'Getting out and getting away': Women's narratives of class mobility. *Feminist Review*, 63(1): 3–24.

MediaGuardian. (2009) Diversity in the media: How the industry reflects the society we live in. *The Guardian*, 23 November 2009.

Mirza, H. S. (2006) 'The *In/visible* journey: Black women's lifelong lessons in higher education'. In C. Leathwood and B. Francis (Eds), *Gender and Lifelong: Critical Feminist Engagements* (pp. 137–152). London: Routledge.

Oliver, M. (1990) *The Politics of Disablement*. London: Macmillan.

Panel on Fair Access to the Professions. (2009) *Unleashing Aspiration: The Final Report of the Panel on Fair Access to the Professions*. London: HM Government.

Puwar, N. (2004) *Space Invaders: Race, Gender and Bodies out of Place*. Oxford: Berg.

Reay, D. (1998) Surviving in dangerous places: Working-class women, women's studies and higher education. *Women's Studies International Forum*, 21(1): 11–19.

Robinson, K. H. and Jones Díaz, C. (2006) *Diversity and Difference in Early Childhood Education: Issues for Theory and Practice*. London: Open University Press.

Skeggs, B. (1995) Women's studies in the 1990s: Entitlement cultures and institutional constraints. *Women's Studies International Forum*, 18(4): 475–485.

Squires, J. (2008) Intersecting inequalities: Reflecting on the subjects and objects of equality. *The Political Quarterly*, 79(1): 53–61.

Walkerdine, V. (2003) Reclassifying upward mobility: Femininity and the neo-liberal subject. *Gender and Education*, 15(3): 237–249.

The Work Foundation. (2007) *Staying Ahead: The Economic Performance of the UK's Creative Industries*. London: DCMS.

Section 3

Boundary Conditions

11
Diversity: Problems and Paradoxes for Black Feminists

Sara Ahmed

What does it mean to embody diversity? This is a question I have learned to ask myself over time. It's an unsettling question. The turn to diversity is often predicated on the numbers game, on getting more of us, more people of colour, to add colour to the White faces of organisations. So if we are the colour, then we are what gets added on. Whiteness: the world as is it coheres around certain bodies. We symbolise the hope or promise that whiteness is being undone.

Our arrival is read as evidence of commitment, of change, of progress. Our arrival is noticeable. I am speaking of whiteness in a seminar. And someone in the audience says, 'but you are a professor', as if to say if Black women become professors then the whiteness of the world recedes. If only we had the power we are imagined to possess, if only our proximity could be such a force. If only our arrival was their undoing. I was appointed to teach 'the race course', I reply. I am the only person of colour employed on a full-time basis in the department. I hesitate. It becomes too personal. The argument is too much to sustain when your body is so exposed, when you feel so noticeable. I stop, and do not complete my answer to the question.

When our appointments and promotion are taken up as signs of organisational commitment to equality and diversity, we are in trouble. Any success is read as a sign of an overcoming of institutional whiteness. 'Look, you're here!', 'Look, look!' Our talk about racism is read as a form of stubbornness, paranoia or even melancholia, as if we are holding onto something (whiteness) that our arrival shows has already gone. Our talk about whiteness is read as a sign of ingratitude, of failing to be grateful for the hospitality we have received by virtue of our arrival. It is this very structural position of being the guest, or the stranger, the one who receives hospitality, which keeps us in certain places, even when

203

you move up. Diversity becomes both a problem and a paradox for those who embody diversity. This chapter contributes to the growing literature on what diversity might mean specifically for Black feminism (Jones, 2006; Mirza, 2006).

What's my story? Like you, I have many. I started out as an academic in a 'very White' university in the North West of England. I was in Women's Studies, having applied for a job in 'Black feminism'. The amazement of getting that job, of there being that job to get. And yet, it was not comfortable, far from it. They interviewed four Black feminists for that job. The audience at the talks was all White. We socialised afterwards, the four of us standing out in a house among White people. Even the carpets were white: no red wine allowed, as if to say, no colour permitted that will leave a stain. We were shimmering colour in all that whiteness. Standing out like a sore thumb, you might say. To stand out is to be sore point, before anything can happen. The desire for you to embody diversity (which can feel like a desire both for you and for what you embody) comes from the right place (race needs to be made integral to women's studies, the core course should be on race). And yet it creates its sore points. If you embody race for them, then they do race through you, which can be a way of not doing race. You can also express their commitment to the very idea of intersectionality. You are the point where the lines meet. A meeting point becomes a sore point.

I am co-director of the Institute for Women's Studies. We can't really do much about race equality, says the Dean in a meeting with Heads of Departments. Rage can interpellate us; it can get through even our best defences. It's too difficult, he says. I send him an email. Saying that you can't do anything about it is how racism gets reproduced, I say. The belief that racism is inevitable is how racism becomes inevitable, I point out. (One of the favourite arguments made by senior management was that the university was 'very White' because of its geography – and that you can't do anything about geography.) Do something about it, he says. It shouldn't be up to me, I reply. And yet, I cannot stay silent. I speak out, I speak up. How quickly we can be interpellated: it is the right reasons that get us there, even if that's not where we wish to get.

Having spoken up, I end up on the race equality team. I am doing something, and of course I am glad about that, but it is an uneasy gladness. We are writing a race equality policy. There are two academics on the team, both Black and Minority Ethnic, or BME as they like to call us. We write the policy. In discussions among our group, we take as our starting point that we need a policy because of inequalities, because of whiteness, because of the hard work of challenging sedimented privilege. We talk about how the word 'diversity' doesn't do this, and we use other words alongside this word, stickier words as I would describe them, like 'racism', 'whiteness' and 'inequality'. We submit our policy. According to the Equality Challenge Unit (ECU), the university 'does well'. We are good at race equality, says the new vice chancellor, his face beaming, as he addresses university staff at a meeting. I did not share the good feeling. The document that documents racism is used as a measure of good performance. When race equality becomes a performance indicator, you know you are in trouble.

I am Director. We are always at the end of a line, struggling, as a Women's Studies department for the right to exist. We are the jewel in the crown, says the Dean, at the same time that he announces we won't get any 'new blood posts' and that we have to leave our large offices at the front of the building for small offices at the back. Never quite viable, no matter what you do. Not being proper is not just about discipline. To be not proper is not only to lack discipline, but also to lack discipline in the wrong way. Anyway, we have to do something. We have to save Women's Studies. Always, it is a saving mission. A rescue mission. So much energy for the right to stay. A colleague approaches me from the Management School. She invites me to co-direct a research project on diversity in education, under the auspices of the would-be Centre for Excellence for Leadership (CEL), funded by the Department for Education and Skills. I seize the opportunity. It is a chance and it feel like a lifeline. Rescuing Women's Studies took me there (unfortunately that part of it did not work), and the world of diversity was opened up. As a text-based researcher by training, I embraced new techniques (talking to people, going to events with the task of documenting the event for others). I was taught important lessons about how institutional worlds as life worlds take shape around some bodies and not others.

This chapter presents what I learned from doing this research project, which is to say, what I learned from re-inhabiting the diversity world as a Black feminist. I interviewed 20 diversity practitioners in British and Australian universities. In the UK, I attended numerous conferences on diversity and race equality set up by organisations such as the Commission for Race Equality (CRE). And I worked as a member of a team, a diversity team. What I want to explore in the chapter draws on my research but also on my own experience as being a member of this team. What happened to the research became a mirror for what the research was about: the unhappy consequences of embodying diversity. It was the experience of doing this research project that led me to writing about happiness and the politics of 'happy diversity', as well as to reflect more on the emotional work of diversity work. This chapter amounts to a series of rather scattered reflections from the field. To scatter is the right kind of verb for this kind of work: to scatter is to throw here and there, as well to disperse. The field of diversity is a field that is dispersed, where things are scattered, and where we do not quite know how to inhabit its ground.

Doing diversity

The diversity world is a world that coheres around diversity. As a word, we could say, the word 'diversity' does things. The word 'diversity' appears in documents that document the university as having a certain existence. Race equality documents (such as the one I was involved in writing) often describe the university as having not only certain principles, but also certain qualities, characteristics and styles. Through such documents, universities are constituted as if they have these qualities. Diversity enters such documents not only as something the university is committed to, but also as a quality the university already has, by virtue of the kinds of staff and students that already exist within the organisation.

Take the following opening sentence from a race equality policy: 'The University values the richness of the diversity of its students, staff and members of the local communities in which it operates.' The discourse of valuing diversity is of course mainstream, and hesitates between discourses of economic value (the business case for diversity) and moral value (the social justice case). This model of diversity reifies difference as something that already exists 'in' the bodies of others (we are diverse because you are here). Our difference becomes their diversity. It is this model of diversity as something others bring to the organisation that we can see at work in the use of visual images of diverse organisations: images of 'colourful' happy faces, which show the diversity of the university as something it has embraced.

Diversity is cited in documents that describe educational missions, and becomes a way of imagining organisations as having certain attributes. It is also a term that is used within organisations by diversity and equality practitioners. How do practitioners mobilise the language of diversity? How does the institutional desire for diversity relate to what practitioners do? Many practitioners are very critical of how diversity is used by their organisations. As one practitioner put it: 'I think the concept of diversity, in the way that it is now used in equality, rather than diversity as a word, which I don't really think it has much relationship to, I think it's used as a complete and utter cop-out. I think it's a dreadful concept.' Indeed, this practitioner felt so strongly about 'the cop-out' of diversity that she refuses to describe herself as an equality and diversity practitioner, even though her job title involves both terms. She goes on to describe 'diversity' as a cuddly concept that extends the university's self-image as being good:

> So now we'll talk about diversity and that means everybody's different but equal and its all nice and cuddly and we can feel good about it and feel like we've solved it, when actually we're nowhere near solving it and we need to I think have that, well diversity as a concept fits in much better with the university's idea of what its doing about being the great benefactor.

We could describe diversity as a politics of feeling good, which allows people to relax and feel less threatened, as if we have already 'solved it', and there is nothing less to do. I ask another practitioner why she thinks that the word 'diversity' is appealing. She argued that it is because:

> it obscures the issues.... It can, diversity is like a big shiny red apple right, and it all looks wonderful. This is an example actually a member of staff came up with in my focus group about gender issues, she says but if you actually cut into that apple there's a rotten core in there and you know that it's actually all rotting away and it's not actually being addressed. It all looks wonderful but the inequalities aren't being addressed.

Again, the suggestion here is that the appeal of diversity is about looking and feeling good, as an orientation that obscures inequalities, like the obscuring of a rotten core behind a shiny surface. As such, diversity as a term has a marketing appeal; it allows the university to sell itself, by presenting itself as a happy place, a place where differences are celebrated, welcomed and enjoyed. Diversity becomes a brand, and a form of organisational pride. Not only does this rebranding of the university as being diverse work to conceal racism, but it works also to re-imagine the university as being anti-racist and even beyond race: as if the colours of different races have 'integrated' to create a new hybrid or even bronzed face.

And yet, this practitioner also acknowledges that there are some benefits to diversity, in the sense it can 'start to engage people'. It is now a given how diversity might make people feel good, that it can be a useful term, as it allows people in: once they are 'in', by implication, then we can do different things, or even use a different set of terms. It is precisely how diversity might work to conceal racism that might make it a term that can do things. Indeed, most practitioners describe their work as a question of 'what works', of using whatever language works for the different audiences they speak to. Diversity is used by some precisely because it's a 'cuddly' term, which allows people to engage more easily with this kind of work. In other words, the appeal of the term for organisations might be what makes the term useful *as an appeal* for practitioners.

But what kind of appeal does diversity make? And what is the relation between diversity and whiteness? In one of my interviews, we discussed a research project on perceptions of the university that had been funded as part of the university's commitment to race equality. What did the research reveal?

> OK yes. It was about uncovering perceptions um, about the xxx as an employer.... xxx was considered to be an old boys network, as they called it and white male dominated and they didn't have the right perceptions of the xxx in terms of what it offers and what it brings to the academia. I think most of the external people had the wrong perceptions about the xxx.

> And I mean, quotes, there were such funny quotes like librarians they were sitting there with their cardigans you know. Um, and things like that, they were shocking reports to read really about how people, external people, perceive the xxx so we have to try to achieve you know, we have to try to make the xxx an attractive employer.

The politics of diversity has become about what we could call 'image management': diversity work is about generating the 'right image', and correcting the wrong one. I was quite interested in what it meant to be shocked by this image, given what I knew of the staffing profile of this university. What organises this shock is the presumption that the perception is what is wrong. According to this logic, people have the 'wrong perception' when they see the organisation as White, elite, male, old-fashioned. In other words, what is behind the shock is a belief that that the organisation does not have these qualities: that whiteness is 'in the image' rather than 'in the organisation'. Diversity becomes about *changing perceptions of whiteness rather than changing the whiteness of organisations.* Doing well, or a good performance, would then be about being perceived as a diverse organisation.

The term 'diversity' is appealing as it does not necessarily challenge organisational culture, even if it allows a change in appearance. To add 'diversity' to a mission statement, hence does not necessarily add anything, other than that just put an educational mission in different terms. The word still has baggage, and still gets associated with people who 'look different'. As Nirmal Puwar points out, 'In policy terms, diversity has come overwhelmingly to mean the inclusion of people who look different' (2004, p. 1). Ironically, the hope of putting diversity into university documentation is that this word will keep these associations, however problematic they may be. The point would not be to constitute racial others as the origin of diversity, as what adds colour to the White face of the university. Rather, insofar as diversity signifies the presence of racial others, then it might expose how organisations are orientated around whiteness, around those who are 'already in place'. The happy smiling face of diversity would not then simply rebrand the university, but point instead to what gets concealed by this very image: the inequalities that are behind it, and that give it its surface appeal.

Being diversity

What does diversity mean for those of us who look different, and who come, in the very terms of our appearance, to embody diversity? What does 'being diversity' do? As I have suggested, diversity can work as a branding exercise, a way of re-imaging the organisation as 'being diverse' through having us, those who embody diversity for them. Diversity becomes a technology of happiness: through diversity, the organisation is represented 'happily' as 'getting along', as committed to equality, as anti-racist. Your arrival is thus a happy occasion for the organisation. But you must smile – you must express gratitude for having been received. If your arrival is a sign of diversity, then you are a success story. You turn an action point into an outcome.

Our diversity team experienced the consequences of being a turning point. We were as it were an outcome, a tick in the box. We were continually reminded that we were the recipients of generous funding. We were 'indebted'. The gift economy is a powerful one. In this case, the gift given is used as evidence of the organisation's commitment to diversity and equality. We had a good team, a mixed team, White and Black feminists working together. Working together and learning from each other, I would say. But as a team we were also an object of desire. We were the 'diversity team' *to* them and *for* them. We embodied diversity for the organisation. They want your picture, of course. Photographs of Black and White people working together is a happy picture for the organisation. Happy hybridity – that was us, for them.

We are at a meeting for the research projects. The director of the organisation is present. We speak, we talk about our research, drawing on our interviews. They are all so interested. We are very committed to diversity, the director says, again and again. Sometimes the repetition of good sentiment feels oppressive. What are they trying to convince us of, I wonder. Enthusiasm can be oppressive, I learn. The occasion becomes *about* the enthusiasm of the White management. They have funded us, we rely on their commitment. Each expression of enthusiasm is a reminder of our debt. I know how we are supposed to respond. We are supposed to be grateful. We are supposed to thank them and be humbled by their generosity. We are good objects at this point, but you know this is precarious. You know it's conditional on returning their commitment in the right way. What do they want? Will we do what they want?

Their commitment does come with conditions and the task is to make the conditions explicit. We learned that the condition of their commitment is that we would speak about their commitment in glowing terms and not speak about anything that exposes the conditions of their commitment. As such, a condition of commitment becomes a demand to use happy words and prohibits unhappy words. In one instance, the diversity officer talks to a newspaper, and uses the words 'institutional racism'. A report follows that uses that word. The director is 'outraged' and sends off an email: 'CEL would never accuse a college of institutional racism', she says. I am stunned. Institutional racism is a term used to describe how racism structures organisations, I respond. Of course, there is 'institutional racism' in the sector. What have we been talking about? The commitment to diversity gets translated into a prohibition on the use of the word 'racism'. It is almost as if the reward for organisational diversity is a moratorium on that word. We are suspended from the right to use the term 'racism' if organisations have committed to diversity, whatever that commitment says or does.

Racism becomes something bad that we can't even speak of, as if to describe x as racist is to damage or even hurt x. I have discussed in earlier work how the language of institutional racism has become psychologising, as if the institution is now the bad person, who needs therapy to get over it, despite the fact that the language of institutional racism was intended to avoid psychological models (Ahmed, 2004a). We can see the risk of the psychologising of organisations. The organisation becomes the subject of feeling, the one who must be protected, the one who is easily bruised or hurt. To speak of racism is to introduce bad feeling. It is to hurt not just the organisation, re-imagined as a subject with feelings, but also the subjects who identify with the organisation, the 'good White diversity' subjects, to whom we are supposed to be grateful. The speech act, 'we would not accuse you of racism' can be translated into, 'I am not racist' insofar as the 'I' that would not accuse the 'you' of racism, has already identified with that you (=happy whiteness).

The word 'racism' is very sticky. Just saying it, does things. Constantly, I am witnessing what the word 'racism' does. We speak of racism in our papers, which we give at a research meeting to an audience made up of other project teams. I can feel the discomfort. It is hard to know sometimes whether feelings are in the room or are a matter of our orientation; the impressions we have of the room by virtue of the angle at which we are placed. I feel uncomfortable, let's say that. We stop, someone asks a question about class. It happens over and over again. We speak about racism, and they ask questions back to us about class. Not just class but something more specific: they ask the same question about the complicity of middle-class Black professionals almost as if they have to re-imagine Black subjects as the ones with relative privilege. They displace the attention. Discomfort shows the failure to fit.

After this particular session, someone comes up to me and puts her arm next to mine. You wouldn't really know you were any different to me, she says. We are almost the same colour, she says. No difference, no difference. Talk about racism becomes a fantasy that invents difference. She smiles, as if our proximate arms are a kind of solidarity, and I say nothing. Turning away, I want to scream. Being diversity feels like one big scream.

I am speaking to one of my interviewees about racism. We are talking of those little encounters, and their very big effects. It is 'off tape', we are just talking, recognising each other, as you do, in how we recognise racism in those everyday encounters you have with people who can't handle it, the idea of it. That's what they always say, she says to me. That you always reduce everything to racism. Racism becomes your paranoia. Of course, it's a way of saying that racism doesn't really exist in the way you say it does. As if we had to invent racism to explain our own feeling of exclusion, as if racism was a way of not being responsible for the places we cannot go. It is a form of racism to say that racism does not exist. We know this.

But I am thinking more about paranoia, and thinking about good reasons for bad feelings. I guess the problem is that I do feel paranoid even if I know that this paranoia is reasonable. I do have a kind of paranoid anxiety about everything. I am never sure when x happens, whether x is about racism or is a result of racism. I am never sure. And because I am never sure, because I have never been allowed to be sure, then x is lived as always possibly about racism, as what explains how you inhabit the world you do. Racism creates paranoia, that's what racism does. Whiteness is reproduced both by the fantasy of paranoia (it doesn't 'really' exist), and by the effect of the fantasy of paranoia, which is to make us paranoid. Our feelings become its truth.

We kept speaking about racism. We must, and we do. I think of it as the kernel of our findings: for Black staff in the diversity world, the recognition of the ongoing nature of racism is constantly blocked. Organisations wanted to talk about diversity *rather than* racism. Diversity becomes a technology for not hearing. We 'need to hear' about good practice, as hearing about good practice is good practice (people are better if they feel better). We need to be useful. We need to tell people what to do. We need toolkits and bullet points. We need to hear about positive experiences. The underlying assumption was that we have to focus on what is good, for things to get better. But what if 'the good' – good feeling, good practice, positive stories – is what keeps our attention away from what is bad, from what hurts, from what gets under the skin, that big scream that you never quite manage to make. In order to avoid people feeling bad, we have to make them feel good, by speaking about diversity. Our hurt and rage is blanketed under the warmth of diversity.

We kept speaking about racism. It never amounted to screaming, but it was the closest we could get. We wrote our report. We offered critiques of good practice. We said no to toolboxes, and gave accounts of racism. It doesn't take long for the enthusiasm to shift into hostility. The director is 'disappointed' in the diversity research. We need more 'positive stories'. There is too much theory. There is too much focus on racism (surely you are exaggerating, how can there be so much?). The attacks feel personal. We are constantly targeted, singled out, made into a case. They never publish our report.[1]

I was so angry. I wrote so many letters. I never sent them. It was a reasonable anger, but I experienced just what some of the practitioners I spoke to call 'the brick wall'; you come up against the organisation, and all that happens is that you get sore. The wall keeps its place, so it's you that gets sore. Embodying diversity is a sore point for Black feminists, but the soreness of that point is either hidden from their view (if we go along with the happiness of the image, which sometimes we must do) or attributed to us (as if we talk about walls because we are sore). So yes, diversity is a happy image, of people who 'look different' just getting along. Happiness becomes a condition of membership: you have to be happy *for them*. You cannot speak about racism; that's too unhappy as it causes them to lose their right to happiness, resting as it is on an ego ideal of being good and tolerant. You certainly should not speak of whiteness, which would implicate them in the force of your critique. You have to stay in the right place to keep your place. Can we do something with the sore points?

Angry Black feminists

Doing and being diversity work taught me about the distribution of good and bad feeling. Some bodies are assumed to be the origin of bad feeling, as getting in the way of the good feelings of others. This is why when I hear people say 'the bad feeling is coming from "this person" or "that person"' I am never convinced. My scepticism is shaped by lifelong experiences of being an outspoken Black feminist, at odds with the performance of good feeling, whether at home or at work, always assumed to be bringing others down, for example, by pointing out sexism or racism in other people's talk.

Just take the figure of the 'killjoy feminist'. Does the feminist kill other people's joy by pointing out moments of sexism? Or does she expose the bad feelings that get hidden, displaced or negated under public signs of joy? Does bad feeling enter the room when somebody expresses anger about things, or could anger be the moment when the bad feelings get brought to the surface in a certain way?

There is a relationship between the negativity of certain figures and how certain bodies are 'encountered' as being negative. Marilyn Frye argues that oppression involves the requirement that you show signs of being happy with the situation in which you find yourself. As she puts it, 'it is often a requirement upon oppressed people that we smile and be cheerful. If we comply, we signify our docility and our acquiescence in our situation' (1983, p. 2). To be oppressed requires you show signs of happiness, as signs of being or having been adjusted. As a result, for Frye, 'anything but the sunniest countenance exposes us to being perceived as mean, bitter, angry or dangerous' (p. 2). For an oppressed person not to smile or to show a sign of being happy is to already be recognised as negative: as angry, hostile, unhappy and so on. I suspect Frye is describing a very familiar situation for many of us. You are 'already read' as 'not easy to get along with' when you name yourself as a feminist. Frye herself alludes to such experiences, when she says, 'This means, at the very least, that we may be found to be "difficult" or unpleasant to work with, which is enough to cost one's livelihood' (pp. 2–3).

Of course, within feminism, some bodies more than others can be attributed as the cause of unhappiness. We can place the figure of the feminist killjoy alongside the figure of the angry Black woman, explored so well by writers such as Audre Lorde (1984), bell hooks (2000) and Aileen Moreton-Robinson (2003). The angry Black woman can be described as a killjoy; she may even kill feminist joy, for example, by pointing out forms of racism within feminist politics. She might not even have to make any such point to kill joy. Listen to the following description from bell hooks:

> a group of white feminist activists who do not know one another may be present at a meeting to discuss feminist theory. They may feel bonded on the basis of shared womanhood, but the atmosphere will noticeably change when a woman of color enters the room. The white women will become tense, no longer relaxed, no longer celebratory.
>
> (2000, p. 56)

It is not just that feelings are 'in tension', but that the tension is located somewhere: in being felt by some bodies, it is attributed as caused by another body, who thus comes to be felt as apart from the group, as getting in the way of its enjoyment and solidarity. The Black body is attributed as the cause of becoming tense, which is also the loss of a shared atmosphere. hooks shows how as a Black feminist you do not even have to say anything to cause tension. The mere proximity of some bodies involves an affective conversion. To get along, you have to go along with things that might mean for some not even being able to enter the room.

To speak out of anger as Black woman is then to confirm your position as the cause of tension. Black woman's anger gets in the way of the social bond; it injures or hurts the feminist group. As Audre Lorde describes: 'When women of Color speak out of the anger that laces so many of our contacts with white women, we are often told that we are "creating a mood of helplessness", "preventing white women from getting past guilt", or "standing in the way of trusting communication and action"' (1984, p. 131). The exposure of violence becomes the origin of violence.

The Black woman must let go of her anger for the White woman to move on.

Some bodies become blockage points, points where smooth communication stops. Our anger becomes a blockage point. We need a yes here. We need to say, yes, Black people are angry: we are angry about racism, about forms of violence and power that are hidden under the signs of civility and love. We are angry and yet Black anger is also a fantasy that allows the dismissal of what we might have to say. Your reasonable thoughtful arguments are dismissed as anger (which of course empties anger of its own reason), which makes you angry, such that your response becomes read as the confirmation of the evidence that you are not only angry but also unreasonable!

To put this another way, Black feminist anger is attributed. So you might be angry *about* how racism and sexism diminish life choices for women of colour. Your anger is a judgement that something is wrong. But then in being heard as angry, your speech is read as motivated by anger. Your anger is read as unattributed, as if you are against x because you are angry rather than being angry because you are against x. You become angry at the injustice of being heard as motivated by anger, which makes it harder to separate yourself from the object of your anger. You become entangled with what you are angry about because you are angry about how they have entangled you in your anger. In becoming angry about that entanglement, you confirm their commitment to your anger as the truth 'behind' your speech, which is what blocks your anger, stops it from getting through.

Political work becomes harder when your feelings are so proximate to their fantasy. Recently, I published a paper on whiteness in the journal *Feminist Theory*, which also included a paper by Suneri Thobani (2007).[2] I had previously written about Thobani's important critiques of the war against terrorism and the politics of how she was dismissed as an angry Black woman (Ahmed, 2004b). In this special issue, Thobani's paper offered a critique of Phyllis Chesler, Zilla Eisenstein and Judith Butler for how they were complicit with imperialism (albeit in very different ways). The journal published alongside her paper a response from Chesler. I could not believe they could publish this kind of response by a White feminist to a Black feminist in a special issue of a feminist journal on whiteness. The response drew on racist vocabularies with quite extraordinary ease. I went from disbelief to shock to rage. And then resignation. It will be a good pedagogic tool, I say to a Black feminist colleague at a conference. It will show students how racism works in academic practices. I don't convince myself. I know very well we have no need for any such tools. We have too many already.

What does Chesler say? She describes Thobani's paper as 'ideological, not scholarly' and as trying 'to pass for an academic or even intellectual work' (p. 228). She describes Thobani's paper as 'angry and self-righteous declaration of war' (p. 228). She suggests that ' "white" folk have sorrows too' and then suggests that Thobani 'is perfectly free to criticise, even to demonize the West, *in* the West because she is living in a democracy where academic freedom and free speech are (still) taken seriously' (p. 230). The familiarity of these kinds of statements is exhausting. When I read it, I just thought of Audre Lorde, and how I wished she was here to help us describe the moment. Even description gets hard at this point.

The Black woman isn't a real scholar, she is motivated by ideology. The Black woman is angry. She occupies the moral high ground. The Black woman declares war by pointing to the complicity of White feminists in imperialism. The Black woman is racist (and we hurt too). The Black woman should be grateful, as she lives in our democracy. We have given her the right to speak. The Black woman is the origin of terror, and she fails to recognise violence other than the violence of Whites against Black. After reading Chesler's response to Thobani, I turned to her book, *The New Anti-Semitism*. One sentence more than any other got under my skin: 'I have known utterly charming, truly enchanting Muslims. *Yes, prick them and they will bleed*' (Chesler, 2003, p. 15 [emphasis mine]). Racist speech is most powerful in such expressions of love: the Muslims bleed, yes, which seems a way of saying they are human, but implies quite the opposite: there must be a doubt that they are not human, for it to be even a question as to whether 'they will bleed' like we do. The doubt as to whether 'they will bleed' is the instrument of violence, of the will to make them bleed. Yes, prick them and they will bleed.

Witnessing Chesler's response to Thobani teaches us about racism and the politics of anger. In a way, we might learn to claim and validate our anger, even as we appreciate how anger is then read in a way that blocks being heard. Within Black feminism, the passion of anger is crucial to what gives us 'the energy' to react against the deep investments that exist in forms of racism as well as sexism. Nowhere is this clearer than in the work of Audre Lorde, specifically in her critiques of racism against Black women. As she writes so powerfully:

> My response to racism is anger. I have lived with that anger ignoring it, feeding it, learning to use it, before it laid my visions to waste for most of my life. Once I did it in silence, afraid of the

weight. My fear of anger taught me nothing.... Anger expressed and translated into action in the service of our vision and our future is a liberating and strengthening act of clarification.... Anger is loaded with information and energy.

(1984, p. 127)

Here, anger is constructed in different ways: as a response to the injustice of racism; as a vision of the future; as a translation of pain into knowledge, and as being loaded with information and energy. Crucially, anger is not simply defined in relationship to a past, but as opening up the future. In other words, being against something does not end with 'that which one is against'. Anger can open the world up. Lorde has talked precisely of how White feminists refuse to hear her anger by returning this anger in the form of defensiveness (1989, p. 124). Angry Black women need to stay angry; even though speaking anger involves risks and costs, even if we fail to get through other people's defences. This is not to say that we can only be angry – anger is creative, and it gives us room to do other things. And nor is it our duty; I am not obliged to keep hitting that wall, sometimes I will, and sometimes I wont. But not to speak anger because it is pointless is not the answer. After all, even if we use softer language, we are already sore points. We might as well do things with those points.

Some bodies become sore points, points of trouble, where communication stops. To speak about racism is to labour over sore points. Other bodies become bearers of the promise of happiness; the good White subjects who will offer us their love. Just play their game, they say. Just be happy. To embody diversity is to play their game. As my experience of being a member of a diversity research team taught me, to embody diversity is to be prohibited from even speaking about racism, as if to say, just get over it. But we can't get over it. We can't get over racism. It's not over. To get over it before it's over would be to keep things in place. We must be the trouble they claim us to be, we must become the cause of their trouble. It's time for us to reclaim our place as angry Black feminists, even as we inhabit different places. The angry Black feminist, who insists on, speaks about racism, who is not happy with diversity, can do things. We don't even know yet just what she can do. We need to be bad at embodying diversity. We need to fail to be happy for them. We need to stay as sore as our points.

Notes

1. Our report was never published by CEL, and despite numerous emails requesting information about this, we were never given any account of this decision.

The report can be downloaded from my website: http://www.goldsmiths.ac. uk/media-communications/staff/finaldiversityreport.pdf. Please disseminate widely.

2. When I first read the special issue, I considered writing a letter of protest to the journal. However, in this case, it felt like the wall was too much. I am writing about it now, in a paper I am writing as a Black feminist for Black feminists. We have to choose when and where to make our points.

References

Ahmed, S. (2004a) Declarations of whiteness: The non-performativity of anti-racism. *Borderlands*, 3(2): 1–54.

Ahmed, S. (2004b) *The Cultural Politics of Emotion*. Edinburgh: Edinburgh University Press.

Chesler, P. (2003) *The New Anti-Semitism: The Current Crisis and What We Must Do About It*. San Francisco, CA: Jossey-Bass.

Chesler, P. (2007) Response. *Feminist Theory*, 8(2): 227–234.

Frye, M. (1983) *The Politics of Reality: Essays in Feminist Theory*. Trumansburg, NY: The Crossing Press.

hooks, b. (2000) *Feminist Theory: from Margin to Centre*. London: Pluto Press.

Jones, C. (2006) Falling between the cracks; What diversity means for black women in the academy. *Policy Futures in Education*, 4(2): 145–159.

Lorde, A. (1984) *Sister Outsider: Essays and Speeches*. Freedom, CA: The Crossing Press.

Mirza, H. (2006) Transcendence over diversity: Black women in the academy. *Policy Futures in Education*, 4(2): 101–113.

Moreton-Robinson, A. (2003) 'Tiddas talking up to the white woman: When Huggins et al took on bell'. In M. Grossman, P. Morrissey and C. Cuthbert (Eds), *Black Lines: Contemporary Critical Writing by Indigenous Australians*. (pp. 66–77). Melbourne, VIC: Melbourne University Press.

Puwar, N. (2004) *Space Invaders: Race, Gender and Bodies Out of Place*. Oxford: Berg.

Thobani, S. (2007) White wars: Western feminisms and the 'war on terror'. *Feminist Theory*, 8(2): 169–185.

12
Talking About 'Diverse Genders and Sexualities' Means Talking About More than White Middle-Class Queers

Damien W. Riggs

Introduction

In the week leading up to beginning work on writing this chapter, I had the pleasure of spending time at my family's holiday house located in Goolwa, South Australia. Goolwa is located on the lands of the Ngarrendjeri people, the First Nations people whose sovereignty over the lands continues despite the ongoing effects of colonisation. I have been visiting Goolwa since I was a small child, and have a strong sense of affinity for the township and those that neighbour it. On this trip I revisited some of the sites that hold the strongest resonance as signifiers of what Goolwa represents to me. Specifically, the accumulation of almost a life's worth of memories of Goolwa make it for me a place of family, of connectedness to others, of closeness to the sea, and an openness of space that is not so readily apparent in the city of Adelaide where I live. At the same time, however, Goolwa is also for me a place of solitude, separation and in some ways almost alienation from all the things listed above, albeit alienating in ways that hold the potential to engender personal growth, rather than inhibiting this. Yet at the heart of my affinity for the environs of Goolwa lies a space now prohibited; that of Kumarangk/Hindmarsh Island. An explanation of this prohibition is thus warranted.

The island, located within clear sight across the Murray River from Goolwa, has over the past two decades been a contested site in the ongoing colonisation of Indigenous lands. Historically (i.e. since the colonisation of the surrounding areas in the mid-1800s), the island was primarily accessible to the general public via a ferry service. In the mid-1990s, however, there began a push for the building of a bridge between Goolwa and Kumarangk/Hindmarsh Island. This push (primarily driven by investors in a marina on the island but also supported by the then Labour government) was met with considerable resistance by the Ngarrendjeri, who stated that connecting the mainland to the island was counter to Ngarrendjeri beliefs about the formation of the land and its meaning for Ngarrendjeri cultural practices. Specifically, a group of Ngarrendjeri women claimed women-only cultural knowledge that a priori precluded the building of the bridge. Yet when the women justifiably refused to present this knowledge publically (on the grounds that it was for women only), and when the inquiry formed to investigate the matter refused to adopt protocols that would respect the knowledge held by the women, the outcome was that the bridge was built. Of note is the fact that the building of the bridge required amendments to laws that otherwise protect Indigenous cultural practices.

So what does the building of the bridge mean for me as a non-Indigenous person? After the building of the bridge, Ngarrendjeri elder Tom Trevorrow stated publically that 'We may use the bridge to access our land and waters but culturally and morally we cannot come to terms with this bridge' (in ABC News, 2010). As someone who is not Ngarrendjeri, however, this statement does not entitle me to access the island via the bridge, a lack of entitlement that I take as both important and legitimate. During my recent visit to Goolwa, I walked with my children across the barrage that also links the island to the mainland (a linking that is sanctioned by the Ngarrendjeri). As I crossed the barrage, I reflected upon why I had such a strong desire to be able to access the island. For me, the island has a particular quality of separation, of isolation, and a character that is truly unique, partly I think because it presents itself to me in many ways as unknowable, and has done so since I was a child. At the same time, it holds many memories of my childhood: trips over on the ferry, visits to the Murray Mouth lookout, and drives around the island. Reflecting on missing the island enabled me to glimpse something of what it must mean to have not just 30-odd years of connection to a place, but tens of thousands of years of connection to a place, as is the case for the Ngarrendjeri people: of family after family living, practicing and visiting there, of ancestors being buried there, and of creation stories being founded there. In attempting to comprehend this 'glimpse', I could see both how little I actually was able to comprehend about what the building of the bridge must mean for Ngarrendjeri people, but also how much I need to continue to sit with my lack of comprehension and the glimpse of understanding I gained.

Speaking about this 'glimpse' with Dylan Coleman, a Kokatha woman whose traditional lands are located on the Eyre Peninsula, some 1,000 kilometres from Kumarangk/Hindmarsh Island, brought home to me even more clearly how wide an impact the building of the bridge had upon diverse groups of Indigenous people. Coleman shared with me the fact that while geographically the land of her people is at a considerable distance from the land of the Ngarrendjeri, the Seven Sisters Dreaming story runs across the land from the west coast of Australia over to and through Kumarangk/Hindmarsh Island, on its way passing through Kokatha country. This is significant, given that knowledge of the Seven Sisters Dreaming story formed part of the ground upon which the group of Ngarrendjeri women challenged the building of the bridge. What was at stake in the building of the bridge, then, was not just a 'little island' (which itself should have been enough justification), but rather a whole series of interrelated facts about the land across Australia as known by Indigenous people, which would be negatively impacted by the building of the bridge.

The case of Kumarangk/Hindmarsh Island thus illustrates both the immense and violent force behind the colonial machine, but also the significance of the ongoing resistance of Indigenous people and the fact of Indigenous sovereignty that accompanies this. That Indigenous knowledges could be represented as 'fabricated' or even as a 'hoax' during the inquiry into the building of the bridge demonstrates the power accorded to non-Indigenous ways of knowing to determine what will count as knowledge and how knowledge claims are assessed. Yet, at the same time, the fact that Ngarrendjeri people continue to speak back to dominant regimes of power, and continue to challenge non-Indigenous claims to knowledge, highlights the fact that colonial power is never complete: it forever fails to achieve its aim of writing Australia as a space available for the taking, as a *tabula rasa* open to inscriptions that would seek to refuse the existence of other, incommensurable, ways of understanding the land.

Of course the reader may well ask why I have opened this chapter in this fashion: how does my narrative do anything other than re-inscribe a White fantasy of belonging in the space of another? And further, how do I, in my writing, do anything other than play the role of the 'ethnographic ventriloquist' (Huggins and Saunders, 1993), speaking both about and for Ngarrendjeri culture? My response to these self-imposed rhetorical questions is what shapes the remainder of this chapter, as I attempt to outline some of the issues – both ontological and epistemological – that shape my narrative above, and how they informed my teaching of a topic on gender and sexuality to a group of social work students in 2010. In teaching the topic, I sought to work with the students to develop an understanding of 'diverse genders and sexualities' that both resisted the anthropological gaze upon 'other cultures', while also firmly placing hegemonic western understandings of gender and sexuality in a broader global and historical framework. In order to outline my approach to this teaching, in the following sections I consider the who, what, how, when and why of representation that shaped the topic.

Where we stand

As my narrative above indicates, the matter of where we stand is of vital importance to how those of us identified as non-Indigenous people live in a country that continues to prosper from the 'illegal possession' of land (Moreton-Robinson, 2003). Where we stand is important in at least three distinct ways. First, the question of where we stand is important for the issue it raises as to who the presumptive 'we' denotes. In the instance of my class on gender and sexuality, the 'we' was a group of non-Indigenous, primarily White, students who had elected into the topic. My reading of the group was that these were a group of relatively liberal students who had a desire to know more about issues of gender and sexuality as they pertain to social work, but that through their liberalism they, at least in part, felt they were already somewhere along the track to engaging in an inclusive approach to gender and sexuality.

Second, and following on from the first point, is the fact that in being a class of non-Indigenous students lead by a non-Indigenous lecturer, we were all standing on land in which we had some form of stake, but to which we had an ethically suspect claim to belong. This was an important starting place, as it would have been far too easy for us all to perpetuate the assumption that the 'we' was constituted by a group of 'well-meaning' people who, in talking critically about gender and sexuality, were somehow outside the operations of colonisation that afford us the government-granted right to stand on the land and speak. That we acknowledged that we stood on Kaurna land, and that we spoke about this standing and what it meant for us to do so, was thus an important aspect of both the opening session of the topic, but also in the weeks that followed as we sought to unpack the differential impact of the built environs upon varying groups of people.

Third, the question of place has specific implications not only in terms of whose land we were standing on (and on whose land I work in Adelaide, and upon whose land I stay when I visit Goolwa), but also from whose land the built environs are *made*. Coleman (2010) speaks of the modernity of buildings in the city of Adelaide – modern in the greater scheme of Indigenous ownership of the land – and the materials from which they are made. She speaks of the fact that not only do such buildings sit on stolen land, but that they are also made of materials that are stolen too. To sit inside the buildings at my university and to teach within them is thus to think about what it means to have the luxury of often unwittingly being surrounded by another person's property that has both been appropriated, but which nonetheless carries with it the sovereignty of the people from which it is taken. As I looked out the windows in the teaching room, and as I now look out the windows of my family's holiday house, I see not simply the environs and the land that is not rightfully mine, but I also see the windows through which I look, the sands from which they are made, and the stories that those sands hold. Importantly, to 'see' country in this way is not about evoking an idealised 'pre-colonial' landscape, in which myself as the colonial subject invents a fantasy of a world without colonisation (Chow, 1994; Riggs, 2004). Rather, my point here, drawing on Coleman's work, is that the colonial past is very much the colonial present, locked up as it is in both the material and psychical relations that shape the spaces we all move in.

Who is standing

Of course where we stand is almost inseparable from who is doing the standing, as denoted above in my discussion of the 'we' who were standing in my gender and sexuality class. In the narrative that I opened this chapter with, I am clearly located not simply as a non-Indigenous person, but as a non-Indigenous person who enjoys the privilege of a 'holiday house'; someone who is university educated, someone who has paid employment and someone who can 'holiday' away from such employment and reflect upon their life. In other words, I speak from a very privileged position. But how does one speak from such a position, and do so with the aim of critically deconstructing that position, without engaging in what Sara Ahmed (2004a) refers to as the 'non-performativity of anti-racism'? In her work, Ahmed speaks of the problem that arises when White people who 'admit' their whiteness treat this admission as inherently critical. Instead, she suggests that there must be a 'double turn'; that in turning towards our own whiteness, those of us who identify as White must simultaneously turn away from ourselves and towards those who have long seen, spoken of, and critiqued whiteness.

In regards to the question of who is standing, and in reference to my gender and sexuality class, the task we engaged in was to find ways of looking at who we stand as *through our relationships to other people*. This involved, as Sanjay Sharma (2006) notes, a focus both on the 'concrete other' (i.e. the actual people upon whose disadvantage our privilege rests), and the 'ontological other' (i.e. the other as a category against and through which our sense of self is formed). To stand as a non-Indigenous Australian, and moreover to teach as a non-Indigenous Australian to non-Indigenous students, is to acknowledge that who we stand as is always a consequence: it is always a product or outcome of an ongoing series of historical relations between actual colonisers and actual Indigenous nations and peoples, as well as the ongoing social hierarchies in which these categories are made to matter. As such, and as Ahmed (2006) again notes, it is racism that produces race, not vice versa. In the context of a colonial nation such as Australia, it is colonialism itself – and its accompanying practices of empire that were informed by a possessive investment in land and a logic of patriarchal White sovereignty (Moreton-Robinson, 2004) that treats others (in this case Indigenous people) as objects to be dispossessed – that produces the hierarchical power relations in which I am made to matter as a non-Indigenous person (Fanon, 1967).

Perhaps part of what I am suggesting, then, is that indigeneity, or one's status as an Indigenous person (or not), functions as a superordinate category in Australia. In stating this, my claim is not per se to argue for a ranking of identity categories; indeed, much of my focus in teaching the gender and sexuality topic was on intersectionality theory (Crenshaw, 1991) as a means for understanding the complexities of identity. Rather, my point is that, in a nation founded on colonisation, and in a nation that continues in many ways to deny the ongoing effects of genocide and dispossession, whether or not one identifies as Indigenous has a particular set of consequences for identity formation, even if this isn't readily apparent to, or indeed is wilfully denied by, many non-Indigenous people. Thinking about who is standing thus requires us to think about the ontological claims that accompany this. I will return to this point later in the chapter, but it is important to note here that within the topic on gender and sexuality I drew upon Beryl Curt's (1994) notion of the individual as a 'fold' of the social to highlight how the latter always already produces subjectivities according to existing social cultural hierarchies, and through which such subjectivities are rendered intelligible. Thus, as Alison Ravenscroft (2003) suggests in her analysis of the work of Kathleen Mary Fallon (a White lesbian woman who has written publically about being a foster carer of an Indigenous child), 'she is the colonising subject and she acts against this and she is the colonising subject and...' (p. 241). Here, Ravenscroft clearly marks the both/and nature of colonising subjectivities: that in being formed through a relationship to ongoing histories of colonisation, non-Indigenous people – even those who engage in an anti-racist praxis – are inextricably bound up in the effects and affects of colonisation. Who speaks, then, is always an effect of power, one that brings with it a particular injunction to consider the representational components of colonisation, as I discuss in the following section.

Before going on to discuss how we represent the places upon which we stand, however, it is important to note a further point about who is standing. As I stated earlier, my class was comprised of non-Indigenous students. This demands the question of why this is the case – why is the student body in all of the topics I teach almost entirely comprised of non-Indigenous students, especially given the fact that government reports continue to indicate that, since the early 2000s, the numbers of Indigenous students enrolled in university courses are increasing (e.g. Schwab, 2006). The answer to this question lies in the fact that such reports indicate that while the numbers of Indigenous students enrolling in higher education are increasing, the nature of such enrolments is limited in at least three ways: (1) Indigenous students typically enrol in 'new universities' (which are seen as less prestigious than older universities, have high numbers of students taught by low numbers of staff and are often funded at lower levels than older universities); (2) Indigenous students may often fail to complete degrees or may undertake non-award degrees; and that (3) for those students who undertake award degrees, these are typically in the humanities or arts. Thus, while the numbers of Indigenous students enrolled is increasing, this does not necessarily translate into a significantly greater number of Indigenous people with higher degrees, or degrees that straightforwardly translate into higher numbers of Indigenous people who are able to gain employment as a result of their degree. As Schwab notes, some of these outcomes may be intentional choices made by Indigenous students that are informed by their cultural and worldviews. However, for many Indigenous students, their higher education 'choices' are still curtailed by the impact of racism, finance, family responsibilities and the effects of intergenerational trauma arising from genocide and dispossession. The who that I see in my classrooms, then, is not simply about who I see (i.e. primarily White middle-class students who will go on to reasonably well-paid professional careers), but also who I *don't* see (i.e. Indigenous students for whom educational outcomes may be considerably disparate to those of non-Indigenous students). This point about who actually enrols in my gender and sexuality topic has considerable implications for how I represent non-western standpoints within the topic, as I discuss in the following section.

How we represent standing

Who is standing and on whose land were thus central questions within the gender and sexuality topic, ones that required ongoing examination and ones that framed how the subsequent pedagogic material was presented. From my perspective, taking a traditional approach of 'once there was this and now there is that' would only have served to retain a focus on the 'what' of colonisation, but not the 'why' and 'how' of colonisation. Focusing instead on the latter allowed us to discuss colonisation as a structuring logic that shapes our very capacity to see what is before us. Much like my reflections upon my desire to visit Kumarangk/Hindmarsh Island again, looking at who we speak as and how we speak (i.e. what authority sanctions us to do so) was an important component of actively seeking to explore how, in the very act of speaking of ourselves, it was potentially possible to catch a glimpse of all that lay outside our frame of reference.

Yet in terms of affect, 'catching a glimpse' doesn't necessarily produce anything beyond a sense either of guilt, or possibly helplessness, for non-Indigenous students. What we had to do, in relation to both our discussions of colonisation and heteronormativity, was to consider what we could do ethically with these glimpses. In this regard, there are many models evoked by non-Indigenous people that are claimed to foster a sense of belonging to land, yet all of which I would suggest involve acts of appropriation or colonisation. For example, and as Sonja Kurtzer (2003) notes in relation to her analysis of non-Indigenous Australian Kim Mahood's claims to 'becoming Indigenous' (claims made also by Germaine Greer), such claims only serve as yet another form of theft of Indigenous knowledges. What we as a class had to do instead was to take up Ahmed's (2004a) challenge to make a double turn: to examine how western, non-Indigenous knowledges are formed through a relationship to both concrete and ontological others. Importantly, however, in developing such an approach we had to carefully tread the line between speaking *of* the other's knowledge, and speaking *for* the other's knowledge (particularly given, as noted above, that the class was almost entirely comprised of White middle-class students). And this was one of the launching points for the class: how do incommensurable differences between differing knowledges potentially prevent us from truly understanding the position of another, yet at the same time how does the location of such incommensurabilities within a broader social context shaped by hierarchies require at least an attempt to engage in an encounter with the other.

How we engage in a representation of the other, then, becomes just as important as where we stand and who we stand as. Indeed, these issues are thoroughly intertwined, as my weaving back and forth between them in this chapter would indicate. This was brought to my attention again recently in a viewing of Jeni Thornley's (2008) documentary *Island Home Country*. In the documentary, Jeni, a non-Indigenous woman, speaks of 'not knowing' about the brutal colonisation of Tasmania, where she grew up. In response, she returns to Tasmania to learn about its history, and in so doing speaks to local Indigenous women. These women challenge Jeni in regards to how she represents Indigenous people, and in particular how she represents Truganini, an Indigenous woman who it was long claimed was the 'last of the Tasmanian Aborigines'. Representing ancestors, the Indigenous women suggested, even if to think critically about colonial histories, is still an act of appropriation, and one that is unlikely to be sanctioned by the families of the people represented. This gave me pause to reflect upon my own use of the six-part documentary series, *First Australians,* in my teaching of the gender and sexuality topic, and in particular my use of the episode that portrayed the life of Truganini. My intent in using the episode had been to demonstrate that gender is always already racialised; that as Truganini and her people were being forced off their lands or forced to work for (and thus in many ways become complicit with) the colonial regime, White women in Australia were enjoying a wide range of privileges that came at the expense of Indigenous people. Again, then, reflecting on my use of the documentary reminded me of how fraught it is to rely upon representations of concrete others to engage in the work of reflexively challenging privilege.

The question this leads me to ask, then, and again following Ahmed (2004b), is how do we work with students to facilitate the attachment of meanings in ways that encourage new associations between concepts, but which don't do so through appropriation? And perhaps put more strongly, how do we create spaces that block particular (stereotyped) ways of knowing about the other, but which open up other ways of thinking? Within the topic on gender and sexuality, I attempted to do this by employing a critical constructionist approach that, perhaps counter-intuitively, treated constructionist claims as fact: not through a form of critical realism or via recourse to cultural relativism per se, but rather through an approach that was grounded in the very fact of difference. In other words, as opposed to promoting the view that 'all cultures are different' (which typically still leaves dominant group cultures as the norm), or stating that race or gender or sexuality (for example) are social constructions, I attempted to convey to students an understanding of both the 'fact' of incommensurable cultural differences, but also to emphasise that 'seeing' cultural difference as we do in the west is the product of a very particular regime of looking; one that is proprietal, judicial and most often colonising. To apprehend the other, in this fashion, is to *have* the other (Torgovnick, 1990).

One of the ways in which I developed this approach, and as I have written about elsewhere (Riggs, 2009), was to centre Indigenous sovereignty as a fact, albeit one for which non-Indigenous people cannot speak. In so doing, we discussed as a class the 'obvious' facts (i.e. that there were over 200 Indigenous nations prior to colonisation, that each of these have their own sovereign claims to land, their own creation narratives, their own beliefs about gender and sexuality), but we also discussed the fact that our 'knowing' of these facts will always already be limited by our position as non-Indigenous people. In a sense, then, this approach adopts what Fiona Nicoll (2004) advocates as one of 'falling out of perspective': instead of attempting to assert a position of knowing (or conversely, to deny any knowledge), non-Indigenous people can instead state that there is something we cannot know, even if at the same time we can know something of it. What we can know is that Indigenous people have a sovereign right to their land, and further, that Indigenous people hold what Aileen Moreton-Robinson (2003) refers to as an 'ontological relationship to land' (which I take to mean that Indigenous people embody a relationship to their land through which they carry their sovereign title to the land, even if they may not be on it). What we can know of this is that this sovereignty has never been ceded, and that non-Indigenous claims to land must always be understood as existing in a relationship to the ongoing fact of sovereignty. A critical constructionist approach here is applicable precisely for its capacity to accept that ownership and rights are themselves social categories, in which (at least in the west) particular ways of being are privileged or made to matter, but that this does not mean that there are not other ways of understanding the world that are both incommensurable but also inalienable. The thinking about how non-Indigenous people (including myself and my students) can understand our location in Australia and our gendered and sexualised identities thus required us to take this critical constructionist framework and use it to examine which models of the self are typically privileged when we talk about gender and sexuality.

Which model of the self

Sharma's (2006) work is useful in attempting to grapple with issues of difference and identity. He proposes the figure of the rhizome as way of understanding relationships, by placing 'both the inside/outside in the same field of immanence. The outside (difference) is *not* a function of the inside (identity); rather, it is *difference* that makes the inside possible and is conceived instead as a "multiplicity" (or a singularity) that is irreducible' (p. 212). Such an approach, Sharma suggests, allows for a definition of the self that does not rely upon a negation of the other. In other words, rather than simply perpetuating the master/slave logic, it is possible to acknowledge both how this logic structures western thought, but how it is nonetheless an imposition upon a set of differences that need not always be distinguished in such ways. Greg Thomas (2007) makes this point well in his Pan-African account of African subjectivities, where he suggests that 'There are never, ever merely girls and boys, men and women, without race and class. Analytically speaking, there are instead a legion of genders and sexualities, so to speak; and they cannot be reduced to the anatomy of any one white elite' (p. 68). Similarly, and as Carolyn Epple (1998) notes in her work on the Navajo nádleehí, within a Navajo world view the meanings attached to clothing or jewellery do not automatically map across onto a reading of gendered differences. As Epple suggests, terms such as 'berdarche' or 'two-spirit' fail to capture a Navaho worldview in regards to differences between bodies, and instead reduce nádleehí bodies to being 'just like' transgender people in the west.

Indigenous sistergirls in Australia too have written and spoken about the ways in which western concepts of gender do not match up with Indigenous understandings of identity. Kooncha Brown, for example, in her documentary and writing (2004, 2005), speaks of the ways in which sistergirls were viewed within Indigenous cultures prior to colonisation, where in some cultures sistergirls were included and valued while in others this was not the case. Importantly, while Brown does not paint an idealised image of the inclusion of sistergirls within Indigenous cultures, she nonetheless emphasises the negative effects of colonisation upon sistergirls, including the enforcement of stereotyped traditional gender roles upon Indigenous communities by colonisers, the forcing of gendered violence upon sistergirls (such as rape or sex work), and the higher risk that this now places sistergirls for contracting sexually transmitted diseases (STDs). Again, then, the voices of sistergirls reminded us in the gender and sexuality class both that there are experiences of gender and sexuality that exist outside the west, and that these cannot be easily (or usefully) represented within the standard categories available within the west. That those of us who live in the west inhabit a range of identity categories that historically were developed in opposition to (or indeed drew upon) those encountered as part of colonisation is not doubtable. But the assumption that it is the other that differs from the normative western self (treated as the centre) is thrown into question when we consider cultural practices that precede and exceed western colonial inscription.

When it comes to talking about the White western self, and particularly in regards to gender and sexuality (as I have done elsewhere, see Riggs, 2010), Sharma's (2006) use of the rhizome is again productive. Through the figure of the rhizome, we can very much see how the White heterosexual middle-class Australian self is constructed as the normative centre, but we can also see how that occurs as a result of the location of this identity at the intersection of a range of categories that simultaneously, rather than cumulatively, produce a site of privilege that always sits alongside the figure of the ontological other. Yet at the same time, the status of this identity position as also non-Indigenous draws our attention to a founding problem in terms of its absolute authority. Indeed, this founding problem for White identities in Australia is perhaps usefully represented by the German term for multiple/intersecting identities – 'Mehrfachzugehörigkeiten' – which, as Gabi Rosenstreich (2007) suggests, refers to a sense of multiple belongings, rather than identities (p. 136 f5). The fact that any configuration of the non-Indigenous self has both many sets of claims to belonging, yet at the same time lacks any constitutive claim to belonging, is perhaps the hallmark of non-Indigenous identities in Australia (Nicolacopoulos and Vassilacopoulos, 2004). Certainly in my own life and in particular in my experiences at Goolwa, while at times (when I have lived and worked in Goolwa and its environs as an out gay man) I have experienced an odd mixture of inclusion and exclusion from other non-Indigenous people, I have at the same time always had a sense of uncanny connection to Goolwa as a place: uncanny for the fact that while I have so many memories of being there, I also know that it is not 'my place'; that more so than in the city of Adelaide I feel a distinct sense of being on someone else's land. Thus, while I have worn many different hats at different times during my life visiting Goolwa, I have never worn one that made me feel totally at home. This, I think, is a good thing, and is actually what appeals to me about Goolwa, as it both reminds me of what I am grasping for, and gives me a starting place from which to comprehend the unattainability of what lies beyond my reach.

Again, then, the figure of the rhizome reminds us that the White western self is as much a product of western discourses of race, difference and sameness as is any other. Importantly, however, this is not to slip into a discourse of 'white people are different too', as Ahmed (2006) warns against. Rather, it is to recognise that the constitutive structures of White western notions of self-bind White people to a vision of gender and sexuality that can't simply be undone by recourse to an 'exotic other' in order to forever and always prop up a normative White self. And it is in the recognition of this that lies the possibility of locating western notions of gender and sexuality within a broader cross-cultural framework that doesn't simply treat 'whiteness' as but one of many cultures, nor does it claim to be able to adequately speak for the concrete other. Instead, my point here is that the 'rules', if you like, of western discourses of gender and sexuality, are relatively readily explicable; that this can then be used to examine how such discourses are constituted through and against competing discourses, thus allowing for the fact of difference to stand while not reducing it to a western model or interpretation.

Why all this matters

While writing this chapter I have repeatedly felt the need to pre-empt the question of how these wider discussions relate to the teaching of a course on gender and sexuality. For me, the most simple answer is that my university requires the 'inclusion' of Indigenous content across all courses, yet to date this has been patchy and typically undertaken in a way that yet again places Indigenous issues on the periphery. Of course, and as Ahmed (2006) notes, this raises the problem of tick boxes; that on the one hand any given institution may demand a set of minimum requirements for inclusion of Indigenous content, but on the other may utilise a wider, vaguer, more aspirational notion of inclusion that still fails to move beyond whiteness as the norm. Indeed, as Ahmed suggests, we could 'even describe the "tick box" as a spectre behind this law: the tick box is what we want to avoid in interpreting legislation, *and yet it is also what the legislation requires or even puts in place.* Moving beyond compliance becomes a matter of compliance' (2006, p. 19).

My approach to teaching social work students has always been to try to move beyond a tick box approach, while also providing students with practical skills for when they enter the workplace. A seemingly impossible task! Why all that I have covered in this chapter matters, then, is because it represents one attempt at moving beyond tick boxes that nonetheless provides critical thinking skills that allow students to recognise that the concrete other *does* possess knowledge, that such knowledge is not a product for consumption nor an object that can be easily incorporated, but that it will nonetheless structure their engagement with those different to themselves. Underpinning my attempts at undertaking this teaching has been a desire to instil in students the injunction to avoid rendering the challenges facing dominant groups in working with those in marginalised positions as the work of those who are marginalised. Understanding the position of the other, or at the very least comprehending that such a position exists and is valid, requires a move beyond a benevolent or paternalistic social work, and towards one in which concepts of 'self-determination' or 'cultural-competency' have some actual meaning outside of neoliberal parlance. To expect that those who are marginalised will 'explain themselves' represents the most insidious rhetoric of self-determination, just as a tick box approach to 'learning about other cultures' is a counterproductive means to developing competence for working cross-culturally. My response in the gender and sexuality topic was to create a space where new meanings could be developed and attached to the terms 'gender and sexuality'. In so doing, my intent was that students would not only see not only the diverse enactments of gender and sexuality *within* western cultures, but that they could also place western expressions of gender and sexuality within a broader global framework that decentred the west without claiming to speak for the other.

Why this all matters is thus a very fair question to keep asking. For me, there lies a propensity within social work to believe that 'doing good' stems from 'meaning well'. As colonial, paternalistic, benevolent discourses about Indigenous people demonstrate, however, this is rarely the case. That the students I work with might possibly see themselves as both agents of change and potential weapons of oppression is thus, in my opinion, vital. And that they may challenge those they then work with to reconsider their own roles as agents of change and potential oppressors is equally important. That the contingency of western knowledge about gender and sexuality can be highlighted only to be decentred (but not replaced with a new, appropriated, centre) is thus perhaps the why that drives my teaching.

Concluding thoughts

To return to my opening narrative, it is useful to think again about how what was in effect a loss that I was voicing (albeit one that I accept as a fair piece of collateral damage on my behalf as a non-Indigenous person), can produce some sort of ethical response. How, in other words, do we recognise the loss experienced by another, without taking it as our own, or refusing it as not being our problem? And how do we at the same time create a space in which we can ethically speak of our own losses? Indigenous scholars and activists across Australia have repeatedly said that the process of reconciliation need not be one of guilt-mongering, nor need it be an act of contrition. Yet time and time again those on the left seem to act as though this is what is called for, and those on the right seem to rally against this alleged call. Instead, perhaps what is called for is a simultaneous recognition of what was lost, what remains, and what can even possibly be gained. In regards to the former, what was lost was the possibility of creating a nation founded upon a treaty that recognised and was principled by the sovereignty of Indigenous nations. What was lost (or more precisely, violently stolen) for Indigenous nations were lives, the effects of which continue. And what was lost for non-Indigenous people was the possibility of having a sense of belonging that isn't founded upon colonising violence. What remains, is the fact of Indigenous sovereignty, the fact of Indigenous ownership of land, the fact of racialised colonial hierarchies and their ongoing role in structuring the Australian nation, and the ongoing search for some way to call Australia home. As to what can be gained, this is perhaps the hardest to answer. For my journey around Goolwa, what I gained was the possibility of envisioning a life in which a nice neat tick box isn't the desirable outcome. Owning one's self, being one's self to the exclusion of others, that is but one way of being. Gaining a sense of self that takes into account one's own loss, and that is indeed accountable for the loss of others, might be something worth having, even if it requires a radical decentring of the non-Indigenous self and the ways of being that inform it.

References

ABC News. (2010) Ngarrindjeri in Symbolic Walk Across Hindmarsh Island Bridge. http://www.abc.net.au/news/stories/2010/07/06/2946354.htm [accessed 14 June 2011].

Ahmed, S. (2004a) Declarations of whiteness: The non-performativity of anti-racism. *Borderlands ejournal*, 3. http://www.borderlands.net.au/vol3no2_2004/ahmed_declarations.htm [accessed 14 June 2011].

Ahmed, S. (2004b) *The Cultural Politics of Emotion*. London: Routledge.

Ahmed, S. (2006) The non-performativity of anti-racism. *Borderlands ejournal*, 5. http://www.borderlands.net.au/vol5no3_2006/ahmed_nonperform.htm [accessed 14 June 2011].

Brown, K. (2004) 'Sistergirls' – Stories from Indigenous Australian transgender people. *Aboriginal and Islander Health Worker Journal*, 28: 25–27.

Brown, K. (2005) 'Sistergirls' – Stories from Indigenous Australian transgender people documentary.

Chow, R. (1994) 'Where have all the natives gone?' In A. Bammer (Ed.), *Displacements: Cultural Identities in Question* (pp. 125–151). Bloomington, IN: Indiana University Press.

Coleman, D. (2010) '*Mazin' Grace*: Transformation through an Aboriginal literary text. Paper presented at the *Future Stories/Intimate Histories Symposium*, Adelaide, SA, 10 December.

Crenshaw, K. (1991) Mapping the margins: Intersectionality, identity politics, and violence against women of color. *Stanford Law Review*, 43: 1241–1299.

Curt, B. (1994) *Textuality and Tectonics*. London: Taylor and Francis.

Epple, C. (1998) Coming to terms with Navajo nádleehí: A critique of *berdarche*, 'gay', 'alternate gender', and 'two spirit'. *American Ethnologist*, 25: 267–290.

Fanon, F. (1967) *Black Skin, White Masks*. New York: Grove Press.

Huggins, J. and Saunders, K. (1993) Defying the ethnographic ventriloquists: Race, gender and the legacies of colonialism. *Lilith*, 8: 60–70.

Kurtzer, S. (2003) 'Wandering girl: Who defines "authenticity" in Aboriginal literature'. In M. Grossman (Ed.), *Blacklines: Contemporary Critical Writing by Indigenous Australians* (pp. 181–188). Melbourne, VIC: Melbourne University Press.

Moreton-Robinson, A. (2003) 'I still call Australia home: Indigenous belonging and place in a white postcolonizing society'. In S. Ahmed, C. Castañeda, A. Fortier and M. Sheller (Eds), *Uprootings/Regroundings: Questions of Home and Migration* (pp. 131–149). Oxford: Berg.

Moreton-Robinson, A. (2004) The possessive logic of patriarchal white sovereignty: The high court and the Yorta Yorta decision. *Borderlands e-journal*, 3.

Nicolacopoulos, T. and Vassilacopoulos, G. (2004) 'Racism, foreigner communities and the onto-pathology of white Australian subjectivity'. In A. Moreton-Robinson (Ed.), *Whitening Race: Essays in Social and Cultural Criticism* (pp. 32–47). Canberra: Aboriginal Studies Press.

Nicoll, F. (2004) 'Reconciliation in and out of perspective: White knowing, seeing, curating and being at home in and against Indigenous sovereignty'. In A. Moreton-Robinson (Ed.), *Whitening Race: Essays in Social and Cultural Criticism* (pp. 17–31). Canberra, ACT: Aboriginal Studies Press.

Ravenscroft, A. (2003) A picture in black and white: Modernism, postmodernism and the scene of 'race'. *Australian Feminist Studies*, 18: 233–244.

Riggs, D. W. (2004) 'Idealising place: Art, appropriation and the "pre-colonial landscape" '. In B. Wadham and S. Schech (Eds), *Placing Race and Localising Whiteness* (pp. 123–132). Adelaide: Flinders University Press.

Riggs, D. W. (2009) The ground upon which we stand: Reading sexuality *through* race. *Lesbian and Gay Psychology Review*, 10: 42–46.

Riggs, D. W. (2010) On accountability: Towards a white middle-class queer 'post identity politics identity politics'. *Ethnicities*, 10: 344–357.

Rosenstreich, G. (2007) 'The mathematics of diversity training: Multiplying identities, adding categories and intersecting discrimination'. In A. Broden and P. Mecheril (Eds), *Re-Präsentationen: Dynamiken der migrationsgesellschaft [Re-Presentations: Dynamics of the Migration Society]* (pp. 131–159). Düsseldorf: IDA NRW.

Schwab, R. G. (2006) *Indigenous Participation in Higher Education: Culture, Choice and Human Capital Theory*. CAEPR Discussion Paper No. 122. Canberra, ACT: Centre for Aboriginal Economic Policy Research, The Australian National University.

Sharma, S. (2006) Teaching diversity – Im/possible pedagogy. *Policy Futures in Education*, 4: 203–216.

Thomas, G. (2007) *The Sexual Demon of Colonial Power: Pan-African Embodiment and Erotic Schemes of Empire*. Bloomington, IN: Indiana University Press.

Thornley, J. (2008) Island home country. *Anandi Films*.

Torgovnick, M. (1990) *Gone Primitive: Savage Intellects, Modern Lives*. Chicago: University of Chicago Press.

13
Knowing Your Way Within and Across Classed Spaces: The (Re)making and (Un)doing of Identities of Value Within Higher Education in the UK

Michelle Addison

Introduction

Asking what exactly work is, where it takes place, who does it and for what benefits is a complex minefield raising concerns about the construction, recognition and remuneration of labour, implicating class positioning and power relations. Despite this, current debates about identity arguably place work itself as peripheral to how people now make sense of their lives (Kirk and Wall, 2011); some argue that individuals are no longer fixed or defined by the work that they do, instead being free to construct their identities. Yet, as has been widely highlighted, distinctions based on ethnicity, sexuality, class, disability, gender, age and religion are increasingly important in defining the role of 'worker' (Adkins, 2004; McDowell, 2008; Taylor, 2009, 2011).

In this chapter, I offer a discussion about the construction of and performance (mis)alignments in employee identities, located within a UK-based Russell Group higher education institution (HEI). In this Economic and Social Research Council (ESRC) funded study, I draw on qualitative accounts with employees about their attempts to 'fit in' with the circulated neoliberal image of the institutional brand constituted via vibrant, aspirational, 'complex and diverse' (University Vision 2021; http://www.ncl.ac.uk/documents/vision2021.pdf), 'well-rounded' and 'good' individuals (Taylor, 2008, p. 158). Employees are seen to accrue, produce and consume 'academic excellence' (university website, 2011)[1] for a price and a profit: 'knowledge has always been our business' (University Vision 2021). With this new business model is the imperative to cultivate a unique selling point and a differential advantage over wider competition. This chapter explores how institutional branding is embodied by employees both within and across classed spaces at work and around particular people, and crucially, how 'fitting in' in an 'elite' HEI is not straightforward. Although Evans (2010) did not focus on branding of HEIs in her study, her research about working-class girls studying at a comprehensive school in a South London Borough pays particular attention to feelings of being out of place inside 'elite' institutions; I too am also interested in emotion signposts discussed by my participants and how, as Evans discusses, they come to register as '. . . very much a part of the visibility of the exclusive past of these social spaces which were demonstrably not designed for women, ethnic minorities or working-class people' (2010, p. 58). In this chapter, I deploy Skeggs' class framework regarding the (re)production of 'subjects of value', enabling an exploration of how class is continually remade via different processes of 'inscription, exchange, evaluation and perspective' (2004, p. 3). Here I show how interviewees in my research discuss their own and others' classed performances of a hegemonically 'valued worker identity'.

For university employees, managing classed performances at work did reap rewards for some, as well as deeply felt injuries for others. I ask who can make claims to this value worker identity, and who is left out? In new times for higher education (HE), how does the intensified neoliberal turn to marketing and branding of the university institution affect the construction of worker identities? Within this, there are connections between the good and valued worker as problematically synonymous with a 'happy' worker. Performing 'value' and being the 'happy worker', even when one does not feel happy is a complicated task; as such, I give attention to this performative emotion practice, which papers over fissures between the self and the valued worker identity. The circulation of a 'valued worker identity' points to renewed inequalities where some employees find themselves in a good position to make claims to a valued worker identity, while others do not. What happens to those employees who can't, won't or don't 'fit'? Despite savage educational cut-backs, we are told that change represents increased opportunities for competition in a 'future' educational system, where adaptable employees can be flexible to market 'needs' and to intensified student expectations: the adaptable individual moves fluidly through space and place even in times of 'crisis' (Taylor, 2009, 2011).

The centrality of the agentic, choosing individual has been queried as a site, and subject, of renewed sources of exclusion and inequalities

(Adkins, 2002). In research on leisure industries, Adkins (1994) discusses the performance of femininity in the workplace to illustrate how a reflexive orientation to gender, while supposedly eroding categories – given that both men and women are positioned as able to switch on or off a 'feminine performance' – actually serves to naturalise gender attributes of femininity to particular women, with some 'performances' going unrewarded. Reflexivity reconfigures classification processes, which, far from negating inequalities, serve to privilege the standpoint of the 'modern, reflexive, individual' as someone who not only knows the 'rules of the game' but also writes them. The problem, then, is that these technologies of knowing and 'telling the self' are made available to some bodies more than to others, legitimating a dichotomy between who is *knower* and what is *known* (Taylor, 2010). Therefore, only certain identities are configured as reflexive and it is these individuals who are made visible.

Social differences of class, gender, age and ethnicity are embodied in the workplace: processes of classification impact on not only *who* does what sort of waged work but also *what* kind of worker is valued (McDowell, 2008). Certain social attributes come to be mapped onto bodies, and it is the valuation of these inscriptions onto bodies in the workplace which is crucial in understanding divisions of labour and the positioning of certain people as more or less suitable for particular types of waged work, reproducing a 'hierarchy of suitability' and re-inscribing inequalities. Skeggs (1997, 2004) has developed a comprehensive framework for understanding how social distinctions, particularly class and gender, are sites of struggle and under constant production; I draw upon such ideas in this chapter on employee identity and performance (mis)alignments, as located within a UK-based Russell Group HEI.

Methods

This research draws on a small, preliminary, qualitative study of employees (n = 9) working at a Russell group HEI in the UK: (including an electrician, research manager, receptionist, liaison manager, business development manager, senior managers and a research associate) aged between 30 and 60 years old). This preliminary exploratory study feeds into a broader postgraduate study with a dataset of 31 interviews with employees working in four areas in this HEI (Estates, Management, Business Development and Academic). In this preliminary study, I use semi-structured interviews to explore how employees' make sense of workplace interactions and the emotional labour entailed. Back (2007) discusses how the researcher must learn to listen more carefully and astutely to what is being left out and unsaid in their contact with interviewees. This involves an 'openness'– a skill that the researcher has to work to cultivate. Certain people are able to weave a story through time and space with reflexive ease, and there are others who find telling the self more troubling. The latter are often omitted from research; it is the forgotten people, the erasure of those who don't come to 'count' for very much at all, the ordinary people, who Back marks out as the Sociologist's project (see also Taylor and Addison, 2009).

I endeavoured to pay attention to the voices of ordinary people, both those who have perhaps come to be positioned as 'elite' both reflexively and structurally in this HEI, as well as those who are smaller and somewhat marginalised. I paid close attention to the emotional signposts that guide their – and my own – stories. The locatedness of the researcher in space and history is also significant, Skeggs (1997, p. 18; Skeggs and Wood, 2009) argues that the researcher is not separate and removed from what is researched, being instead 'implicated in relations of knowledge'. While Skeggs supports and defends the role of experience in informing how theory comes to be constructed, she also notes the problems associated with experience as an analytical category in which being is assumed to equal knowing. Who gets to speak is already marked by the researcher. How participants in the research come to represent their experience is already located historically and spatially and, as such, some may not have the resources to be heard. In this study, employees were asked to self-define their class position using their own historicised 'schemes of perception' (Bourdieu, 1984, p. 373), meaning that both objective and subjective identifications with class similarities and differences are deployed in this study (Taylor, 2008): five participants identified as working-class and four as middle-class based variously on the respective values they personally inscribed regarding where they lived growing up; the jobs their parents did; their own jobs and educational attainment; their accent and way of dressing; knowledge of social and cultural practices, as well as their own values and beliefs. In asking participants in my study to talk about how they understand, negotiate, identify and resist class practices (social, cultural and economic) and how they permeate their own embodied histories I am mindful of Taylor's words of caution in her study of working-class lesbians' experiences of school: recalling memories about class can be a raw emotional process for participants and can impact on their sense of self and worth, bringing with it a renewed, and sometimes painful awareness of what is (im)possible and (un)achievable (2007, p. 350).

In doing my research, I also acknowledge that my own embodied history as a working-class woman who has lived all her life in the researched region has a bearing upon how I interpret my findings. Although I share some classed and classing 'schemes of perception' (Bourdieu, 1984, p. 373) and similar emotional experiences with the working-class participants in my study, I also wrestle with my advantaged position in accruing and producing knowledge vis-à-vis these interviews. My own situatedness as a postgraduate, and a previous employee, in this HEI increases my knowledge of and movement between classed spaces here, thus complicating my own positioning. My own positioning within this HEI is not straightforward but it has meant that I have been able to hear and observe how voices from some employees are sometimes overshadowed, forgotten or erased both during and after social relations with those in a position of power. It is these kinds of stories that touch on classed practices that I am particularly interested in and have guided my research.

Given the limited size of the sample, the findings here are only intended to be illustrative, serving to raise important questions about future directions of research inquiry regarding feelings, practices and identities of value within the workplace. The intention here is to draw attention to somewhat partial and incomplete accounts of otherwise unattainable access to supposedly 'ordinary', yet complex human experiences of 'fitting in' in the workplace.[2] So, while I am not deliberately leaving out other practices of inequality rooted in intersecting social differences (sexuality, race, disability, age, etc.), I am limited in the scope of my study and I am only in a position to argue that my research shows specifically that classed and gendered practices (talking posh, having the *right* knowledge, wearing the right clothes, moving comfortably between certain spaces and people) continue to reproduce the figure of the 'valued worker identity' in this HEI.

'Subjects of value' and the 'valued worker' in HE

Value is generated and attached to particular bodies and not others through differently legitimated symbolic systems, which enable some people to be recognised, accepted and marked as respectable, defining 'who can be known and how' (Skeggs, 2004). Identity is shaped by how we come to know and recognise value as it marks, sticks to and slips off some bodies as a classed and gendered process. Skeggs' (2004) framework focuses on processes of inscription, exchange, evaluation and perspective that constitute systems of classification. Perspectives on class are (re)produced across a variety of historical contexts and fields through different systems of knowledge: truth, representation, rhetoric and opinion. Perspective is a 'knowledge position' we adopt in relation to a particular issue or person; this is always about having a particular vantage point that adheres to a particular way of interpreting and representing people and/or events as they unfold (Skeggs, 2004). Dominant perspectives on class can come to eclipse all other perspectives and work to the benefit of particular groups of people. Processes of *exchange* are also examined in this framework: a relational transaction that generates value. How we come to generate value is central to understanding processes of classification such as class, gender and race; it is the role of relationships and perspectives that enable the generation of value in exchange to take place (Skeggs, 2004). By giving attention to exchange, consciousness in the systems of power that operate between people and groups is raised, highlighting how some come to extract value, be seen as valued and resist being deemed as valueless (Skeggs, 2004).

Some individuals resist the value that is ascribed to their bodily attributes, and thus challenge the dominant symbolic order. In Skeggs' study (1997), young working-class women were seen as wrong, failed and failing, negatively valued through hegemonic symbolic classification systems. Yet they made many attempts to contest negative valuations of their bodies as being naturally 'too fertile', 'too sexy', 'too excessive'; this resistance became more difficult when these negative valuations were institutionalised, authorised and legitimated across education, social welfare, the media and so on. This naturalisation and fixing of social differences makes it very difficult, if not impossible, to escape historical attributions and attachments. Acquiring the 'right' resources and mobilising these through the key mechanism of legitimation is important to the realisation of value. As McDowell notes in her studies of workplace performances, social difference is inscribed on particular bodies, recognised and valued to 'produce an embodied performance that meets the demands of employers' (2008, p. 49). These practices are not limited to the service sector (Adkins, 1994; Hochschild, 1983; Mann, 1999; McDowell, 2008) and are permeating knowledge-based organisations as they are transformed via a neoliberal economic policy: as Lynch notes 'universities have been transformed increasingly into powerful consumer-orientated corporate networks' (2006, p. 1) involving a manifest return to exclusivity and 'élitism' via 'marketisation and commercialisation' (2006, p. 2). Embodying what it means to be 'elite', as part of an emerging desirable 'worker identity' is problematic and hinges on how particular bodies are inscribed with value. The corporatisation of worker identity in HE is linked with the increasing strategic branding of these HEIs (Pettinger, 2004). In order to compete in a global marketplace for research funding, student admissions, citation listings, staff recruitment and Research Assessment Exercise placements, HEIs are tasked with establishing their unique selling points, captured in a corporate brand, in order to survive the twenty-first-century education cull (Chapelo, 2010; Hemsley-Brown and Goonawardana, 2007; Taylor, 2011).

In a time where the role of HE is changing and is subjected to intensified market forces and devastating cut-backs 'with the rise of the New Right, neoliberal agenda' (Lynch, 2006, p. 1), the impact these current changes are having on employees in the education sector is significant. The commodification of knowledge, and marketisation of education, explored through everyday practices in HEIs, produces a 'relatively silent colonisation of the hearts and mind of academics and students' and worryingly inculcates 'a deep alienation in the experience of constantly living to perform' (Lynch, 2006, p. 7). The ramifications of such a culture are wide and unrelenting, with HEIs announcing departmental closures, redundancy and withdrawals from areas of research in which they cannot be deemed 'excellent' (Watson, 2010). Academics are facing unprecedented colonisation of their roles as educators, researchers and public critics. This makes workers on lower-scales who don't 'perform' the 'successful academic' much more vulnerable, contradicting the idea of inclusivity, which positions the HE brand as a 'place for all' (Taylor, 2008, 2009). We must also consider the wider remit of staff who operate within a HEI. This culture of quantification, which divides the excellent HEIs from the supposedly *not* excellent, amounts to swift closures and redundancies that affect *all* staff, not just academics. This is not to say that academics are automatically positioned in HEIs as privileged workers and other employees are situated against them in a worse position; rather I would argue for a consideration of the differently pressurised workers in a new economy of appraisal and competition.

Leathwood and Hey (2009) are concerned that the emerging neoliberal culture effaces true value in HE, (re)producing an overly rationalised culture. Workers are constantly required to prove their value and worth by being productive successful employees; it is only particular bodies that are seen as able to fit with the neoliberal brand of HE at the expense of social differences, which is devalued as wrong rather than 'diverse'. There are many embodied forms of pain, pleasure and fear in HE (Leathwood and Hey, 2009; Taylor, 2009), as employees come to negotiate and resist new emerging workplace subjectivities that (mis)align with the HEI corporate brand and notion of the 'valued worker identity'. But what exactly is the corporate HE brand and how is it structured by and through the valued worker identity? Chapelo (2010) queries what constitutes a 'successful' brand among UK HEIs, looking at how institutions use branding to communicate a message about image and values in order to attract others to the institution and promote loyalty. Managing impressions of the university, that is, associations, emotions and what 'types' of people are linked to the university, in order to communicate a unified and recognisable message to others, is fundamentally the purpose of HEI branding (Bunzel, 2007; Taylor, 2008). The brand is deeply embedded in social relations, workplace practices and corporate structure, keeping legitimised notions about 'value' recirculating. People are very important to the constitution and circulation of the corporate brand message in HEIs; the value of the brand is to a large extent contingent on the person who is legitimated as suitable to fill the category of valued worker identity.

Interviewees discussed how they were expected to behave in this HEI. Ravi spoke with a certain confidence and knowledge about a way of 'doing things' here, an etiquette that is closely aligned with representing exclusivity, difference, even 'poshness' – an attribute that he feels is constitutive of the university brand:

> Here, right at the university there is etiquette, . . . you have this kind of *posh* brand you see, and you're trying to maintain this kind of *poshness* or, erm, the *value* of the brand. Because we want to rise *above* the rest. [. . .] you know, we are the *posher* brand, we have to maintain this integrity . . .
>
> (Ravi, Development Manager, middle-class)

This perspective on what comes to be valued and what is valueless circulates through different systems of knowledge of how to embody the 'good' and 'well-rounded' individual (Taylor, 2008, p. 158) within an HEI aspiring to capture in an all-encompassing brand 'academic excellence' and 'elite' status (Evans, 2010; Lynch, 2006). Ravi speaks from a position of power in which he claims that *being* posh is integral to the intrinsic value of the brand, both how it is perceived by co-workers and by potential customers, clients and the general public. However, embodying this poshness and enacting this etiquette is not a position that is accessible to everyone in this workplace. As we will see later, not everyone is able to represent the posh brand and make claims to a valued worker identity as their bodies become laden with differently valued inscriptions, which position them awkwardly in a very complex class system that establishes their worth as individuals against others and relevance to the university brand of poshness.

Exchanges of value

Being able to take up a valued position in this workplace is not straightforward. In my study, processes of inscription repeatedly attach value to employees' bodies in classed and gendered ways, especially when wearing what was deemed to be inappropriate clothing. Ravi, in conveying the symbolic value of this HEI's brand, makes comparisons with the brand 'Jack Wills', which is a high-end, expensive clothing and home ware line marketed at a younger, affluent 'university crowd'. Ravi describes his workplace as being akin to a 'Jack Wills dressing room'. Importantly, the circulation of what comes to represent value is reproduced across time and embedded in culture; not everyone in this HEI is included in the metaphoric 'Jack Will's dressing room', with working-class women in particular marked out by scathing attacks on their inability to embody a valued appearance or to represent the desired university branded message. Ravi pays particular attention to how working-class women come to represent what not to *be* (Lawler, 1999); he subjects certain female employees to processes of surveillance of a highly sexualised nature, marking certain women as 'whores' because they have come to work in the 'wrong' clothes that would be suitable in the 'Bigg Market', a highly classed and denigrated leisure space in Newcastle upon Tyne's city centre, attracting a supposedly working-class clientele:

> 'Look honey, look in the mirror in the morning and if you look as though you can fit in in the Bigg Market on a Friday night, then you are wearing the wrong clothes to come to work in', you can't say that here. If you say that here, that person can take you straight to HR, cos you're practically calling them a whore.
>
> (Ravi, Development Manager, middle-class)

Being able to identify those who do not belong in the HEI is a powerful position that Ravi lays claim to. He does note that because of gender and sexual discrimination policies regulating these judgements, he has to be discreet about how he impresses these views on others.

Other ways of marking out employees and so shaping, recognising and making claims to the 'valued worker' was through accent. Jill, a research manager, draws attention to the performative aspects of trying to inhabit a valued position; she describes how she consciously changes her voice to 'put on', as she says, a *posh* accent in order to 'fit in' with wider expectations of what practices are valued in this workplace. Interestingly, Jill also gives attention to those who cannot authentically *do* a posh accent, marking these performances out as flawed and *failing*. The complexity of this performance is conveyed as Jill both values the 'posh accent' but openly admits that she has to 'put it on' – a required class performance that is both valued and pretentious. Although she does not refuse this performance, instead actively participating in its reproduction, she conveys a sense of ambivalence about 'losing' her normal accent and reshaping it to converge with people whom she recognises to be powerful and important in this HEI. Making visible these systems of power that operate in exchanges between people is important in understanding where people come to be positioned within a hierarchy of worth (Skeggs, 2004). This is exemplified in the scenario between Jill and a senior management figure outlined below; this conversation attaches value to particular bodies and voices, reproducing a hierarchy of worth in the workplace

> ...this is *totally* wrong...I know it's wrong. But say if it is somebody who is say the Pro-vice Chancellor or something, I would say 'oh, heelloo' (laughter)! Ridiculous! [...] And I know, a *local* accent, some people think that that is a *dreadful*, dreadful accent (laughter) [...] And you feel that that's the appropriate thing to do...cos they're important and they speak 'Queen's English', you know, that's what you have to aspire to, cos that's what they want to hear. [...] I know *I* do it, and I *know* I do it, I don't purposefully do it, but I *know* I'm doing it. I could *hear* myself! I wasn't my *normal* 'local accent, it was...er...trying to be posh, and I think when you sometimes hear certain people doing that, it sounds terrible! (laughter)
>
> (Jill, Research Manager, working-class)

Ravi talked about his surprise at encountering co-workers with these localised accents at this HEI and positioned them outside of the valued worker identity. Certain accents were seen as not 'right' and never would be; one particular broad, local accent in the area was perceived as 'dreadful', 'basic', not 'well-read', 'weird' and not 'fitting in' with the university 'posh brand'. Joan, a receptionist, similarly describes how an employee would be perceived as failing if they spoke with a strong accent and dialect. Like the working-class women in Skeggs' study

(1997), Joan too has acquired knowledge of the systems of classification that may harm how she is viewed at work; she complexly identifies as working-class but *knows* that there are aspects of being working-class that do not have transferable or recognisable value in workplace exchanges with other employees, and so she painfully tries to lose or make invisible these particular classed attributes. Joan goes on to describe how being a valued employee requires acting 'middle-class' in order to convey feelings of confidence, entitlement and self-assurance. Joan specifically makes reference to the valuelessness of working-class accents, which she believes to be particularly evident among female cleaners at the HEI who did not *know* how they should act. Joan also talks about the inappropriateness of other co-workers who continue to use their valueless accent as being resistant and subversive of the 'good impression' they should, like her, be making. As someone who also has a 'local, working-class accent', Joan somewhat humorously advised me to improve myself and 'get on' by demonstrating the 'correct' embodiment of a valued worker to save me from making the same mistakes as some of her co-workers. In equipping me with knowledge of the classificatory system in operation at this HEI, Joan provided a 'what-not-to-do':

> If you go into work and go 'Why aye hinny, how ya dyin like?' (laughs) 'Alreet pet?' ... it doesn't give a good impression. You have to say, 'Hello there, how can I help you?'
>
> (Joan, Receptionist, working-class)

Even with such explicit, 'helpful' guidance, it is important to acknowledge that not every individual who has a local accent, like my own, for example, is always positioned as working-class. Some very middle-class people of course, do have regional accents – so there are important class slippages here in that two people can share a very similar accent and be classed very differently depending on how they are each positioned in relation to other forms of class inscription, for example, such as clothes, spatial belonging, and knowledge of the operating classification systems. Class is not simply or wholly signified by 'local' accents but rather, it is coupled with other ways of reading and doing class (Taylor and Addison, 2009).

Resistance and surveillance

Employees who embodied an undesirable working-class upbringing, signalled by their accent, clothes, gestures and knowledge of workplace practices, at times laboured to lose this classed identity by neutralising an accent, dressing 'up', and feigning cultural knowledge. These practices were subject to scrutiny and were sometimes viewed as failing, or via a thinly veiled humour. Similarly, the Jack Wills brand (http://www.jackwills.com/Jack/Brand.aspx), which Ravi compared with the HEI brand, also deploys similar judgements about 'copycats' that are not the 'real deal'; this practice of copying or counterfeiting is tightly policed and marked out as fraudulent and inferior. This policing of the integrity of the brand is also noticeable within this HEI, in that employees talked about looking out for counterfeiters and copycats among their co-workers.

Nonetheless, some participants were able to resist valuelessness. Tony talks about feeling pressured and coerced to work on himself in order to be recognised as at least attempting to be seen as a valued worker. Tony spoke about this as being a fruitless practice as he would never be able to escape 'who he is'; he was resistant to investing energy in trying to be more 'middle-class', a performative practice that was at odds with his classed history and would mean 'not being true' to himself. He recognised that endeavours to be 'something that he was not' is signposted by 'bad feelings' and generates further bad feeling. This refusal to work on himself so that he would be seen as a valued worker and be a happy match with the HEI brand was often met with conflict as other co-workers sought to coerce, or police his behaviours, marking him as a 'troublemaker' who was upsetting the happy equilibrium sought by and for good, 'valued workers'. For them, being a valued worker also meant looking like a 'happy worker' and appearing happy was read as being morally good:

Tony: Well, if you go against the grain ... If somebody said to me 'ah, yes you may be right but, I'd rather you did it this way, I'd say, well no, I can't. Cos if I was forced into doing that I wouldn't feel true to myself, would I?' [...] I would feel as though I would be letting myself down, what's the other word ... well, just not being true to yourself.

Michelle: So if you are not true to yourself, how are you feeling?

Tony: I would feel *baaaaadddd. Wouldn't I?*

Michelle: How would your body feel?

Tony: It would probably play on my conscience. And I wouldn't be able to sleep ... if I'd ... done something against the grain.

(Tony, Electrician, working-class)

Some working-class participants spoke of becoming more practiced over time at presenting valued classed performances in the workplace; these employees tended to have worked at the HEI for a considerable duration. Eve describes how trying to appear to be a happy worker in her previous role at the HEI was a pretentious activity that left her feeling drained and unfulfilled. She was able to negotiate her struggles and reject her accrued bad feelings by leaving her job altogether in search of another, an option not open to some workers faced with the same pressures to work on the self. In telling her story about resisting pretentious performative practices, she also makes a claim to a valued subject position that is perceived as authentic and sincere:

> Oh, it's never comfortable acting! *Bloody* hate it, you know? But er…I think it became a self preservation thing. Cos you know, I didn't want to take all that baggage home, on a night time, you know? Cos I had another life, you know. But you know, I can't be doing the acting, no. So there you go. I really, *really*, hate it and I just like to deal with my reality. So I am not at all comfortable with it. But thankfully it didn't last long cos I made a determined effort to get out of it.
>
> (Eve, Project Accounts Manager, working-class)

Classed and gendered performances of how 'not to be' the valued worker are also captured in Joan's discussion of female cleaners working in this HEI; these women are marked as working-class for having a strong accent, smoking ('fag hanging out of her mouth'), being over familiar with clients and behaving without middle-class manners of politeness – and ultimately *being* a cleaner. Joan recognised that these women would be seen by the 'high powered, company manager' as out of place and rude, demonstrating classed practices that would be regarded as disrespectful to the manager's entitled high 'status'. Joan feels that this process of judging working-class women, and ascribing value that is read off their bodies and behaviours by company managers, positions them as always unable to convey the *right,* middle-class image constitutive of the valued worker at this organisation. As we saw earlier, Joan also takes up a working-class identity and is conscious that she too may be seen in the same way as the working-class cleaners, a 'misfit' with the corporate brand; she conscientiously works on her presentation of self in the office, painfully subscribing to and reproducing a classificatory system that values more middle-class practices in order to consistently try to inhabit a valued subject position at work that is uncomfortably always out of her reach. These efforts to inhabit the valued worker identity, for Joan, requires almost constant surveillance of and work on the way she tries to be seen by others when she is on display as a receptionist at work:

> ...[the cleaner] wouldn't be there long because they would have to give a certain *impression* at reception...er...whereas some people might find it funny, if you get somebody from a company, a company manager...who is high powered and er...turns over millions of pounds a day...they wouldn't expect you to act like that at reception *at all*. They would want somebody who is going to say 'Ah, so you want to see such and such, I shall phone them now...would you like to take a seat? [...] To them...it is *their* status that they feel they are entitled to because of their standards in life. They wouldn't be expecting someone with a fag end hanging out their mouth, you know, like 'here's ya cuppa', and chuck it at them.
>
> (Joan, Receptionist, working-class)

Symbolic violence and the 'happy worker'

The appearance of being a happy worker was repeated over again in this study; this emotion framework deployed practices that paper over any disjunctures between the self and the valued worker identity. The participants talked about feeling shame, ridicule and a sense of being made invisible; they felt as though they were judged as being without *worth* as a result of falling short of an enforced valued worker identity, this being a form of symbolic violence. *Being* happy hides the symbolic violence. Some of the participants in my study talked about a need to appear to be the 'happy worker', even when they did not feel this way, because they recognised that this was the good, legitimated and approved position to occupy within the HEI. I would suggest that performing happiness disguises – and embeds – these feelings of shame and indignity, what Tony calls 'bad feelings', which arise out of not being true to oneself and instead being judged by co-workers for not quite successfully or convincingly inhabiting the 'right way of being and doing' (Bourdieu, 1983, p. 511).

In Ravi's discussion below, he draws attention to his ability to move in and across differently classed and gendered spaces that are policed in terms of how the employee is expected to dress, talk and behave around certain people, in order to get 'the transaction done', which he confidently and assuredly delivers. In what he recognises as middle-class space, Ravi talked about being 'proper' in terms of politeness and respect, whereas in a working-class space he reported being able to 'F' and blind with another co-worker quite comfortably without fear of repercussions. This sets Ravi at a powerful reflexive advantage, comfortable with his position in work as the embodiment of the happily valued worker, compared with other employees in the organisation such as Joan who has no choice but to be 'Mrs Nice', that is 'Mrs Happy', all the time even when she is disrespected and de-valued in her role:

> I am a fish that can swim in any waters. The thing is... is that I've worked in... different places in industry... when I have sat across tables from Chief Executives, to working in organisations on the shop floor all the time... And you *learn* to go up and down to each level that you need to. And genuinely, I learned... that if I need to... in order to communicate with somebody I need to 'F' and blind then... if that's what it needs... If I need to be *proper* with somebody I will be, it's whatever gets the transaction done at the end of the day.
>
> (Ravi, Development Manager, middle-class)

Ravi is able to move with reflexive ease within and across classed and gendered spaces and around particular people because of how his embodied identity is inscribed with value, coupled with his accrued knowledge of how things are done around here. However, as we see in Joan's account, she is positioned much more rigidly within the HEI. Joan talks about being expected to learn how to embody the valued worker as soon as employment is taken up at the university and for her, unlike Ravi, these workplace practices are non-negotiable, even if she does at times feel like crying or 'being nasty back', she cannot. She must be nice, she must at least look happy:

> You have to act... in a professional manner... that you *learn*... when you first start working there. So you learn the right way to dress, the right way to greet people in that office environment and that's part of controlling your emotions as well. So if someone is nasty to you at the reception window, which has happened before, you can't be nasty back. You have to be Mrs Nice, *all* the time.
>
> (Joan, 45, Receptionist, working-class)

The importance of at least *trying* to appear to be happy at work is described by Tony, who comments on how a female colleague refused to laugh at his jokes, a practice he often engaged in, feeling that this helped others to forget or refuse the hurt felt through inequalities, stereotypes and injustices at work. Tony felt he was helping others to just *be* happy and he felt affronted and hurt when this female colleague refused to even pretend to appear happy and engage in *his* subversive practices through humour. To him, this co-worker demonstrated a muted and serious disposition, which he described as typical emotional behaviour of women who were menstruating. There was also an element of provocation embedded in the retelling of this story to me, a female researcher. It felt as though I was being 'set up' by Tony so that I would respond in an emotionally defensive way in order to vindicate his judgements and positioning of women as emotionally reactive, overly sensitive and 'hormonal'. This is a reversal of the trouble maker, one who refuses to play a different kind of game at work aimed at putting on a 'brave' face and seeing the 'funny side' of inequality:

> Tony: (laughter) well, normally we would laugh and carry on about it. Or either she was under pressure, or under stress or whatever . . . she might not have seen the funny side of it. But women are funny creatures, aren't they?
>
> Michelle: Why? Why is that?
>
> Tony: (laughter) cos they go all funny (laughter) *hormonal*, that's what I'm on about! (he gestures at the researcher)
>
> Michelle: Hormonal? An interesting word, what do you mean?
>
> Tony: Well you know what I mean! (laughter)
>
> Michelle: Honestly, I don't . . .
>
> Tony: (laughter) when their hormones are all to pot. (laughter) You might as well . . . (laughter) . . . be talking to a brick wall when a woman . . . when a woman is on her period! (laughter)
>
> (Tony, Electrician, working-class)

In my study Tony occupied a very complex and awkward position where he openly refused to take up middle-class practices that constituted the valued worker identity enforced by his bosses. Yet he tried to mend the tensions this refusal gave rise to among his co-workers by trying to use humour to help make people happy, thus making claims to a subversive position of value within the organisation. An open rejection by others of his attempts to use humour to ease tension and take up a position of value, like the female co-worker above, caused him deeply felt hurt, which he struggled to make sense of ('well, women are funny creatures, aren't they?'). Tony talked about being on good terms with many of his female colleagues, some of them he called friends, who he enjoyed talking with, 'winding up', and sharing personal stories to pass the time and make them laugh; however, on this occasion he told me that his jokes based on 'harmless', mild sexist stereotypes ('well it's cos you're a woman!') upset another female co-worker who had confided in him that she was experiencing a difficult time doing her job and fitting in at work. Afterwards, when he had learned of her feelings about what he had said, he was sincerely troubled by this, saying that 'I really never meant to hurt anyone.'

Conclusions

Many researchers have raised important concerns regarding the intensified marketisation of HEIs as a revitalised neoliberal turn bringing forth an 'academic capitalism'. Watson (2010) demonstrates how the emphasis placed on discourses of 'excellence', 'transparency', 'accountability' and research 'impact' is reshaping the construction of successful HE identities in light of new branding exercises within institutions (see Taylor, 2008; Wakeling, 2010). There is continued questioning of our investments in particular notions of the 'successful academic', asking, what does this take and who can do it? (Hey, 2004 and Taylor, 2009). A successful academic is constituted via dress, a way of being, publications, teaching, ranking in the citation index and winning grants, to name but a few. The neoliberal, competitive working culture in HEIs in the UK also impacts on the wider remit of staff, from receptionists to cleaners. Employees are being forced to align themselves with their HEI's strategic, market objectives, in order to more closely 'fit' with the corporatised brand; this branding gives precedence to a hegemonic, employee identity that values and fits with a particular 'posh' performance, a position, as we have seen, that is only available to particular bodies and not others.

As a new employee, one inherits a brand package that instructs one how embodied performances *should* be done in this particular space (Pettinger, 2004); this can sometimes be at odds with one's own embodied history of class and gender. The valued worker identity endures as employees police practices, monitoring their own performances as well as others to mark out those who are counterfeiters, fakes and failing.

This ensures that the 'integrity' of the HEI brand continues as viably 'posh' and of value even in precarious times.

Making claims to a position of a 'valued worker' involves classed and gendered practices that some employees were able to enact with ease, whereas others found this activity more troubling. Some employees developed subversive strategies as a coping mechanism; they refused the classed and gendered position of the 'valued worker identity' and used humour to claim a differently valued subject position, whereas others left their job altogether. For other employees, attempting to inhabit the role of the valued worker identity, even when this became shameful and uncomfortable and generated 'bad feelings', was their only option. Showing these 'bad feelings' at work was not usually acceptable. Instead, some workers became adept at papering over these disjunctures, disguising 'bad feelings' with performances of the happy worker, even when all was not well.

Performing 'value' or being the happy worker, even when one does not feel happy, is a complicated task indeed. It is when this performance of the happy worker becomes obligatory that acts of symbolic violence can be very damaging and concentrated on particular people at work who are unable to inhabit the valued worker identity. Some of the female, working-class employees in my study felt they did not have the same power as other more middle-class employees to negotiate or refuse classed and classing practices; these women talked about continuing to perform happiness around certain people even when bad feelings are accrued. This is not to deny that these struggles do not lead to other acts of subversion (e.g. Tony's satirical humour; Eve leaving her job). However, many inequalities and injustices based on classed and gendered practices of dress, accent and knowledge of how to be in the workplace are made invisible by the compulsion to always subscribe to a narrative of the 'happy worker = good worker' even when one is *not* happy: not many people want to be the unhappy *troublemaker* who challenges why they are experiencing complex feelings about inequality at work (Ahmed, 2004, 2010). People are differently positioned to be able to claim this valued worker identity in what McDowell (2008) calls a 'hierarchy of suitability'; some people take up this identity comfortably, while others experience hurt, tension and refusals and accrue 'bad feelings'. These 'bad feelings' are not permissible at work, they equate with the bad worker who is out to make trouble, so the narrative of the happy worker is invoked and aligned with being good: being good at work means being *happy* (Ahmed, 2010). I would question whether the good worker actually feels happy and what kind of person is positioned as a troublemaker if they draw attention to their experience of being unhappy at work. While some employees in this study such as Ravi, a self identifying middle-class male, find themselves in a good position to make claims to a valued worker identity, happily fitting in with ease and moving within classed and gendered practices, others such as Joan, a self-identifying working-class woman, do not and subsequently find themselves unhappily pushed to the margins through managing and policing their workplace performances. Eve, working-class, stated that finding another job was easier than trying to force herself to be happy and fit in here. Tony, also working-class, felt situated in an awkward position of resistance and as a 'troublemaker' because he was not happy with or willing to enact the figure of the 'good' and 'valued' worker. Others, like the spectre of the female, working-class cleaner were ambivalently 'fixed' in place with little value attached to their worker identity – nobody I interviewed knew whether these particular women were actually happy in this HEI and whether it even mattered. These practices of exclusion and effacement of particular individuals, produce the 'different subjects' of education, as a classed and gendered embodied encounter.

Notes

1. For confidentiality the specific name of the university has been removed: such phrasing is nonetheless apparent in a range of university websites.
2. This study has abided with the ethical standards of the Economic and Social Research Council and the British Sociological Association; all names in this research have been replaced with pseudonyms and ages have been marginally changed.

References

Adkins, L. (1994) *Gendered Work: Sexuality, Family and the Labour Market*. Bristol: Open University Press.

Adkins, L. (2002) *Revisions: Gender and Sexuality in Late Modernity*. Philadelphia, PA and Buckingham: Open University Press.

Adkins, L. (2004) Passing on feminism: From consciousness to reflexivity. *European Journal of Women's Studies*, 11(4): 427–444.

Ahmed, S. (2004) *The Cultural Politics of Emotion*. Edinburgh: Edinburgh University Press.

Ahmed, S. (2010) *The Promise of Happiness*. Durham, NC: Duke University Press.

Back, L. (2007) *The Art of Listening*. Oxford and New York: Berg.

Bourdieu, P. (1983) The field of cultural production, or: The economic world reversed. *Poetics*, 12: 311–356.

Bourdieu, P. (1984) [1977] *Distinction*. London: Routledge and Kegan Paul.

Bunzel, N. (2007) Universities sell their brands. *Journal of Product and Brand Management*, 16(2): 152–153.

Chapelo, C. (2010) What defines 'successful' university brands? *International Journal of Public Sector Management*, 23(2): 169–183.

Evans, S. (2010) 'Becoming "somebody": Examining class and gender through higher education'. In Y. Taylor (Ed.), *Classed Intersections: Spaces, Selves and Knowledges* (pp. 53–71). Surrey and Burlington: Ashgate.

Hemsley-Brown, J. and Goonawardana, S. (2007) Brand harmonisation in the international higher education market. *Journal of Business Research*, 60: 942–948.

Hey, V. (2004) Perverse pleasures – Identity work and the paradoxes of the greedy institutions. *Journal of International Women's Studies*, 5(3): 33–43.

Hochschild, A. (1983) *The Managed Heart: Commercialisation of Human Feeling*. Berkeley, CA, Los Angeles, CA and London: University of California Press.

Kirk, J. and Wall, C. (2011) *Work and Identity: Historical and Cultural Contexts*. Houndsmill, Basingstoke and Hampshire: Palgrave Macmillan.

Lawler, S. (1999) 'Getting out and getting away': Women's narratives of class mobility. *Feminist Review*, 63(3): 3–24.

Leathwood, C. and Hey, V. (2009) Gender/ed discourse and emotional sub-texts: Theorising emotion in UK higher education. *Teaching in Higher Education*, 14(4): 429–440.

Lynch, K. (2006) Neo-liberalism and marketisation: The implications for higher education. *European Educational Research Journal*, 5(1): 1–17.

Mann, S. (1999) Emotion at work: To what extent are we expressing, suppressing, or faking it? *European Journal of Work & Organizational Psychology*, 8(3): 347–369.

McDowell, L. (2008) *Working Bodies: Interactive Service Employment and Workplace Identities*. Oxford: Wiley-Blackwell.

Pettinger, L. (2004) Brand culture and branded workers: Service work and aesthetic labour in fashion retail. *Consumption, Markets and Cultures*, 7(2): 165–184.

Skeggs, B. (1997) *Formations of Class and Gender: Becoming Respectable*. London: Sage.

Skeggs, B. (2004) *Class, Self and Cultures*. London: Routledge.

Skeggs, B. and Wood, H. (2009) 'The transformations of intimacy: Classed identities in the moral economy of reality television'. In M. Wetherall (Ed.), *Identity in the 21st Century: New Trends in Changing Times* (pp. 231–249). Houndsmill, Basingstoke, Hampshire: Palgrave Macmillan.

Taylor, Y. (2007) Brushed behind the bike shed: Working-class lesbian experiences of school. *British Journal of Sociology of Education*, 28(3): 349–362.

Taylor, Y. (2008) Good students, bad pupils: Constructions of 'aspiration', 'disadvantage' and social class in undergraduate-led widening participation work. *Educational Review*, 60(2): 155–168.

Taylor, Y. (2009) Facts, fictions, identity constrictions: Sexuality, gender and class in higher education. *Lesbian and Gay Psychological Review*, 10(1), Special Issue: 38–47.

Taylor, Y. (2010) Stories to tell? Reflexive (dis)engagements and (de)legitimized selves. *Qualitative Inquiry*, 1–9: 633–641.

Taylor, Y. (2011) *Letter Home? Distances and Proximities.* http://sociologyandthecuts.wordpress.com/?s= letter+home

Taylor, Y. and Addison, M. (2009) (Re)constituting the past, (re)branding the present and (re)imagining the future: Women's spatial negotiation of gender and class. *Journal of Youth Studies*, 12(5): 563–578.

Wakeling, P. (2010) 'Is there such thing as a working-class academic?' In Y. Taylor (Ed.), *Classed Intersections: Spaces, Selves, Knowledges* (pp. 35–52). Surrey and Burlington: Ashgate.

Watson, C. (2010) Accountability, transparency, redundancy: Academic identities in an era of 'excellence'. *British Educational Research Journal*, 37(6): 955–971.

14
Facts, Fictions, Identity Constrictions: Sexuality, Gender and Class in Higher Education

Yvette Taylor

In this chapter I aim to provide some (personal, professional) insights into the negotiation of Higher Education (HE), combining classed, gendered and sexual positionings as significant to this experience. I have been somewhat guarded in writing this piece, in thinking about whether it would be a useful addition or a personalised 'complaint', a case of another academic taking up too much space (Taylor, 2010a). In still struggling with (personal and research) articulations, I'd like to explore the 'critical differentials' (Gabb, 2004) in processes and experiences of being at and becoming in university (Evans, 2010; Taylor, 2011; Taylor and Scurry, 2011; Evans, this volume). Which versions of ourselves (sexual or classed) get to be, and get to speak: who can have voice and legitimacy within this (Adkins, 2002; Skeggs, 2002)? My concern is in making visible varied stories as well as the absence of (legitimate) tales, where the ordinariness of privilege can also be made evident in such articulations and silences (Taylor, 2009). I aim to focus upon the substantive – and frequently neglected – issue of intersecting sexual and classed lives. Identifying as working-class and 'queer' in academia is a fraught and challenging process (Binnie, 2011; Taylor, 2005a, b); such challenges, can never fully be achieved or completed as (only) 'mine' if the potential to situate claims beyond the personal (and beyond identity) is taken seriously. But how to take these claims and conditions seriously? Higher educational institutions (HEIs) produce guidelines on 'dealing with' and even capitalising upon diversity (frequently invoking legal compulsion, employment worth and cultural variety) (see Ahmed, this volume). This is arguably heightened in the current UK educational climate[1] where elite institutions may now be in the curious position of marketing their own 'elitism' *and* 'diversity', while post-1992 institutions are positioned as 'failing' to deliver on what is now a strange brand of 'diverse' elitism (Taylor, 2011, 2012). In being that thing (diversely 'elite'?), I was recently asked to provide my 'diversity story' by a lesbian, gay, bisexual and transgender (LGBT) staff-student group, for the purposes of university marketing: 'let them know we are here, we are queer!' But one may consider how many white, middle-class, middle-aged heterosexual men are approached in university branding of diversity. Even LGBT organisations can endorse an instrumental inclusion of diversity. 'Diversity' is seen to make 'good business sense for all employers, particularly when the economic climate is tougher,' (David Shields, Stonewall Director of Workplace Programmes, www.stonewall.org.uk). HEIs, as increasingly 'enterprising' seek out and sanction 'diversity' as an institutional capital, while effacing unequal experiences and institutional-interpersonal 'mis-fits'.

Many have pointed to the structuring of education as it solidifies, rather than challenges, social divisions. In referencing such research, and in combining this with personal positioning and tension, I seek to highlight the complexities of 'coming out' in relation sexuality, gender and class, where the constrictions of academia often mean that there is little space to do so. Being 'diverse' for and in the institution can be an awkward premium and a personalised pain, an enduring 'sore point' that harms while diversity is hastened as promise, cure and capital (Ahmed, this volume). This is my small attempt at highlighting disjunctures in diversity rhetorics and realities, in 'coming out' in academia, seeking and even disrupting (un)comfortable spaces.

Behind the university door

So – consider this:

A young female lecturer starting out in her career sits behind her closed office door (observe her dangling on the bottom rung of academia, while ambivalently hopeful, if not expectant or certain of upward climbs). While students bunch and buzz outside, emails are monotonously checked, ever received and she pauses to reflect upon the space she now inhabits with its various freedoms and constraints (swivel office chair, ok computer, not the biggest office ...). Snippets of student chatter is overheard; behind her door they are pausing over whether to choose her course this semester – who knows what she's really like (one of them, one of us)? How young is she (who does she think she is)? Where does she come from (funny accent)? And what about that hair cut, those clothes (a lesbian??!!). Suspicion, excitement and a dose of caution gather in the corridor; pens linger over her sign-up sheet – what have she and these students signed up for? An official 'diversity and equality' email arrives in her inbox, all mainstreamed and official. The university welcomes, actions, promises; an inclusive certainty, a new agenda, a line on 'sexual minorities'.... While she reads and searches, a voice from outside authoritatively declares 'She IS a lesbian'. Her course, herself – a matter of fact? A threat? An absence? What should she do? She opens the door, heads to the printer, picks up the email, and a few looks along the way...

Opening and closing those same academic doors, many feminist researchers have spoken about the ways that feminists frequently occupy an insider/outsider positioning within academia, often mapped out and connected by political and personal affiliations, pains and contradictions (Jackson, 2004). Diane Reay (1998) has, for example, detailed both the explicit and insidious markers of class within HE, generating a series of doubts and certainties in working-class and middle-class existences. Such class divisions cannot fit with the story of good diversity when the middle-class are the normative measure against which others are supposed to 'aspire' and move towards (Evans, 2010; Taylor, 2008). Other feminist writers have discussed such divisions and intersections, on being *Outside in the Teaching Machine* (Spivak, 1993) and *Labourers in the Knowledge Factory* (Tokarczyk and Fay, 1993), where academics from working-class backgrounds speak of being out of place, without space and unable to return 'home', actively forcing themselves to 'fit' in strange places (Hey, 2001, 2004; Skeggs, 1995, 1997; Wakeling, 2010).

Class is known materially, culturally and emotionally marked in embodied dispositions (see 'funny accent'), resources (economic, social and cultural capital), entitlements (expectations realised through resources) and knowingness (confidence and legitimacy). Classed intersections happen in the spaces we can or cannot occupy, the boundaries – geographical, material, emotional – regulating these, the rendering of people in or out of place and the productions of subjectivities and spatialities. In posing hard questions such as 'What (or who?) are we doing this for?' (Robinson and Ferfolja, 2001) and 'Who are you calling queer?' (Vicars, 2006), authors writing about sexuality in teaching contexts – like those writing about class – illustrate the damaging effects, of not quite belonging, alongside the authorisation of 'wounding words', 'failed' embodied performances and prevailing heteronormativity (Grace and Hill, 2001; Mintz and Rothblum, 1997). Attention to why, how, where and when class, gender and sexuality *still* matter brings into focus the structured, situational and intersectional nature of identity accomplishments and refusals within – and beyond – academia (Taylor, 2007). These facts of identity, experience and opportunity travel with us, allowing us to consume and take up space – some more readily or greedily than others.

Speaking of HE as a particularly greedy or demanding institution, Valerie Hey (2004) critically assesses regimes of knowledge production, distribution and control, where political and personal elements of identity (such as being a feminist, a lesbian, working-class) are erased, to be replaced by the demands of a 'productive' professional identity. In contrast, certain subjects are positioned as already 'fitting-in', entitled and mobile in relation to occupation choice and occupational change, where the abundance of 'choice' flows into the realm of how and who to be (at work): to be someone becomes a declaration of worth, investment and reflexive potential, reliant on positioning others as immobile, fixed and failing (Addison, this volume; Evans, this volume). The question then concerns which positions, claims and identities can and should be staked out within 'greedy institutions' that increasingly expect more: more output, more time – and more of our 'selves' as indicators or embodiments of 'diversity' (Berglund, 2006). Here the valuing of diversity is packaged as offering unlimited benefits, fostering creativity and innovation, also achieved (or displaced) through successful (private) management of precarious subject positions ('queerness'). Diversity becomes flexible, something that is done in and out of margins and mainstreams.

In 'flexible' times, when resources and energy are nonetheless stretched to the limit, spaces of creativity, 'outness', even subversion are arguably more marginalised, even as equal opportunities and diversity agendas are incorporated and 'mainstreamed'. The ideal of 'employability', displayed in management manuals, in diversity documents and promotions material, reactivates certain knowledges and skills, while allowing a presentation of these 'assets' as merely self-realisations of individual capacity (Addison, this volume). Divisions continue within the university environment itself, often reproduced despite the work of 'coming out', in managing precariousness, and getting on with it. In contrasting professional and personal levels, some simply do not have to 'come out' at all but rather fit in and easily align with institutional arrangements and expectations.

Seeing and being seen: academic outness

So,

What do you imagine of this 'young academic'? What does she look like, short hair besides? (It does matter, not least to her.) Dressing for work is mostly a causal affair, the wardrobe proud in its choice provisions: jeans, vests, jeans, vests. If this is dressing for success, should she hang up the vest, get another costume (are long sleeves safer)? She strolls along the corridor, out-fit on, suited people pause in awe of her: a) hardiness ('a vest in winter, do you not get cold?!') b) stupidity ('you're a student no more') c) good taste (unlikely). In the comments, criticisms and doubtful praise, the feminism she knows is disappeared. She glances down, she IS clothed. This wasn't meant to be subversive...

Many times in many places, including on the written academic page, I 'come out' in signalling class and sexual identity (Taylor, 2005a, 2007). Sometimes my identifications are defensive retorts, sometimes obvious truths, often markers read and understood by those in the know, encoded and revealed by embodied appearance and accent. Social class is a contested category, combining the material, cultural, emotional and spatial, and this contestation often confuses, where sexuality 'rescues', my research (and myself); what is seen as boring and rather outdated is seemingly (but uncomfortably) redeemed by the exciting and the queer. Class is not a 'difference' that can be easily incorporated into a queer research framework or institutional practice, where notions of deconstruction and diversity sit uneasily alongside that which often is still not named, complicating ideas of multiplicity and situatedness inside and outside of academia.

In situating these political locations and intersections, class is repeatedly 'dislocated' and 'given up': how then to hold on to it, to recognise continued intersections and unequal effects? The connections that I chart in my research are also personal passions and pains, unsolved by the rolling of eyes, academic or otherwise, as I 'come out'. But it may seem that queer working-class academics (and students) are rudely refusing to acknowledge recently bestowed privileges and newly acquired educational mobility, resisting a re-packaging along more advantageous routes (Binnie, 2011). Are they falsely identifying as working-class, where research projects and other academic exercises become a romanticised means of holding on to previous empathies, previous lives and ultimately past experience, a way of connecting with *real* working-classness, while further entrenching themselves in (middle-class) academia? In being positioned between privilege and disadvantage, via non-existence, academics and students, from working-class 'backgrounds' continually risk being positioned as fraudulent in 'coming out'. Why tell this story to a sceptical audience? Even sympathetic audiences/institutions may commodify it and make it theirs.

In *Is There Such Thing as a Working-Class Academic?*, Paul Wakeling (2010) suggest another version of telling – if not resourcing – the self; the autobiographical tradition of academics reflexively writing about class in academia (Tokarczyk and Fay, 1993). Considering the *lack* of reticence among academics from working-class families to discuss these matters, Wakeling plays with the idea of class as essential, even immortal (rather than dead) where no amount of social mobility can scrape away the traces of birth class. He seeks to locate academics' 'objective' class position and to present an analysis of the testimonies of academics from the working-class, where subjectively 'feeling' working-class may not be enough to *be* working-class. There is, Wakeling suggests, a danger of self-indulgence, embarrassment and awkwardness in 'coming-out' on paper, or even in performing an academic 'strip-tease': but perhaps consider if his questioning title would make sense as a pointer to the (im)possibility of the middle-class academic? There would perhaps be no question mark, no contradictions to map, feel or query, with middle-classness being the 'fact' to others 'fictions'.

So, while pondering the knowledge constructions and assertions in communicating *working-class lives*, another consideration involves the construction, assertions and mis-communications of *middle-class lives*, spaces, selves and knowledges (Taylor, 2009, 2010a): when are these made explicit and queried? Must they negotiate writing themselves out, while putting or writing themselves in? Rather than 'playing up' and pointing to class and sexual identity as embodied only by some, it is possible to problematise middle-classness and heteronormativity, to ask why this is currently downplayed in academia (never subject of – just to – 'diversity') (Taylor and Scurry, 2011). The focus and burden on the disadvantaged to come out, to reveal themselves and make their difference and their position known, could be potentially displaced by considering how privileged positions are inhabited, done and undone; displacing the importance of the 'coming out' imperative.

Ever repeated, never heard?

At the end of her course she distributes module feedback forms, welcoming 'constructive criticism' (Teaching Certificate now completed). How will they rate her? The service provided, polished enough? Or excessively threatening, a step out of place? Sociological analysis embodied as 'personal', academic authority condemned as 'niche'. Pressure and promotion, as a personal problem. She's read the guidelines 'Dignity at Work' but these words on the page are more insidious. Although she's situated feminism(s) in their political, social, historical context, teasing out complexity and tension, she sees that 'it' (like her) has been reduced as a conspiracy, as a conspirator, as anti-men (her all-female class protest and fear). She conspires, she challenges. And she gets tired.

Queer employability consists of managing and precariousness, requiring risk awareness instead of a reliance on social securities. In this context, thought is required as to what it could mean to encourage heterosexual educators to reflect on their 'coming out' strategies and the ways in which they manage heterosexism, within the classroom. There are challenges in being a lesbian academic and navigating homophobia in the HE workplace, including in the classroom, the corridor and lecture hall. The dilemmas I have encountered include: the degree to which I am open about my sexual identity with students; choosing appropriate moments to come out (and managing the ways these will be read and responded to as inappropriate); and challenging heteronormative and homophobic viewpoints at the same time as encouraging students to engage in discussion around a range of complex issues. Attempting to create a non-heteronormative classroom can involve a range of strategies, such as incorporating sexuality into the curriculum and supporting LGBT students (Ryan-Flood, 2009; Taylor, 2011). Yet efforts to challenge heteronormativity within HE settings can themselves reveal how identity and space are mutually constituted, reconfigured and re-embedded: I come out and they, perhaps you, don't have to.

Róisín Ryan-Flood (2009) explores the heteronormative space of the classroom and how to manage students' heterosexism and homophobia. It is important to make sexualities and genders visible in the classroom, so that they are not 'the elephant in the room' (see Riggs, this volume). Perspectives on coming out vary by context of teaching (classroom environment, topic), and Ryan-Flood outlines strategies such as mentioning her research interests but leaving students to 'read between the lines' in compulsory courses, and 'coming out' through declarative statements in optional gender and sexuality courses. Sometimes 'reading between the lines' is injurious and insulting, as made vivid in a partly adapted (to preserve anonymity) response from student feedback: '...I realize sociology is predominantly a women's subject, hence the large amount of girls enrolled in the topic. But I have never come across a module leader with such a dislike towards boys...I'm sure having gone to a private school and studying "class" didn't effect her opinion of me but felt the slightly obvious feminist views and condescending attitude towards men was a bit too blatant. There needs to be a re-think in her approach towards the men in class as equals, not below women...' (student feedback, 2009). That these words feed back to module leaders as part of institutional regulation of 'standards' itself speaks to the careful weighing-up of pros and cons that can be involved in classroom environments, where to 'come out' (or not) is a live dilemma; silence and articulation, tensions and contradictions, claims and denials, are all part of the intersectional slippages that are negotiated in academia – and by some ('blatant feminists') more than others.

Conclusion: no place like home?

She's split her week in three in multi-tasking fashion – admin (1 day), teaching (2 days), research (2 days), a triple burden or efficient mandate depending on weekend seepage. Logging in earlier and earlier, logging off later and later, she notices that 'diversity' has been re-cast, thrown out of the inbox, downgraded as a privilege, an add-on, an indulgence. Her colleagues have also stretched the week and themselves; they've found that there's always more to do and good intentions combine with guilt, failure and urgency ('this is my RESEARCH day!!!') What responsibility does she have to come out, fighting and forceful? To get out, enraged and embittered? She catches her own reflection in her office window, dark skies outside, office light on inside. She clicks her heels, three times over, and returns home.

Personalised (and spatialised) disjunctures and mis-fittings can act as realisations and re-articulations of the long-standing feminist declaration of the 'personal as political', while political actualisation requires a move beyond individual placement, beyond individual reflexivity – and tiredness – alone (Skeggs, 1997). The issue of 'who gets to talk' is partly about what we ask and how we hear: I start with my own (dis)identifications and (mis)positioning, though these offer, perhaps, an awkward story (Taylor, 2010b). This is not, however, meant as solely personalised confession, whereby research reflexivity is achieved in 'coming out' on paper. I resist the temptation to write in all of these moments as personal slights, emphasising instead the value of interrogating such moments as ongoing research encounters. The sole situation of the researcher is often overdone and in probing at whose story has weight, I will include interrogation of my own positioning and investments – this is certainly relevant, yet 'where I am' in this may also be viewed as deliberately absent and present.

Beverley Skeggs (2002) argues for the turning away from self-telling, and authorising oneself (being), in order to instead prioritise research reflexivity in practice (doing), albeit noting that lesbian, gay and feminist politics have used similar self-telling strategies in order to make political claims. The institutional context and classing of such 'stories' is crucial here to her contention, where it becomes 'a matter of positioning and access to the means of telling. It is also about the ability to be heard' (2002, p. 352). Feminist research has insisted on practices that involve a 'self-situating' to avoid overarching universalism, yet an easy insertion of identity categories ('lesbian', 'working-class') may risk neglecting what resources are required to tell (legitimate) stories, tending towards 'self-promotion' rather than signalling responsibility and accountability in and throughout research(ing). Lisa Adkins (2002) also makes this point, criticising the misplacement of researchers' introspective reflexivity as signalling 'good' research, positioned against a 'bad' lack, which also fails to consider uneven distributions of reflexivity in relation to class and gender. In seeking to situate 'selves' and engage with multiplicity (that queer invites), I also seek to attend to the 'complexities' and 'complications' in articulating varied – and unequal – positions (Taylor, 2009, 2010b). Fear of claims-making and misrepresentation may be refocused in listening to convergences and differences, to hear lived experience as a challenge to renditions of classlessness, and commodified 'diversity' (Ahmed, this volume; Taylor, 2011).

And yet the queer academic is encouraged, hastened, to change her academic 'five key words' when she declares that 'lesbian' and 'working-class' are still reappearing on the mainstreamed page. The pause – and repetition – is suggestive of what becomes excessive knowledge, a messy contribution, a 'past' that should – even if embodied – be given up for projections into another, different, academic future. But the queer academic(s) insist; in advancing approaches we won't just be moved on, displaced, in the call to the new and the mobile. Where research provides the spaces for lives to be narrated, it should be attentive to the opening and closing of dialogue and to the subject positions mobilised or refused in academic encounters. There is still much that needs to be said, and there are still some voices that remain unspoken or unheard; the positions of the privileged are also neutralised in the frequently 'additive' rhetoric (and benchmarking practice) of diversity policy in educational institutions.

Note

1. This research was conducted in an established red-brick university that is a member of the elite UK Russell group. Widening participation issues are

different in 'new' post-1992 universities but in this new educational climate of Conservative-Liberal fees, it is these institutions that have longstanding commitments to 'widening participation' as a tangible everyday reality that are now rendered more vulnerable. In contrast, elite universities may be in a position to offer limited student bursaries through the National Scholarship Programme, without altering their overall white, middle-class composition.

References

Adkins, L. (2002) Reflexivity and the politics of qualitative research. In May, T. (Ed.), *Qualitative Research in Action*. London: Sage

Berglund, E. (2006) Exhausting academia: In defence of anthropology, in search of time. *Journal of the World Anthropology Network*, 1(2): 25–35.

Binnie, J. (2011) 'Class, sexuality and space: A comment'. In Y. Taylor (Ed.), Special issue: Sexuality and class. *Sexualities*, 14: 21–26.

Evans, S. (2010) 'Becoming "somebody": Examining class and gender through higher education'. In Y. Taylor (Ed.), *Classed Intersections: Spaces, Selves, Knowledges* (pp. 53–72). Farham: Ashgate.

Gabb, J. (2004) Critical differentials: Querying the contrarieties between research on lesbian parent families. *Sexualities*, 7(2): 171–187.

Grace, P. and Hill, R. (2001) Using queer knowledges to build inclusionary pedagogy in adult education. Adult Education Research Conference Proceedings. http://www.edst.educ.ubc.ca/aerc/2001/2001grace.htm [accessed April 2006].

Hey, V. (2001) The construction of academic time: Sub/contracting academic labour in research. *Journal of Educational Policy*, 16(1): 67–84.

Hey, V. (2004) Perverse Pleasures – Identity work and the paradoxes of greedy institutions. *Journal of International Women's Studies*, 5(3): 33–43.

Jackson, S. (2004) Crossing boundaries. *Journal of International Women's Studies*, 5(2): 1–5.

Mintz, B. and Rothblum, E. D. (Eds) (1997) *Lesbians in Academia*. London: Routledge.

Reay, D. (1998) 'Always knowing' and 'never being sure': Familial and institutional habituses and higher education. *Journal of Educational Policy*, 13(4): 519–529.

Robinson, K. H. and Ferfolja, T. (2001) 'What are we doing this for?' Dealing with lesbian and gay issues in teacher education. *British Journal of Sociology of Education*, 22(1): 121–133.

Ryan-Flood, R. (2009) Putting yourself on the line: Pedagogy, homophobia and the elephant in the classroom. *Lesbian and Gay Psychology Review*, 10(1): 8–12.

Skeggs, B. (1995) 'Women's studies in the 1990s': Entitlement cultures and institutional constraints. *Women's Studies International Forum*, 18(4): 475–485.

Skeggs, B. (1997) *Formations of Class and Gender*. London: Sage.

Skeggs, B. (2002) 'Techniques for Telling the Reflexive Self' in May, T. (Ed.) *Qualitative Research in Action*. London: Sage

Spivak, G. C. (1993) *Outside in the Teaching Machine*. London: Routledge.

Taylor, Y. (2005a) The gap and how to mind it: Intersections of class and sexuality. *Sociological Research Online*, 10(3): 1–24.

Taylor, Y. (2005b) Classed in a classless climate. *Feminism and Psychology*, 15(4): 491–500.

Taylor, Y. (2007) *Working-Class Lesbian Life: Classed Outsiders*. Basingstoke: Palgrave Macmillan.

Taylor, Y. (2008) Good students, bad pupils: Constructions of 'aspiration', 'disadvantage' and social class in undergraduate-led widening participation work. *Educational Review*, 60(2): 155–168.

Taylor, Y. (2009) *Lesbian and Gay Parenting: Securing Social and Educational Capital*. Basingstoke: Palgrave Macmillan.

Taylor, Y. (Ed.) (2010a) *Classed Intersections: Spaces, Selves, Knowledges*. Farnham: Ashgate.

Taylor, Y. (2010b) Stories to tell? (de)legitimised selves. *Qualitative Inquiry*, 16(8): 633–641.

Taylor, Y. (2011) Accessions: Researching, designing higher education. *Gender and Education*, 23(6): 777–782.

Taylor, Y. (2012) 'Good students, bad pupils: Constructions of "aspiration", "disadvantage" and social class in undergraduate-led widening participation work'. In T. Hinton-Smith (Ed.), *Issues in Higher Education Widening Participation: Casting the Net Wide?* Basingstoke: Palgrave Macmillan.

Taylor, Y. and Scurry, T. (2011) International and widening participation students' experience of higher education, UK. *European Societies*, 13(4): 583–606.

Tokarczyk, M. and Fay, E. A. (Eds) (1993) *Working-Class Women in the Academy: Labourers in the Knowledge Factory*. Amherst, MA: The University of Massachusetts Press.

Vicars, M. (2006) 'Who are you calling queer?' Sticks and stones can break my bones but names will always hurt me. *British Educational Research Journal*, 32(3): 347–361.

Wakeling, P. (2010) 'Is there such a thing as a working class academic?' In Y. Taylor (Ed.), *Classed Intersections: Spaces, Selves, Knowledges* (pp. 35–52). Farnham: Ashgate. www.stonewall.org.uk [accessed 17 October 2009].

Index